TENNESSEE

Gardener's Guide

TENNESSEE
Gardener's Guide

Judy Lowe

COOL
SPRINGS
PRESS

Nashville, Tennessee
A Division of Thomas Nelson, Inc.
www.ThomasNelson.com

Published by Cool Springs Press, a Division of Thomas Nelson, Inc., P. O. Box 141000, Nashville, Tennessee, 37214.

Lowe, Judy.
    Tennessee gardener's guide.-- 3rd ed.
      p. cm.
    Includes bibliographical references (p.   ).
    ISBN: 1-888608-95-1 (pbk. : alk. paper)
    1. Landscape plants--Tennessee. 2. Landscape gardening--Tennessee.
    3. Gardening--Tennessee. I. Title.
  SB451.34.T2 L68 2001
  635.9'09768--dc21

                                  2001004622

First printing 2001
Printed in the United States of America
10 9 8 7 6 5 4

Managing Editor: Billie Brownell
Horticulture Editor: Dr. Willard Witte, Assoc. Prof., Univ. of Tennessee (retired)
Copyeditor: Tama Fortner
Designer: Sheri Ferguson
Production Artist: S.E. Anderson

On the cover: Iris, photographed by Robin Conover

Visit the Thomas Nelson website at www.ThomasNelson.com

Table of Contents

Dedication and Acknowledgments 6

How to Use This Book 7

Welcome to Gardening in Tennessee 8

Annuals 17

Bulbs 47

Grasses 64

Groundcovers 82

Perennials 96

Shrubs 135

Trees 169

Vines 199

Water Gardens 217

Gardening Basics 226

USDA Cold Hardiness Zone Map 248

Frost Data 249

More About Roses 251

Made in the Shade 253

What's in a Name? 256

Glossary 262

Bibliography 266

Index 267

Meet Judy Lowe 272

Dedication

To my husband, Carlyle, who without complaint watched the Atlanta Braves alone night after night and who never said a word as the unpruned shrubs grew taller and taller, while I worked on this book.

Acknowledgments

I owe the deepest debt of gratitude to Billie Brownell, the greatest editor a writer could have. She and Hank McBride have been unfailingly kind, understanding, and patient—even when it would have been easy not to.

Thanks also to Tama Fortner, whose diligence made this book more accurate and who made me sound better than I really do.

Much appreciation is due Dr. Willard Witte, the book's horticultural advisor. He cheerfully kept us up to date with all the taxonomical changes to botanical names and offered invaluable advice.

A very big thank-you to Nell Neal for her tips, and to countless Tennesseans who answered my phone calls and e-mail messages asking for facts, advice, and recommendations This would have been a much different guide—and not nearly as useful—without them.

How To Use This Book

Each entry in this guide provides you with information about a plant's particular characteristics, habits and its basic requirements for active growth as well as my personal experience and knowledge of the plant. I include the information you need to help you realize each plant's potential. Only when a plant performs at its best can one appreciate it fully. You will find such pertinent information as mature height and spread, bloom period and colors (if any), sun and soil preferences, water requirements, fertilizing needs, pruning and care, and pest information. Also, unless otherwise indicated, each plant is appropriate for all Tennessee zones.

Sun Preferences

Symbols represent the range of sunlight suitable for each plant. See page 253 for an explanation of each of these terms. Some plants can be grown in more than one range of sun, so you will sometimes see more than one sun symbol. The symbols are placed in order of my recommendation.

Full Sun   **Mostly Sun**   **Part Shade**   **Full Shade**

Additional Benefits

Many plants offer benefits that further enhance their appeal. The following symbols indicate some of the more important additional benefits:

 Attracts Butterflies

 **Attracts Hummingbirds**

 Produces Edible Fruit

 Has Fragrance

 Produces Food for Birds and Wildlife

Drought Resistant

 Suitable for Cut Flowers or Arrangements

 Long Bloom Period

 Native Plant

 Supports Bees

 Provides Shelter for Birds

 Good Fall Color

Companion Planting and Design

For most of the entries, I provide landscape design ideas as well as suggestions for companion plants to help you achieve striking and personal gardening results from your garden. This is where I find the most enjoyment from gardening.

My Personal Favorite

"My Personal Favorite" sections describe those specific cultivars or varieties that I have found particularly noteworthy. Give them a try . . . or, perhaps you'll find your own personal favorite.

Welcome to Gardening

in *Tennessee*

Tennessee is a great place to garden. We have a long growing season, abundant rainfall, a mild climate in which many different kinds of plants thrive, and most of us are blessed with fertile soils. (Even clay, which many grumble at, is rich in nutrients.) But the same factors that make the Volunteer State a gardener's paradise also present

some of the biggest challenges. Our long growing season generally means that we must fight more insects than gardeners in northern climates. That clay soil holds too much water, which can drown plants' roots. At the opposite extreme, rocky mountain soils drain so quickly that watering may be needed two days after a downpour. While most of our winters are mild, they're rarely predictable—temperatures can fall from 80 to 20 degrees Fahrenheit in a single day. Plants don't like that any better than people do, and because they can't go inside the house to get away as we do, they suffer from such extremes. Rainfall may also be too much—15 inches in March—or too little—$1/2$ inch in the heat of August.

But the pluses of gardening in our state far outweigh the minuses, as any gardener will tell you. It's easy to have a great-looking yard in Tennessee. How? There's no secret to it. Simply match the amount of sunlight and the type of soil in various spots in your yard to plants that like those conditions. That's why this book was written—to help you find the trees, shrubs, flowers, even vines and water garden plants that are right for your yard.

Developing a Green Thumb

Many homeowners believe it's necessary to have a green thumb in order to be a successful gardener. Not so. In reality, it's a matter of learning more about your yard and more about what plants want. It's not enough to buy a Crape Myrtle because you like its flowers if your yard offers no more than 4 hours of sun daily. Crape Myrtle's main need is full sun—provide that and it will be happy in your yard. Similarly, if you put Impatiens in a hot, dry spot that's far from a water faucet, the plants are going to languish or die.

So, before you head to a nursery to buy plants, do your homework. Observe the amount of sunlight and shade in various portions of your yard at different times of day. Dig a few holes to see what the soil is like—black and crumbly, hard and red, rocky, or somewhere in between. Then you're ready to make the right decisions and choose the plants that will be happiest in your landscape. When plants are happy— that is, when they're placed in the conditions they prefer—they grow well, resist insects and diseases better, and look great. And that's what you're aiming for.

Designing Your Landscape

If you've moved into a new house, or if you're starting a new landscape almost from scratch, choose trees first. They're the backbone of your garden; they provide the structure. Avoid the temptation to pick the fastest-growing trees you can find; these are almost always trees that have problems—and you'll regret planting them. Instead, plant trees for posterity. If you want them to grow as quickly as possible, water them regularly and feed them yearly, and they'll grow well.

Your second plant selections should be shrubs, probably a mix of evergreen and deciduous shrubs. Some of these should be flowering shrubs, and it's important to pay attention to when they bloom so that you can have flowers throughout the growing season, not just in spring. (Did you know that your yard could feature shrubs in flower in January? That's one of the joys of Tennessee gardening.)

If you want a landscape that's as carefree as possible, look up the eventual height and spread of any shrub *before* you buy it. That way, you won't spend hours every summer cutting it back because it's too big for the place where it's planted.

Now you're ready for flowers. Annuals will provide the main floral show for the first few years in your new yard. They're colorful, inexpensive, and long blooming. They also fill pots and baskets, as well as flower beds. But you may want to add a border or bed of perennials. Unlike annuals, these plants bloom for a shorter time (sometimes as little as two weeks), but they return year after year.

Then you may be ready to grow up instead of out—with vines, which may be evergreen or deciduous, flowering or not. Many flowering vines are excellent for attracting butterflies and birds. The ones that are native to Tennessee are a natural part of a garden created for wildlife.

If grass is increasingly difficult to grow in shade beneath trees, consider planting a shade-tolerant groundcover to provide texture and color without all the mowing that a lawn requires. Grasses in Tennessee aren't limited to Fescue, Bermuda, Zoysia, and so forth, but increasingly include handsome ornamental species, which provide interest in the garden not only when they're green and growing, but after frost when they've developed plumes and turned tan. If you want an almost foolproof plant—one that isn't bothered by insects or diseases and needs little water once it's mature—a perennial type of ornamental grass is your best bet.

Simple Tricks of the Trade

Practically everyone wants to have a yard that looks great, but many people feel that it's a goal beyond their reach—that it would probably take too much time or require gardening expertise they don't have.

That's a misconception. You don't have to have be married to a green thumb gardener, completely redo your landscape, or spend all your waking hours working in the yard in order to have a piece of property that will make you proud and call forth favorable comments from neighbors and passersby.

All you need are some tricks of the trade. Nothing startling or difficult. In fact, if you've gardened at all, you probably already know—subconsciously at least—many of these "rules" for an easy-to-care-for, good-looking yard. They're simple, but they work.

Rule 1: Use seasonal color and lots of it. Think of the yards that attract your attention in spring as you drive to and from work or errands. They may be waving seas of yellow—with rows of sunshiny Forsythia and golden Daffodils. Or they may be filled with fluffy white clouds of Ornamental Pear blossoms accented by pink Creeping Phlox (often called Thrift in this part of the world) and banks of early Tulips.

In April, a garden that's a mass of Dogwoods and Azaleas is a floral fantasyland, and really, that's all you notice about the property. You don't see if the house needs painting or the lawn could use some edging. Your eyes focus on the colorful flowers. (Of course, once spring is over, so is your yard's moment of glory.)

Rule 2: Masses of any plant are more impressive than one or two single specimens. Similarly, three red Azaleas, planted together, have more impact than one pink, one white, and one red plant. Coordinate your colors carefully. A row of either bright yellow Forsythia or cherry-blossomed Flowering Quince is eye-catching; but alternating the two shrubs in one row creates a jumbled effect. So does alternating Boxwood and Azalea. They look fine till spring, and then the Azaleas' impact is diluted.

In the same way, Tulips that are all the same color, or that are planted so that drifts or blocks of the same color are together and flow into the next color, are considerably more effective than multicolored mixtures.

Rule 3: Flowering trees and shrubs require much less effort on a homeowner's part than do annuals and perennials. You plant them once, keep them watered regularly for two years (until they're established and growing well), fertilize them occasionally, and little more is needed. But they keep blooming year after year—even when you don't do a thing.

Beware, however, of creating a hodgepodge. One Ornamental Peach, two Ornamental Pears, a Spirea, and a Kerria—especially marching across the front of the property like so many decorated soldiers—don't attract much interest because the effect is too busy; there's no unity, no focal point.

Rule 4: Extend the season of color in your yard by planting trees or shrubs that bloom in summer or that have especially colorful fall foliage. Aim for blooms or color from spring until fall—even into winter—by trying some of these plants in your landscape. Deciduous Magnolias, which may be grown as large shrubs or small trees, bloom very early in spring. Kousa Dogwood (*Cornus kousa*) is a beautiful flowering tree that blooms about a month later than the native Dogwood and is generally not subject to anthracnose. Golden Rain Tree has unusual flowers in summer, followed by pods that make a gentle rustle in a breeze. Ginkgo and named cultivars of Red Maple will provide reliable fall color. Witch Hazel will even bring a burst of blooms to your landscape in the middle of winter.

Rule 5: If it's different from what everyone else is growing, it's going to attract attention. You need to be careful, though, to make sure the plant you're considering is hardy in your area or if it's difficult to grow (meaning it may require more TLC than you have time to provide).

As you leaf through this book, you may discover that you haven't heard of some of the plants that are listed—Red Valerian, Loropetalum, Japanese Zelkova, and Sweet Box possibly among them. That's intentional. Many of the plants discussed are old favorites in our state, but others, which grow just as well, aren't as well known as they deserve to be. Consider giving some of them a try in your yard.

Rule 6: When it comes to bulbs, choose the ones that will come back each year and still look good. Daffodils and Crocuses do; Tulips sometimes don't. Daylilies do. So do Bearded Irises, but many of the newer cultivars are subject to many pests and may be harmed by cold weather. Siberian Irises are trouble-free and don't need dividing often.

In the Zone

The U.S. Department of Agriculture has developed a plant-hardiness zone map that divides the country into various sections, according to the average lowest winter temperature encountered there. In Tennessee, as you'll see on the map on page 248, we have two zones: Zone 6, for areas where temperatures rarely fall below -10 degrees Fahrenheit, and Zone 7, where average lows are usually zero to 10 degrees Fahrenheit.

The southern part of Shelby County is further divided into Zone 7b, where winter temperatures are not supposed to often fall below 5 degrees Fahrenheit.

What does this mean to you? To be on the safe side, grow plants—especially the expensive ones such as trees and shrubs—that are rated for your hardiness zone. That way, when Tennessee experiences one of its extra-cold winters that come along every ten years or so, or one of the bad ice storms that occasionally happen, you won't be replacing too many plants.

However, it's human nature that most of us want to push the limits and grow things that are for warmer climates. Southern Indica Azaleas thrive in Memphis—until temperatures fall to zero and below. The same with many strains of Zoysia and Bermuda grass in Nashville. I've been conservative about zones in this book because I don't want readers to spend money on a plant that they lose to cold.

While the zone designations are wonderful as guidelines, they're not a substitute for knowing your own climate. For instance, Knox County is in both Zone 6 and

Zone 7. Use a reliable thermometer to measure if temperatures in your part of the county fall below zero sometimes. Note that the official temperature at the airport will be of no help in telling you exactly how chilly it is in your backyard.

Also recognize that every property has what are called *microclimates*, places where the climate and temperate are slightly different from surrounding areas. The south side of the house and spots next to expanses of paving are going to be warmer.

Northern exposures will be cooler. Large trees and structures may provide shelter that helps retain heat at night. Slopes and especially low spots may be frost pockets that get colder than other nearby areas. Avoid planting spring-flowering plants in these vulnerable locations because their blossoms will frequently be killed by late spring frosts.

Weather often plays an important part in whether or not spring flowers are nipped by frost. An unseasonable warm spell causes trees and shrubs, vines and perennials to bud and begin to bloom sooner than usual. Then, when the weather returns to its normal chilly state, those premature blossoms are hit by frost. There's not too much you can do about this except to try to place susceptible shrubs and trees in protected locations, where they won't be harmed. Or run out and cover them up with a blanket or quilt (never plastic) when frost is forecast.

With perennials and bulbs, you can moderate the climate somewhat with the liberal use of mulch, which protects roots from winter cold. Mulch may also keep the soil cool in spring, to delay blooming until after damaging frosts have ended.

Tennessee's summer weather tends to be hot and humid. Some plants don't like this—Colorado Blue Spruce in Zone 7, for instance, or Firs. They're used to colder climates. If you want a needled evergreen, be sure to select one that's adapted to our climate. Plants with silver or gray foliage are especially vulnerable to heat and humidity. When they've had enough, they collapse—gardeners call this *melting out* or *melting down*. It means that some plants that thrive in the North won't do well in the Volunteer State. But there are so many more that will, that we would never have time—or space— to grow all the plant choices that are available to us.

Creating a Landscape to Be Proud Of

If you have picked up this book out of a desire to beautify the corner where you live, read on—about soil, watering techniques, and fertilizer, as well as exciting plants that may be new to you. All 175 of the plants profiled in this guide have been selected because they'll thrive in your garden. They're practically guaranteed to make you look as though your thumb is bright green, whether you've gardened before or not. Just remember to match the plants to your yard's growing conditions, and you'll create a landscape to be proud of.

Annuals *for Tennessee*

Annuals are the cheerful, uncomplaining workhorses of the garden. Most of them bloom continuously from spring until frost, asking only for regular watering, occasional feeding and—with some types—picking off old flowers as they fade.

Versatile Beauty

It's true that annuals—unlike perennials, shrubs, or trees—must be planted every year, since they live out their life cycles in a year. But that's a small price to pay for such versatile beauty—in flower beds and borders, by the mailbox, or in containers.

Some annuals are perfect for those hot, sunny places in your yard. Others delight in the relative coolness beneath a shade tree. Still others—Wax Begonia is a good example—will be happy in sun, shade, or anything in between.

When you shop for annuals, you'll find some that will trail over the edges of pots, others that emit a pleasant perfume, some (such as Coleus) that are grown more for their intriguing foliage than for flowers, tropical plants that laugh at the hottest weather summer can produce, and more colors than in a rainbow.

Selecting Annuals for Your Yard

When selecting annuals to grace your summer yard, do so on the basis of several factors:

- *Planting conditions:* Check the light, soil, and water conditions in the spot where you plan to plant. Most annuals are sun lovers. If your yard features many trees, look for the ones that prefer shady spots. Only a few will grow in poor soil. For the others— and this is particularly important if you have clay soil—work organic matter (such as finely shredded bark, rotted leaves, peat moss, or compost) into the top 12 inches of soil before planting. Some annuals need moist soil. If your soil isn't moist, avoid those plants or plan to water.

- *Color*: Choose colors that coordinate with your house (maybe matching the shade that the shutters are painted) and other plantings in the yard. Some gardeners like to plant an all-blue garden; others prefer to stick with pastels. Still others enjoy a combination of hot colors. But watch out for gold Marigolds and red-flowered annuals such as Salvia—these generally clash. White and light colors are especially good in areas where you can see them in the evening—around patios, for instance.
- *Mature height*: Most annuals sold today are short—less than a foot tall. To add interest to your flower beds, search out plants that grow smaller or taller than that, placing the taller ones in the backs of the beds and the dwarfs in front.
- *Cut flowers*: In the beginning, most gardeners grow annuals because they look so good in the garden for such a long time. But many annuals may be cut and brought indoors to be placed in vases and arrangements. If you don't like the idea of removing flowers from prominent spots in the yard, plan a special cutting garden in an out-of-the-way spot.

What to Look For

Most gardeners buy annuals as bedding plants. Look for strong stems, and check beneath leaves for any signs of insects. Check the roots—you should be able to see them, but they shouldn't completely cover the soil in a thick web (this is called being rootbound).

If the bedding plants were selected from a greenhouse, they'll need to be hardened off before planting. This is the process of acclimating them to outdoor conditions. (If annuals are taken from a warm, humid greenhouse where they are somewhat shaded from the sun and suddenly have to contend with wind, cold, and full sun, they will struggle.) First, place the plants in a shaded, sheltered spot for a few hours, bringing them indoors at night if outdoor temperatures are below 50 degrees Fahrenheit. Then gradually increase their exposure to sun and other natural conditions until they're ready to live outside. This may take a week in mild weather, or up to two weeks if the weather remains chilly at night.

It's difficult for most people to believe, but annuals that have *not* yet started blooming when you buy them are a better bet for the garden than those that have. The reason is that for the best summer-long performance, the plants need to develop good root systems. If they're putting their energy into producing flowers instead, root growth (so important as the basis of later plant and flower growth) suffers. Many experts suggest pinching off flowers and buds just before you plant.

As noted earlier, you should dig up the soil to at least a foot deep and improve the soil with organic matter. The best times to plant are in early evening and on cloudy days. Water the plants thoroughly several hours before you plan to set them out in the garden. Plant them at the same level they grew in the pots, spacing them as recommended on the label. In hot weather, you may need to provide some shading for a few days, to protect the young seedlings. And remember that those tiny root systems will need frequent watering for the first few weeks after planting; they simply aren't big enough in the beginning to fend for themselves.

Child's Play

Anyone, even a child, can take good care of annuals. Water regularly, fertilize occasionally (frequently for plants in containers, because nutrients are washed out by frequent watering), keep weeds pulled up, and remove faded flowers. Pinching off blossoms that are past their prime is important not just for neatness, but because it causes the plants to bloom more and longer.

Annuals are a joy because they give you an almost instant garden and—best of all—an easy-to-grow garden filled with spectacular color.

Ageratum
Ageratum houstonianum

I started using Ageratum in 1976, America's bicentennial year. Everyone was planting red, white, and blue flower beds, and low-growing blue Ageratum was ideal to place in the forefront of these patriotic beds. While I haven't used those colors together since, Ageratum has remained a staple in my yard. I like the mounded shape of the dwarf varieties, and the fuzzy little flowers last a long time with regular watering and deadheading. Not often available from nurseries, taller Ageratum cultivars can be grown from seed. They make nice cut flowers.

Bloom Period and Color
Pale blue, pink, white, or lavender flowers all summer.

Mature Height × Spread
5 to 30 inches × 6 to 12 inches

When, Where, and How to Plant
Wait until all chance of frost is past to set out plants, 6 inches apart in well-drained soil that has been enriched with compost, peat moss, or finely shredded bark. In my experience, Ageratum does better when shaded slightly than if grown in full sun.

Growing Tips
Never let Ageratum dry out; it likes moist soil. Fertilize twice a month with a water-soluble fertilizer for blooming plants, or twice a season with a pelleted, slow-release fertilizer.

Care
Besides regular watering, the other key to keeping this charming annual blooming is to regularly pinch off the faded flowers. If the blooms turn brown during the hottest part of summer, shear them off with pruners. They'll return, fresh and pretty, when temperatures become more moderate. Watch out for spider mites, which make the leaves look grayish. Hosing down the plants occasionally—especially during dry weather—can prevent spider mites or lessen an infestation. If you feel you need a chemical control, look for a miticide since all-purpose insecticides don't affect spider mites (because they're not technically insects).

Companion Planting and Design
Ageratum is used mostly to edge flower borders. I like it combined with white or pink Cosmos, yellow Marigolds, or Coreopsis. A patriotic combination is white Cosmos in the back, red Snapdragons in the middle, and blue Ageratum in front.

My Personal Favorite
'Blue Lagoon', which forms a mound about 8 inches high and 8 to 10 inches wide, blooms longer for me than any other Ageratum.

Angel Trumpet

Datura wrightii

When, Where, and How to Plant

Wait until the weather is reliably warm (at least May) before planting outdoors. You can also set out potted plants anytime in summer. In our part of the country, this is a plant that's usually grown in containers, but you may plant it in the garden, if you prefer. In either setting, it needs sun for all or most of the day and soil that contains plenty of organic matter. For best results, mix pelleted, slow-release fertilizer with the planting soil.

Growing Tips

Like other tropical plants, Angel Trumpet likes plenty of water and fertilizer. Keep the soil evenly moist and fertilize with a water-soluble plant food made for flowering plants.

Care

Remove faded blooms if they don't drop naturally. Insect and disease problems should be few, but if any occur, consult with the Extension Service about remedies. The fruits—green, knobby balls about 1¹/₂ inches long—as well as the seeds and other parts of the plant are very poisonous, so be careful. If you have a warm, sunny place to put it indoors, you may want to overwinter *Datura*. Otherwise, it will be killed by frost.

Companion Planting and Design

While *Datura* is mostly grown by itself as a specimen plant, try planting a Bougainvillea vine in the same tub as Angel Trumpet, letting it scamper up a string or small arbor.

My Personal Favorite

'Evening Fragrance' has 8-inch white blooms with a touch of lavender against bluish leaves.

There are several plants sold as Angel Trumpet and Datura. All are large, lush-growing, tropical plants with bold foliage and beautiful, trumpet-shaped flowers. The first time I ever saw a group of them in a private garden, it was midsummer and they made me feel as though I were in the jungle. Because the plants had been moved into a greenhouse in winter, they were several years old and covered with blooms— mature plants may have thirty-five to forty daily. And the crowning touch is that they're sweetly fragrant.

Bloom Period and Color
White and violet blooms from summer until fall.

Mature Height × Spread
3 to 5 feet × 3 to 5 feet

Celosia

Celosia argentea plumosa

Celosia isn't for the faint of heart. Not because it's difficult to grow—actually, nothing could be simpler—but because of the spiky, fire-engine-red flowers that, when planted en masse, look as though a fire has started. There are also yellow, orange, and pink hybrids available, but red seems to be the color of choice—even in old-fashioned Cockscomb (Celosia argentea cristata), which produces velvety, convoluted blooms that resemble a rooster's comb on steroids. All tolerate heat and drought, asking no more of a gardener than removing faded flowers.

Bloom Period and Color
Summer to frost in red, yellow, orange, and pink.

Mature Height × Spread
8 inches to 3 feet × 8 to 12 inches

When, Where, and How to Plant
Celosia may be grown from seed inside or outside. Sow seed indoors about eight weeks before you plan to plant outside; sow outdoors two weeks after the average last-frost date. Those sown outdoors won't bloom until July, but they make good replacements for plants that didn't perform well. Set out nursery plants after soil has warmed. Celosia likes sun and tolerates average, well-drained soil, although it prefers fertile soil that holds moisture. Space 9 to 12 inches apart. Mix pelleted, slow-release fertilizer in the planting hole.

Growing Tips
Don't let young plants dry out. Once they're established, you may not need to water except in dry spells. Fertilize twice a month with a liquid plant food for flowering plants.

Care
Should you pinch the stems? Pinching will cause the plant to become bushier. But pinching also makes it so heavy that if you don't stake, it will get beaten over in thunderstorms. Remove flowers as they fade. If a plant turns completely yellow, it's diseased; remove it from the bed and destroy. Otherwise, Celosia should have few pests.

Companion Planting and Design
Plumed Celosia adds a strong vertical accent. Plant white Petunias in front of red-flowered Celosia, or put red Celosia in front of white-flowered Morning Glory.

My Personal Favorites
Celosia argentea 'Prestige Scarlet' produces multiple branches. *Celosia argentea plumosa* 'Apricot Brandy' has gold blooms against green-purple foliage.

Cleome

Cleome hasslerana

When, Where, and How to Grow

Refrigerate Cleome seeds overnight, then plant in a sunny spot in the garden after the last expected frost. Or sow seeds six to eight weeks earlier in a warm, indoor environment for transplanting outdoors after the chance of frost is past. Thin or set plants 18 to 24 inches apart in average, well-drained soil. Avoid windy locations. Fertilize at planting time with a root stimulator and mix a pelleted, slow-release fertilizer into the soil.

Growing Tips

After it has become established, Cleome can tolerate some drought, but it's best to water often enough to prevent wilting—once dried out, it may not grow or bloom well from then on. Fertilize with weekly applications of a water-soluble plant food, such as 20-20-20. Because Cleome reseeds, use only a light mulch around the plants so that the seeds will germinate and produce new plants.

Care

When plants are a foot tall, pinch an inch off the tip of the main stem to encourage branching. The plant attracts few pests, but if aphids appear, spray with insecticidal soap. Occasionally leaf spot will develop. Pick off the affected leaves and dispose of them.

Companion Planting and Design

Plant a group of Cleomes at the back of a flower bed with tall annuals, such as standard Zinnias, in front to mask Cleome's rather leggy stems. It also looks nice with silver-leafed Artemesia at its base.

My Personal Favorites

'Helen Campbell', which grows about 4 feet tall, has glossy white flowers. 'Cherry Queen' is a pretty rose color.

If your grandmother or great-grandmother was a gardener, she grew Cleome. Then flower fashions changed—people wanted to buy bedding plants instead of growing flowers from seed, and they wanted short plants, not tall ones. So lovely Cleome (also called Spider Flower) fell out of favor. But now it's back. And what a good thing, too. In midsummer, when the yard looks tired, Cleome shines, completely unaffected by the heat. In Chinese, the common name of Cleome is "drunk butterflies." Look closely at the airy blooms, and you'll see why.

Bloom Period and Color

Midsummer until frost in shades of pink, rose, purple, and white.

Mature Height × Spread

3 to 6 feet × 1 to 1^1/$_2$ feet

Coleus
Solenostemon scutellarioides

Who would've imagined old-fashioned Coleus as a trendy plant? But in the past few years, that's exactly what has happened. Plant breeders have developed hybrids with leaves in brilliant color combinations that will knock your socks off. And most of these new cultivars—propagated from cuttings instead of seed—don't bloom, saving you the chore of pinching off the tiny flowers all summer. Many will also tolerate a fair amount of sun. When it comes to plants that are versatile and can take the heat, Coleus comes through with shining colors.

Bloom Period and Color
Foliage in shades of red, pink, gold, chartreuse, and bicolors from spring until frost.

Mature Height × Spread
6 inches to 4 feet × 8 inches to 3 feet

When, Where, and How to Plant
Set out plants after all chance of frost has passed in spring. Coleus appreciates moist, well-drained soil; amend soil with organic matter to help it hold moisture. Some varieties tolerate more sun than others; check the plant label to be sure whether shade or sun is indicated. Usually the leaf colors appear more intense in shade or partial shade. Space plants 6 to 18 inches apart, depending on mature size. Mix pelleted, slow-release fertilizer with the soil in the planting hole.

Growing Tips
Feed once a month with a water-soluble fertilizer, such as 20-20-20. Pay special attention to the water needs of Coleus in containers and hanging baskets; don't let them dry out.

Care
Pick off flowers as they appear. Once flowers open, the plants begin a natural decline. Watch out for snails and slugs; ask at a garden center about new organic controls for them. Begin lightly pinching the tips of the stems of upright Coleus when they are 4 to 6 inches tall to encourage branching, and continue pinching occasionally as needed to prevent a leggy appearance. Take cuttings of favorite plants in fall. Grow indoors over winter.

Companion Planting and Design
Grow red Coleus with silver-leafed Dusty Miller. Match other colors of Coleus with perennial flowers or Geraniums of the same shade. Gold and chartreuse Coleus look nice with yellow and green Hostas.

My Personal Favorites
'Trailing Red', which has small leaves and red stems, is good in containers. 'Bellingrath Pink' is red in sun and chartreuse in shade.

Cosmos
Cosmos bipinnatus

When, Where, and How to Plant

Cosmos is easy to grow from seed. Start it indoors six weeks before the last expected frost; sow in single pots rather than flats to prevent disturbing roots during transplant. Or sow seeds outdoors in a sunny spot where they are to grow. Plant in well-drained, poor to average soil. (When grown in soil rich with organic matter, stems will be weak.) Space homegrown or purchased plants 12 to 18 inches apart. Avoid placing tall Cosmos in windy sites. Water with a root stimulator. Mulch lIghtly or not at all to encourage reseeding.

Growing Tips

Fertilize sparingly—one application of a water-soluble plant food made for flowers at midseason is plenty. Once the plants are established, little watering is needed, but soak the soil well each time you do water.

Care

Pinch tall varieties when they reach 12 to 18 inches in height for maximum flowers. Snap off faded flowers to keep Cosmos blooming a long time. The plant has few insects or diseases, but can attract aphids. Spray them with insecticidal soap or a blast of water.

Companion Planting and Design

Cosmos are essential to cottage garden and natural landscape styles. Put shorter types up front; use tall varieties for vertical interest at the rear of the border or bed.

My Personal Favorites

'Imperial Pink' is brightly colored and grows 4 feet tall. *Cosmos sulphureus*, which is available in yellow, orange, and red selections, has sturdy stems and blooms earlier in the season than *Cosmos bipinnatus*.

Cosmos is a cheerful flower that anyone can grow. It has ferny foliage and airy single flowers with yellow disks in the center, much like Daisies, but more delicate. Despite its appearance, you don't have to treat Cosmos with kid gloves. It thrives in poor spoil, rarely needs water once it has developed a good root system, and almost never requires fertilizer. The reward for this neglect is armloads of blooms in your garden and full vases from summer till frost. They're so easy that many highway departments use them along roadways.

Bloom Period and Color

Blooms midsummer to frost in white, pink, rose, and fuchsia.

Mature Height × Spread

2 to 6 feet × 1 to 2½ feet

Geranium

Pelargonium species and hybrids

I can't imagine a summer without Geraniums. I always grow them in clay pots so that I can move them to the porch during long rainy spells, which cause them to stop blooming and sulk. But there are now some seed-grown Geraniums in interesting colors that are inexpensive enough and small enough for planting a bed of just Geraniums. (These seed-grown Geraniums will usually be sold in packs of four or six.) In the cooler areas of Tennessee, you'll also want to try delicate-looking Ivy Geraniums in hanging baskets.

Bloom Period and Color
Spring until fall in red, orange, salmon, pink, lavender, and white; some are mottled or bicolored.

Mature Height × Spread
12 inches to 3 feet × 14 to 24 inches

When, Where, and How to Plant
Purchase plants in spring, and place in the garden or pots after the last frost. All Geraniums prefer morning sun and afternoon shade, but Ivy Geraniums need mostly shade, especially in the warmer parts of the state. Use a packaged potting mix for containers and rich, moist soil if planting in the ground. Amend garden soil with compost or other organic matter to create a rich mixture that also drains readily. Space plants so that air circulates between them—1 to 2 feet apart depending on type. Work a pelleted, slow-release fertilizer into the soil. Mulch lightly.

Growing Tips
Fertilize Geraniums in pots once a week with a water-soluble fertilizer made for blooming plants. Place more pelleted, slow-release fertilizer around bedding Geraniums in midsummer. Don't let the soil dry out.

Care
The key is pinching the tips of young plants regularly to make them branch and thus produce more flowers. If stems rot, dig plants up and remove from the garden. If leaves turn yellow, spray with chelated iron. Keep old flowers cut off to encourage new blooms. Geraniums root easily in fall; take cuttings and overwinter in a sunny windowsill or greenhouse for first flowers next spring.

Companion Planting and Design
Welcome guests by lining the stairs to the front door with clay pots of salmon-colored Geraniums mixed with Dusty Miller, letting variegated *Vinca major* trail over the edges.

My Personal Favorite
'Eyes Right' has pink blooms accented with a red eye.

Globe Amaranth

Gomphrena globosa

When, Where, and How to Plant

Because Globe Amaranth is a heat-loving plant, it prefers to be planted after the weather is consistently warm—usually May. Place in a sunny spot that has average to poor soil that drains rapidly. Space plants a foot or so apart. Mix pelleted, slow-release fertilizer into the soil in the hole. Mulch lightly.

Growing Tips

Once plants have gotten their roots established, water only during dry spells and fertilize seldom, if at all. If you used a timed-release fertilizer when planting, you shouldn't have to feed plants again. But if leaves look pale, apply a water-soluble fertilizer, such as 20-20-20. Globe Amaranth attracts few pests, but stippled leaves can indicate spider mites. Test for them by placing a piece of white paper under the suspected leaf and thump it. If the "dust" that falls begins to move, it's spider mites. Pick off affected leaves and remove severely infested plants. To prevent spider mites, spray water once a week under the lower leaves of the plants. Dried flowers last for years; cut when half open and hang upside down in a dry, warm place.

Companion Planting and Design

Edge a driveway or sidewalk with Globe Amaranth, or fill medium to large clay pots with plants for the deck. It also looks nice combined with white-flowered annuals or perennials.

My Personal Favorites

'Lavender Lady' produces pale violet blooms on a plant about 2 feet tall. The scarlet flowers of *Gomphrena haageana* 'Strawberry Fields' make a wonderful accent in the garden.

When I first fell in love with this plant because of how it laughs at the hottest weather, I knew it would never become a hit unless it got a common name. Fortunately, Gomphrena (pronounced gom-FREE-nuh) is now called Globe Amaranth by everyone but me—old habits die hard. It has a rounded shape and is topped all summer with little ball-like flowers that remind me of the ones on Red Clover. These will dry right on the plant and can be saved for winter arrangements.

Bloom Period and Color

Summer to fall in white and shades of purple, pink, orange-salmon, and red.

Mature Height × Spread

10 to 24 inches × 12 to 16 inches

Impatiens
Impatiens walleriana

Impatiens—or Busy Lizzie, as your Great Aunt Flo probably called them—need no introduction to anyone with a shady yard. This plant is the standby for shade because it's attractive, easy to grow, and covered with flowers from the time you plant it until it's struck down by frost. They're as at home in containers as they are in flower beds. Hybrids are available in a variety of heights, but it's my experience that in a rainy summer, they'll all grow tall. And they make an impressive show!

Bloom Period and Color
Mid-spring to frost in white, pink, lavender, red, orange, and bicolors.

Mature Height × Spread
6 to 36 inches × 8 to 24 inches

When, Where, and How to Plant
Once all chance of frost is past, plant Impatiens in a shady spot about 10 inches apart in garden soil that's been enriched with organic matter. Partial shade is okay, but the more sun, the more you'll have to water. Mix pelleted, slow-release fertilizer into the planting soil. Top with a 2-inch layer of organic mulch.

Growing Tips
Ample water and frequent fertilization are the keys to success with Impatiens. Keep the soil moist and apply a water-soluble fertilizer made for blooming plants every two weeks during the season. Beds of Impatiens under trees respond very well to soaker hoses for irrigation.

Care
Many Impatiens are "self-cleaning"; that is, spent flowers fall off and disappear into the leaves, so deadheading isn't necessary. Few pests appear other than slugs in wet weather and spider mites in very dry weather. Ask at a nursery about barriers to controls slugs, or consult the Extension Service about chemical controls. Keeping the plants well watered during dry spells usually prevents spider mites. Pinch plants back anytime they look leggy; cuttings will root easily to increase your collection. Some Impatiens reseed, but may not come true to their parent.

Companion Planting and Design
Use bright colors to surround trees and liven up a flower bed that contains Ferns and Hostas. Plant white or pastel shades *en masse* for viewing from the patio.

My Personal Favorite
'Victorian Rose' has double flowers and looks nice in hanging baskets.

Madagascar Periwinkle

Catharanthus roseus

When, Where, and How to Plant

Don't rush to get Madagascar Periwinkle outside in spring. It's a heat-loving plant, and its leaves may turn yellow when temperatures remain below 70 degrees Fahrenheit. (If this happens, douse the plants with 1 tablespoon of chelated iron mixed with a gallon of water and the foliage will green up again.) Plant in a sunny area with well-drained soil or in containers filled with potting mix. Groundcover types, such as the Carpet series, do well in hanging baskets.

Growing Tips

When you plant, mix a timed-release fertilizer into the soil, according to package directions, and sprinkle an equal amount on top of the soil in August. Or fertilize once a month with a water-soluble fertilizer for flowering plants. Once established, plants in the garden manage on rainfall. Water potted plants often so they don't wilt.

Care

The flowers drop off when they die, so there is no need to deadhead. To encourage branching, pinch the tips of the stems occasionally. Watch out for slugs and snails, which munch holes in the leaves. These can be picked off by hand when seen or prevented by using barriers, such as copper strips. If mature plants develop yellow leaves during warm weather, this is a sign of disease; remove the affected plants from the garden.

Companion Planting and Design

"Eyed" Periwinkles look nice paired with Snapdragons and Wax Begonias that are the same color as the eyes.

My Personal Favorite

I always plant 'Parasol', which has extra-large white flowers, each with a red eye.

In August, when the temperature and humidity are both hovering around 90, and other annuals look as tired as you feel, pretty Madagascar Periwinkle is still perky. It has a constantly neat appearance, with glossy green leaves and flowers that simply fall off when they fade. And it blooms all summer—in the ground or in a variety of containers. This is the one annual I'm never without. When you go to the nursery, be sure not to confuse it with the perennial groundcover Vinca, which may also be called Periwinkle.

Bloom Period and Color

Spring to fall in white, pink, and lavender. Some are accented by darker eyes.

Mature Height × Spread

4 inches to 2 feet × 8 inches to 1 1/2 feet

Marigold
Tagetes species and hybrids

I'd always grown dwarf Marigolds—because I didn't like to stake the tall ones—until Sanford Deck, the "flower man" at the Senior Neighbors complex in Chattanooga, insisted that I try 'Inca Yellow' Marigolds. Variously called American or African Marigolds, these won't get beaten over by thunderstorms, even if not staked, Mr. Deck claimed. They also have large flowers on shorter plants, a winning combination. I tried them—he was right—and I've grown them ever since, although now I try all the new hybrids as well.

Bloom Period and Color
Summer until fall in shades of yellow, burgundy, orange, and cream.

Mature Height × Spread
6 inches to 3 feet × 10 inches to 3 feet

When, Where, and How to Plant
Marigolds are easy to grow from seed planted indoors one month before you want to plant them outside, or from seed sown directly in average garden soil just after the last frost date. Marigolds like to be planted in the sun. Work in a thin layer of organic matter before planting. Thin seedlings or space plants about 6, 10, or 18 inches apart, depending on the type. Mulch lightly.

Growing Tips
Let soil dry out slightly between waterings, and fertilize once a month or less with a liquid plant food for blooming plants—too much water and fertilizer contribute to too much leaf growth with few flowers and may promote leaf diseases or root rot. Avoid overhead sprinklers and watering late in the day, too. Regular watering at ground level, however, will help prevent spider mite infestations.

Care
Slugs will devour tender young marigolds; use barrier methods to control them rather than pelleted poisons that may attract pets and birds. Pinch plants as they grow to promote branching and more flowers. Keep faded flowers picked off to prolong bloom time.

Companion Planting and Design
Use dwarf varieties along edges of containers that also hold Zinnias, Periwinkle, short Ornamental Grasses, and other plants that appreciate a dry environment. Plant taller varieties in mixed flower and herb beds with other sun lovers.

My Personal Favorites
I wouldn't be without 'Climax' and the Inca II series because of the very large flowers they produce. I go for the clear, lemon yellow ones.

Melampodium
Melampodium paludosum

When, Where, and How to Plant

Melampodium seeds sprout easily; start indoors six weeks before the last expected frost, or seed directly into average garden soil after it warms up. Purchased plants, often in full bloom, make great "instant color" spots in garden beds or pots in full sun. Space transplants or thin seedlings 10 to 16 inches apart and incorporate a pelleted, slow-release fertilizer into the soil. Mulch lightly. Melampodium forgives poor soil and forgetful watering, and grows fastest in hot weather, making it an excellent candidate for late planting and replacement of other annuals.

Growing Tips

Water regularly until plants are established, then encourage their drought-tolerance by allowing the soil to dry out between waterings. Feed once or twice a month with a liquid plant food.

Care

Slugs can be a problem, but their invasion also indicates conditions are too wet. Aphids and whiteflies occasionally appear. Treat these insects with insecticidal soap or an insecticide containing pyrethrin. Melampodium is such a care-free plant that it branches without pinching. The daisy-shaped flowers also dry up and shed readily, then quickly replace themselves without deadheading. Melampodium reseeds prolifically unless thick mulch suppresses the process.

Companion Planting and Design

This is a perfect plant for massing. Try it with Shasta Daisy, orange Zinnias, Black-eyed Susan, a medium-sized Ornamental Grass, or Sunflowers.

My Personal Favorites

My favorites are 'Showstar and 'Medallion' because they bloom so prolifically.

When I was introduced to Melampodium by Stuart Miller of Chattanooga State, I knew it was a "keeper." Enamored of its small yellow blooms and tolerance of heat and humidity, I went around recommending it to everyone. Some people were disappointed because "it grew too big," they said. They wanted dwarf annuals that never reach beyond 8 inches tall or wide. But because I plant extensive flower beds, I like an annual that fills some space—that way I need fewer of them. Less cost and less work!

Bloom Period and Color

Summer in shades of golden yellow.

Mature Height × Spread

8 to 18 inches × 14 to 24 inches

Moss Rose
Portulaca grandiflora

I defy anyone to talk about Portulaca *without mentioning the words "cute" and "perky." Add to that "low-maintenance." This is one tough little plant, thriving in those hot, dry spots that other annuals shun. Its low-growing, fleshy foliage is also covered by some of the most brilliant flower colors around—at least on sunny days; they're not fond of rain or overcast skies. And they stop blooming when autumn days turn chilly. But if you need a carefree summer flower for a difficult place, Moss Rose will deliver.*

Bloom Period and Color
Blooms all summer in white and bright shades of red, yellow, orange, pink, and purple.

Mature Height × Spread
3 to 6 inches × 12 to 24 inches

When, Where, and How to Plant
Moss Rose thrives in warm soil and sun. If starting seeds indoors, keep the room temperature at 70 to 75 degrees Fahrenheit. Begin about four weeks before the last frost date and plan to put them in the garden several weeks after that. Or purchase bedding plants for the garden and hanging baskets on sunny patios. Sandy soil is best, either naturally occurring, amended (always purchase "sharp" sand for gardening) into garden soil, or incorporated into peat-based potting mixes for container growing. Mix pelleted, slow-release fertilizer into the soil when planting. Don't mulch so that the sun can warm the soil.

Growing Tips
Once plants are established, let the soil dry out between waterings. Then, every two or three weeks, use a balanced water-soluble fertilizer, such as 20-20-20 or one that's made for flowering plants.

Care
No grooming is needed. The plants attract few pests, but aphids and thrips may occur. Spray with insecticidal soap to control aphids; insecticides containing pyrethrin will also control aphids and sometimes thrips. If thrips do cause flowers to abort or open with distortions, replace the plants, as this pest can be difficult to control in annuals.

Companion Planting and Design
Use *Portulaca* in sunny rock gardens and wall crevices to add color, or fill the dry space between the driveway and sidewalk with a mix of colors.

My Personal Favorite
'Sundial Peach', an All-America Selections winner, has 2-inch double flowers that stay open a long time.

New Guinea Impatiens
Impatiens hawkeri

When, Where, and How to Plant

Plant 12 to 15 inches apart in good garden soil that has been enriched with plenty of organic material, or place three plants in a 3-gallon tub or container filled with a peat-based potting soil amended with rotted compost. Place the plants where they will receive sun all day, or where they will get only a few hours of late afternoon shade. Fertilize with root stimulator at planting time and mulch well.

Growing Tips

Keep well mulched and well watered; if stems collapse from drought, they do not recover well. Add a water-soluble fertilizer, such as 20-20-20, to the water every other week, alternating with 10-56-0. Feed more often if leaves begin to pale or turn yellow (unless foliage is supposed to be yellow).

Care

Pinch plants once when they are 4 inches tall, then pinch tips as needed to keep a bushy shape. Flowers fall off on their own. You should encounter few if any insects or diseases on New Guinea Impatiens, with the exception of spider mites if conditions are too dry. Spray water on leaves at least weekly to help prevent them.

Companion Planting and Design

Grow New Guineas with Cannas and Agapanthus for instant tropical texture. Or use them to bridge the gaps between blooms in a sunny perennial bed—the same well-drained soil amended with organic matter and the same regular watering practices will sustain both.

My Personal Favorites

'Tonga' has bronze and green leaves and lavender and purple flowers. 'Tango Improved' may be grown from seed.

The flowers of Impatiens and New Guinea Impatiens are somewhat similar, but that is where the likeness ends. New Guineas are grown mostly for their jazzy variegated foliage and the showy colors of their flowers. It's ideal where you want a plant that creates a festive feeling and calls attention to itself—near the swimming pool, for instance. Unlike Impatiens walleriana, New Guinea Impatiens—which were introduced into this country in the 1970s—are not shade plants. While they like a bit of afternoon shade, they do best in mostly sunny spots.

Bloom Period and Color

Summer to first frost with blooms in white, red, pink, and salmon. Leaves are green or red-bronze; some are variegated with creamy yellow.

Mature Height × Spread

12 to 20 inches × 12 to 15 inches

Ornamental Cabbage

Brassica oleracea

It wasn't so many years ago that gardens planted in fall were filled only with vegetables. Now the beginning of football season sends us to nurseries for plants that will provide color in our yards until Christmas and even spring. Ornamental Cabbage and Kale (which has lacy, fringed leaves) aren't as hardy as Pansies, but they have novelty on their side, making them great for anyone who wants something different. As days and nights grow cooler, the coloration of purple-leafed Ornamental Cabbages deepens to almost luminous.

Bloom Period and Color
Fall until a hard freeze, or spring until early summer; grown for fringed leaves of green, white, red, and purple.

Mature Height × Spread
6 to 12 inches × 8 to 12 inches

When, Where, and How to Plant
If you'd like to try growing them from seed, start in summer. Sow seeds in a sunny spot with average, well-drained garden soil; keep the seedbed moist in hot weather by laying a board over the seeds until they sprout. If you buy plants from a nursery in fall, do it as early as possible. The sooner they're planted, the more winter hardy they'll be. Thin seedlings or space purchased plants 1 foot apart; be sure the transplant sits directly at ground level. Water plants frequently until they become established or the ground freezes. Mix a pelleted, slow-release fertilizer into the soil at planting time. Mulch to moderate soil temperatures and retain moisture.

Growing Tips
Water weekly during fall. Add a water-soluble plant food, such as 20-20-20, to irrigation water every three weeks until the ground freezes.

Care
Insects attracted to this plant include cabbageworms, slugs, snails, and cutworms. For the latter three, use barrier methods and plant collars to prevent them. Exclude egg-laying butterflies with insect barrier fabric or spray with *B.t.* to control cabbageworm larvae when they hatch. Grow Ornamental Cabbages and Kales away from edible varieties.

Companion Planting and Design
Ornamental Cabbages make excellent companions to complementary-colored Chrysanthemums and when planted in front of Ornamental Grasses.

My Personal Favorites
'Nagoya' Kale has especially frilly leaves. 'Color Up' hybrid Cabbage—in pink, white, or red—has intense coloration.

Ornamental Pepper

Capsicum annuum

When, Where, and How to Plant

Start seeds indoors using a packaged potting mix; place flats in a very warm (70 degrees Fahrenheit), sunny environment six weeks before the last frost. Home-grown seedlings or small purchased plants cannot stand soil temperatures below 60 degrees Fahrenheit, so wait to plant outside until the soil is warm. Peppers thrive in moderately rich soils that stay evenly moist. Amend sandy and clay soils with organic matter; mulch well. Space plants 10 to 16 inches apart. Work a pelleted, slow-release fertilizer into the soil.

Growing Tips

Use a water-soluble fertilizer, such as 20-20-20, once a week. Peppers' thin leaves and heavy fruiting increase the need for water; container-grown Peppers may need water daily in the heat of the summer to prevent wilting. Plants stunted by lack of water will not fruit.

Care

Whitefly can be a serious pest; spray to control at the first sign of infestation with an insecticide containing pyrethrin. Plants received as gifts in December should be kept in a warm, sunny room until frost-free weather arrives. Repot in a peat-based potting mix and take the plant outside for the summer. Choose plastic pots; their dark surfaces keep roots warmer and more evenly moist than clay pots.

Companion Planting and Design

Grow Ornamental Peppers with Madagascar Periwinkle and 'Wave' Petunias for color all summer.

My Personal Favorite

'Variegata' has white, lavender, purple, and green foliage, with purple peppers that ripen to red.

One summer we were living in a rented house in Johnson City. There was no room for a vegetable garden, although there was a sunny flower bed near the front door. So I decided to grow Cherry Tomatoes and Ornamental Peppers among the annual flowers. This was in the days before edible landscaping made such a splash, so I wasn't sure what the neighborhood reaction would be. It turned out that everyone loved the little round peppers that turned from cream to purple, and they wanted to grow some, too.

Bloom Period and Color

Summer to frost with white or purple flowers followed by peppers that ripen to red, purple, yellow, or orange.

Mature Height × Spread

4 inches to 3 feet × 6 inches to 2 feet

Pansy
Viola × wittrockiana

I've been gardening long enough to remember winters without Pansies. Then two things happened: Gardeners became more interested in having something blooming in their yards year-round. At the same time, people noticed that theme parks—such as Six Flags and Disney World—were filled with colorful flowers every month of the year. Responding to all this, plant breeders developed Pansies that are quite cold hardy. Now most of us can't imagine a winter without perky little Pansies. They won't bloom during winter's coldest weather, but the flowers return quickly during warm spells.

Bloom Period and Color
Fall through early summer in red, yellow, orange, blue, violet, and white; single types and bicolors, many with "faces."

Mature Height × Spread
8 inches × 8 inches

When, Where, and How to Plant
Buy plants in early fall; the sooner they're planted, the more their roots will grow and the hardier they'll be. One problem with most fall-planted Pansy beds is that the plants are spaced too far apart so that you don't get the maximum effect from massing. Pansies won't really grow much, if any, over winter; they'll start growing larger only in spring. But winter is when you want the show, so place Pansies 5 inches apart in well-drained soil that's rich in organic matter. Pansies like sun in winter and partial shade in spring. Water with a root stimulator fertilizer.

Growing Tips
Use a water-soluble fertilizer for blooming plants every other week until the ground freezes. During winter thaws, fertilize again. Pansies require consistent moisture and may need watering several times a week in windy weather. Once plants are established, mulch to protect roots and prevent them from being heaved out of the ground.

Care
Keep old flowers trimmed off to extend the bloom season. Slugs can be a major pest; set up barriers, such as copper strips, to control. Planting too closely, overwatering, and damp weather conditions contribute to an assortment of fungal diseases. Good air circulation and well-drained soil help prevent diseases.

Companion Planting and Design
Grow Pansies with Snapdragons and Foxglove for a bright spring show.

My Personal Favorites
'Jolly Joker' is an eye-boggling orange and purple. The 'Majestic Giant' series has 4-inch flowers.

Pentas
Pentas lanceolata

When, Where, and How to Plant

The recent popularity of Pentas makes it available as a nursery plant, ready for the garden when the soil has warmed up. Or you may sow seeds indoors in a cool (60 degrees Fahrenheit) environment ten weeks before the last frost and plant about three weeks after it occurs. Sun and well-drained, very rich soil make for success with Pentas. Prepare garden or potting soil by adding plenty of compost (and ground bark or rotted sawdust if drainage is a particular problem). Work in a pelleted, slow-release fertilizer at planting. Space plants 6 to 8 inches apart and mulch generously.

Growing Tips

Like most tropical plants, Pentas likes abundant moisture and fertilizer. Water several times a week in dry weather, more often if they're in containers. When the plant is between blooming periods, fertilize with a water-soluble plant food made for flowering plants.

Care

Keep spent flowers picked off. Pinch young plants once to encourage bushy plants with multiple flower heads. As plants grow, pinch to maintain shape; cuttings without flowers root easily in potting soil all summer. Starved and thirsty Pentas grow woody and may not recover; cut them back in hope of rejuvenation. Slugs will eat Pentas, but they will eat other plants first. Few other pests trouble healthy plants.

Companion Planting and Design

Grow Pentas with Petunias, Asparagus Fern, and red Fountain Grass in a huge urn for a special patio centerpiece.

My Personal Favorites

'Pink Profusion' is a pretty color. I like 'Ruby Glow' with yellow Coreopsis.

In our current rush to grow lush-looking tropical plants, Pentas is finally starting to get the attention it should. That's because it's easy to grow, doesn't mind the steamiest summer, and blooms for a long time. Besides, it's pretty. If you want to attract butterflies to your yard, Pentas draws them like a magnet. The round flower clusters—consisting of dozens of tiny, star-shaped blossoms (giving rise to the common names Star Flower and Egyptian Star Cluster)—are often red or pink, adding to the "hot" look.

Bloom Period and Color

Summer in pink, rose, purple, and white.

Mature Height × Spread

14 to 24 inches × 10 to 14 inches

Petunia

Petunia × hybrida

Petunias may seem as familiar as your best friend. But today's choices aren't necessarily your mother's Petunias. New hybrid Petunias are released each year, with many of the newest types being grown exclusively from cuttings. Choose classic Grandifloras for early, big flowers in baskets and boxes, add Multiflora and Floribundas for massing in flower beds, and fill a sunny, dry spot with the smaller flowering, trailing 'Surfinias' and 'Million Bells'. While large Grandifloras are glitzy, the single Multifloras aren't beaten down by rain, which is a valuable quality.

Bloom Period and Color
Spring until frost in white and every shade of red, pink, purple, yellow, and bicolors.

Mature Height × Spread
6 to 18 inches × 12 to 24 inches

When, Where, and How to Plant
Set out plants after all chance of frost has past and on into midsummer. Grow in average garden soil. If well watered, Petunias can grow in full sun, but they appreciate an hour or two of afternoon shade. You may also place them where they're in sun about half a day. Space plants 8 inches apart, slightly closer in containers. Water with a transplant solution, and mix in pelleted, slow-release fertilizer at planting time. Mulch lightly to moderate soil conditions; add more if soil dries out and plants wilt.

Growing Tips
Because Petunias like moist soil, water often enough to keep the bed or container from drying out. Add a water-soluble fertilizer for flowering plants to the water every other week.

Care
Pinch after the first flowers to encourage bushy plants and more blooms. If plants grow leggy, shear back and fertilize to rejuvenate. You may want to do this before you go on vacation so you'll be greeted by newly flowering plants upon your return. Always pinch off faded flowers. Overly dry conditions encourage whitefly infestations, while excessively damp conditions promote botrytis and pythium rots. Ask the Extension Service about controls, or remove diseased plants and replant.

Companion Planting and Design
Grow trailing Petunias like 'Million Bells', 'Surfinia', and the Wave series in hanging baskets or so they spill over a porch railing.

My Personal Favorites
The Madness series stands up well to heat and humidity. I like 'Super Cascade' for really full hanging baskets.

Red Salvia

Salvia species and hybrids

When, Where, and How to Plant

Sow Salvia seeds indoors ten weeks before the last frost date in a sunny, moderately warm environment (65 degrees Fahrenheit). Space purchased plants 6 to 18 inches apart (depending on type) after the chance of frost has passed and the soil has warmed. All types perform best in average, well-drained garden soil that receives sun all or most of the day. Add a pelleted, slow-release fertilizer to the soil at planting time.

Growing Tips

Red Salvias demand consistent moisture, the Texas Sages less so, and Mealycups prefer to dry out between waterings. Fertilize every two weeks during the growing season with a water-soluble fertilizer for flowering plants.

Care

Keep fading flowers picked off Salvias, especially the reds. Once flowers mature, plants fail quickly. Pinch back Mealycups after blooming to maintain the bushy habit and to keep flowers coming. Salvias have few pests, but can develop leaf spot and rust fungus in cool weather. Pick off affected leaves. Leafhoppers and aphids can be a problem in very dry weather. Spray with insecticidal soap or, for severe infestations, ask the Extension Service to recommend a control.

Companion Planting and Design

Use Red Salvias with silver Dusty Miller and white Madagascar Periwinkle. Plant Texas Sage in front of Roses. Give Mealycups space among perennials and bulbs.

My Personal Favorite

Salvia coccinea 'Lady in Red' is, hands down, my favorite annual.

Although Red Salvia—sometimes called Scarlet Sage—is the best known of the annual Salvias, red isn't the only color, and the familiar spiked blooms of Salvia splendens *aren't the only form. Annual Salvias are available in pink, purple, and creamy white;* Salvia coccinea *(Texas Sage) sports delicate red or white and salmon flowers; and Mealycup Salvia comes in white and shades of blue. That's an appealing lineup for a family of plants that's simple to grow, likes heat and sun, blooms from early summer until frost, and attracts hummingbirds.*

Bloom Period and Color

Bright red, pink, purple, and creamy white from late spring through frost.

Mature Height × Spread

10 to 26 inches × 12 to 18 inches

Scaveola

Scaveola × 'Blue Wonder'

Blue flowers are so hard to find—and so coveted by gardeners—that when Scaveola burst onto the scene, it became an instant hit. Not all varieties have true blue blooms—some are lavender or violet-blue—but you'll find shades that range from pale to intense blue. This is a trailing plant that's ideal for hanging baskets and will form a low mat as an unusual annual groundcover. When you head to the garden center for plants, ask for skuh-VOH-luh; sometimes called Fan Flower for the shape of its blooms.

Bloom Period and Color
Blue to violet flowers from late spring until frost.

Mature Height × Spread
4 to 12 inches × 12 inches to 3 feet

When, Where, and How to Plant
Buy plants when they're available at nurseries, and place in a sunny spot after the soil has warmed up. Space 12 to 18 inches apart in well-drained soil that's been enriched with organic matter. Or place two to three plants in a hanging basket. Mix pelleted, slow-release fertilizer with the soil at planting time. Mulch beds with pine straw.

Growing Tips
If this rapidly growing plant is not kept watered, growth and blooming will stop. So don't let the soil dry out. Twice a month for in-ground plants and weekly for those growing in hanging baskets, fertilize with a water-soluble plant food that's made for blooming plants.

Care
As soon as plants have produced 3 inches of new growth, pinch the tips of the stems lightly to promote bushiness. Continue pinching occasionally through midsummer. If you have a greenhouse or sunny indoor spot for plants, cut back a plant or two of Scaveola to induce new growth and pot up the cuttings for growing indoors. Next spring, take cuttings and root them at 70 to 75 degrees Fahrenheit to plant outdoors in May.

Companion Planting and Design
Place pots of Scaveola on top of a wall and let them cascade over. Or pair it with your favorite red- or yellow-flowered annuals—Petunia, Salvia, Celosia, or Sunflower. It's also good for large hanging baskets, trailing 3 or more feet.

My Personal Favorites
'Blue Wonder' and 'Blue Fans' have sky-blue flowers accented by white eyes. 'Blue Shamrock' is the most intense blue I've seen.

Snapdragon
Antirrhinum majus

When, Where, and How to Plant
You don't have to wait until the chance of frost is past to plant; get Snapdragons into the garden as soon as they're available. Amend average garden soil with compost and organic matter to enrich soil and improve drainage. Space plants 6 to 12 inches apart in sunny beds. Or plant in containers with peat-based or soilless potting mix. Water with root stimulator fertilizer and mix a pelleted, slow-release fertilizer with the soil.

Growing Tips
Water frequently until plants are established, then water enough that the plants don't dry out. Use a water-soluble fertilizer for blooming plants every two weeks until the flowers stop in summer. Then cut back the plants by one-third and keep them watered. When new growth resumes, start fertilizing again for fall flowers.

Care
Look for rust-resistant Snapdragon varieties to avoid this common problem; use soaker hoses and leave space between plants for air circulation. Deadhead (pick off faded flowers) regularly to keep the plants blooming. Stake tall varieties to keep flowers clean. Cut them for arrangements when one-third of the flowers are open on a stem.

Companion Planting and Design
For a cottage garden look, mix various shades of Snapdragons. Otherwise, they look best massed in solid colors. Mix yellow Snapdragons with variegated *Liriope* or purple-flowered *Verbena bonariensis*.

My Personal Favorites
'Frosty Lavender Bells' grows 8 to 10 inches tall in sun or shade and has almost cup-shaped flowers. 'Chinese Lanterns' has a cascading habit.

I'm going to let you in on a secret. Snapdragons are in the annuals chapter because that's what the experts call them. But most years in Tennessee, they're perennials. They come back year after year, except when we have an exceptionally cold winter. That means you can have perennial plants at annual prices, since they're sold in six-packs. If you have children in your life that you'd like to interest in gardening, show them how to open the "jaws" of the flowers and let them snap shut again.

Bloom Period and Color
Spring until frost in pink, red, purple, orange, yellow, and white; solids and bicolors.

Mature Height × Spread
6 inches to 3 feet × 1 foot

Snow-on-the-Mountain
Euphorbia marginata

The first time I saw Snow-on-the-Mountain was in Chattanooga. I was in the yard of an inner-city resident whom I'd been told grew beautiful Roses. The Roses were pretty, but my eyes kept coming back to this white and green plant that I didn't recognize. She'd started it from seed that someone had given her, and she shared some seeds with me. Since then it has become a staple for me because of how it stands up to summer heat and drought, all the while presenting a cool-as-a-cucumber appearance.

Bloom Period and Color
Summer through fall; leaves and bracts with white margins in clusters.

Mature Height × Spread
12 to 24 inches × 12 to 22 inches

When, Where, and How to Plant
It's not hard to grow Snow-on-the-Mountain from seed. Start seeds six weeks before the last expected frost, then plant in the garden after the soil has warmed up. Fill flats or peat pots with sterile soil, keep moist and warm, and thin seedlings to one per pot. Grow seedlings in very bright sunlight or under grow lights to prevent stretching. Plants purchased in spring may be larger and "bloom" sooner; all types tolerate poor garden soil and full sun. Space 6 to 18 inches apart, depending on the type. Work in a pelleted, slow-release fertilizer at planting time.

Growing Tips
Use a water-soluble fertilizer, such as 20-20-20, every two or three weeks. The plant is drought-tolerant, but must be watered until it becomes established, so it doesn't wilt. Mulch lightly, if at all, as these native plants reseed readily but are not invasive.

Care
There are few pests in good growing conditions, but leaf diseases may occur in wet or very shady conditions. Remove affected leaves and move the plant to a warmer, sunnier location. Like its relative the Poinsettia, milky sap runs from cut stems; burn the ends to seal them for use in arrangements.

Companion Planting and Design
Grow them alongside Melampodium with Gomphrena and Moss Rose in front, since all like the same conditions.

My Personal Favorite
For a contrast, I like to plant 'Summer Icicle', which grows 18 to 24 inches tall, in front of my Smoke Bush.

Sunflower

Helianthus annus

When, Where, and How to Plant

Although every kindergartner has started Sunflower seeds in a cup of potting soil, they don't always transplant well; success is more assured when you plant seeds outdoors where you want the plants to grow. Wait until the danger of frost is past, and sow seeds in a sunny location. If Sunflowers are in too much shade, they will lean toward the light and need staking. Sunflowers can tolerate just about any kind of soil, but they grow better in soil that's been enriched with organic matter and a handful of 6-12-12 granular fertilizer. Keep soil moist until seeds sprout. Thin to 1 to 4 feet apart, depending on the ultimate size.

Growing Tips

Sunflowers are drought-tolerant and so don't require a great deal of water. But regular watering when rainfall is lacking produces more consistent growth and blooming. In midseason, spread another handful of granular 6-12-12 fertilizer in a circle 6 to 12 inches away from the stem and water it in. Or use a balanced, water-soluble fertilizer, such as 20-20-20, several times.

Care

Many of the new cultivars have multiple heads and bloom longer if deadheaded. Pest problems are few.

Companion Planting and Design

Place shorter varieties with Butterfly Weed, Coreopsis, and Gaillardia. Tall ones look best against a dark background, such as a fence or row of evergreens.

My Personal Favorites

'Moulin Rouge' has deep red flowers and burgundy stems. 'Teddy Bear' has fluffy yellow flowers on 3-foot stems. Goldfinches love 'Italian White'.

Remember when sunflowers were tall and yellow and mostly grown on the edges of vegetable gardens? Boy, have they changed. Now there's a color and size for every yard—creamy white, smoky red, orange, bronze, and red. And flowers vary from 4 inches to more than a foot across atop plants as diminutive as 24 inches high. Fortunately, growing these exciting new sunflowers—perfect for arrangements—is still as simple as child's play. Kids and birds have always loved sunflowers; now the rest of us are catching on.

Bloom Period and Color

Summer to fall in yellow and brown, cream, red, bronze, and orange.

Mature Height × Spread

24 inches to 12 feet × 12 to 24 inches

Sweet Alyssum

Lobularia maritima

Seeing—and smelling—Sweet Alyssum transports you back to a quieter, slower time. This sweet little plant, covered with tiny blooms and giving off a delightful fragrance, has a wonderfully old-fashioned feel. It reminds you of your grandmother's garden, but will be right at home in yours—if you have a sunny spot that's out of reach of the hose. Low-growing, drought-tolerant, and producing a profusion of white flowers that mix with everything, Sweet Alyssum brings the best of the past to the present.

Bloom Period and Color
Spring to frost in white, purple, pink, and light salmon.

Mature Height × Spread
3 to 6 inches × 12 to 18 inches

When, Where, and How to Plant
Alyssum plants are readily available at garden centers, or sow directly in the garden about three weeks before the last expected frost. Amend clay or sandy soils with compost to improve their ability to sustain fine roots and hold moisture. Work in a pelleted, slow-release fertilizer before planting. Thin seedlings to stand 4 inches apart when they are an inch tall; crowded seedlings will be thin with few flowers. Place purchased plants 6 to 8 inches apart.

Growing Tips
Water before the soil dries out completely and add a water-soluble fertilizer, such as 20-20-20, every two or three weeks. Mulch when plants are established to moderate soil moisture conditions.

Care
Alyssum will be more drought-tolerant in light to medium shade and may go dormant in the hottest part of the summer. Shear the plants to rejuvenate them if flowers stop forming. There are few pests except occasional caterpillar larvae. Plants usually suffer little damage. Sweet Alyssum reseeds but is not invasive; pull extra seedlings out and they will not resprout.

Companion Planting and Design
Alyssum grows readily between cracks in sidewalks, in rock walls, and along flower bed edges, especially those next to warm concrete. Plant Alyssum beneath Roses with Artemesia for a cottage garden look.

My Personal Favorites
Deep-pink 'Rosie O'Day' is the most fragrant I've grown. A true edger, it grows only 3 inches tall. 'Snow Crystals', about 6 inches tall, is the most heat-tolerant I've tried.

Wax Begonia
Begonia × semperflorens-cultorum

When, Where, and How to Plant

In spring, after the threat of frost has passed, plant Wax Begonias in pots or flower beds in soil that's rich in organic matter and will stay consistently moist. If that doesn't describe your soil, amend potting or garden soils with compost, rotted leaves, or finely shredded bark. Add a pelleted, slow-release fertilizer at planting time. Mulch plantings well to hold in moisture. Wax Begonias grow lush in partial or full shade, but can tolerate full sun, if watered abundantly.

Growing Tips

Keep well watered. Twice a month, apply a water-soluble fertilizer made for blooming plants.

Care

When plants reach 4 inches tall, pinch off the tips of the stems to encourage branching and a fuller appearance. Any time the plants grow leggy, pinch them back again. If you'd like more plants, cuttings root easily in water or potting soil. Wax Begonias have few serious insect or disease problems. Slugs can attack seedlings; overwatering can promote root rot. Whiteflies and spider mites occur in very dry conditions; cut back the plants, mulch, and water more often to prevent. Call the Extension Service for control advice.

Companion Planting and Design

Edge evergreen foundation shrubs with a row of red Wax Begonias. Place plants in a shady flower bed to provide color in mid- to late-summer, when perennials may have stopped blooming.

My Personal Favorites

'Pizzazz' grows 8 to 12 inches tall and is completely covered with bright rose, light pink, red, or white blooms all summer long. 'Lotto' has the largest flowers.

Is there a more versatile annual than Wax Begonia? I don't know of any. Wax Begonia will grow just about anywhere you put it—from full shade beneath a tall oak to blazing sun by the mailbox. The shiny leaves range from bronze to bright green, providing an accent to red, pink, or white blooms that look at home anywhere in the yard. I don't much care for the name, but I always grow the Cocktail series ('Gin', 'Whiskey', and 'Vodka') because they seem to stand up to full sun best.

Bloom Period and Color

Spring until fall with white, red, and pink flowers.

Mature Height × Spread

6 to 14 inches × 6 to 18 inches

Zinnia

Zinnia species and hybrids

We've come to expect a great deal from annuals. We want them to provide nonstop color from spring until Jack Frost visits in the fall. We'd also like them to be available in a host of colors to go with the other flowers in the yard as well as our indoor décor. Zinnias do all that—and more. There are cultivars that make great cut flowers, that are wonderful bedding plants, and that creep along the ground or hang over the edges of containers. Think of them as a triple treat.

Bloom Period and Color
Summer until fall in solids and bicolors of white, red, pink, orange, purple, yellow, and green.

Mature Height × Spread
6 inches to 3 feet × 12 inches to 3 1/2 feet

When, Where, and How to Plant
Zinnia elegans starts easily from seeds sown directly in the garden once the soil has warmed up (May or later). Sow seeds in a sunny spot, in average garden soil, amended only lightly with compost. Thin so they stand 6 to 18 inches apart, depending on mature size. Plant Narrowleaf Zinnias 8 to 10 inches apart or in containers. Mulch lightly, if at all; let the sun warm the soil.

Growing Tips
Use a water soluble fertilizer made for flowering plants no more than every two weeks. Once plants are established, water enough to prevent wilting, but no more.

Care
Overwatering, overcrowding, and overcast weather promote the leaf diseases that can plague Zinnia; avoid these situations and choose varieties that are resistant. Or ask the Extension Service for advice on fungicides. But remember, they're preventative, not curative. Hot, dry conditions can promote spider mites; cut flowers from affected stems and remove those plants from the stand. Spray with insecticidal soap. Use Zinnias in arrangements; cutting ensures future flowers. Remove faded flowers from *Zinnia elegans* regularly; Narrowleafs need no deadheading.

Companion Planting and Design
Zinnias and Narrowleaf Zinnias are staples of the cottage garden and bring hot colors to tropical plantings. Or make a sunny bed of *Zinnia elegans* with Melampodium, Marigolds, and Gomphrena.

My Personal Favorites
'Cut and Come Again' remains my favorite for cutting. 'Crystal White' and 'Star Gold' are my favorite Narrowleafs.

Bulbs *for Tennessee*

For most people, it wouldn't seem like spring without bulbs in bloom—the tiny purple and golden Crocuses that announce that winter is on its way out, sunny yellow Daffodils that brighten the season from February through April, and finally, the majestic Tulips—in almost every shade of the rainbow—that finish up the spring blooming season.

The Who's Who of Bulbs

But there's more to bulbs than the familiar spring-flowering varieties. This chapter also includes those bulbs' beautiful kin—plants that grow from tubers, rhizomes, and corms, including such summer favorites as Caladiums, Cannas, Dahlias, Lilies, and the "surprise lilies" known as Lycoris.

Just to clarify the situation, a *true bulb*, such as a Tulip, is a complete plant wrapped in a skin. It has swollen leaf scales that protect the flower bud and store food during its rest period. Bulbs store almost all the food needed by the plant in order for it to grow and bloom. A *corm* is similar to a bulb in that it also stores food in fleshy, underground stems. It is flatter than a bulb, and somewhat saucer-shaped. Gladiolus is one plant that grows from corms. A *tuber* is another swollen, underground stem that has buds, or "eyes," which are the flower and growth buds. A Caladium is an example of a popular tuber. A *rhizome* is an underground stem that grows horizontally instead of vertically. Bearded Iris is one example. All of these

47

plants grow much the same way and use food stored in their underground storage units. Some of these are considered cold hardy and some are not.

Preparation Is the Key

The one thing that all types of bulbs have in common is that enjoying them takes foresight on the part of the gardener. In order to have a bevy of bulbs flowering in April, for instance, you have to plant them in fall. Dahlia tubers set out at the end of April won't begin blooming until at least midsummer and often later. So planning and patience are the bywords for bulbs.

That's not to say that bulbs are difficult; just the opposite is true. Spring-flowering bulbs are especially easy—dig a hole, drop a bulb in it, add some soil, and wait till spring. But if you want your bulbs to last more than one season, you should prepare the soil for them, just as you would for any other flowers.

Good drainage is a must for all bulbs; in soil that stays wet, bulbs rot. In ordinary clay soil and in rocky or sandy soil, mix in ample amounts of compost, fine bark, or rotted leaves. In clay soil that remains wet for a day after rain, plant bulbs in raised beds.

While many gardeners plant spring-flowering bulbs in individual holes, when you're putting out a hundred or more, it's easier to dig up the entire bed to the proper depth, pile the soil on the side, space the bulbs in the bottom of the bed, and replace the soil that was removed from the hole.

What is the proper planting depth? The rule of thumb is to place the base of the bulb three times as deep as the height of the bulb and to space bulbs three times their width apart. The planting depths for some common bulbs are as follows: Iris at 1 to $1^1/2$ inches; Arum at $2^1/2$ inches; and Caladium and Crocus at 4 inches. Small Daffodils are planted at 6 inches deep and large ones at 9 inches deep. Dahlias, Grape Hyacinths, Lycoris, and Spanish Bluebells are planted at 5 inches deep; Lilies at 9 inches; and Tulips at 9 to 12 inches.

In heavy clay soil, you may not be able to plant as deeply as recommended, but it's worth making the effort for two reasons—deeper planting discourages rodents from digging up and making a meal of your bulbs, and also, the deeper you've planted them, the longer the bulbs will return. I've had Tulips come back for more than seven years when they were placed a foot deep.

It's not always easy to know which end is up for a bulb; make your best guess and then don't worry about it. Being upside down or even sideways won't prevent it from blooming.

There are many misconceptions about fertilizing spring-flowering bulbs—and acting on some of them can spell failure for your plantings. Here are the dos and don'ts:

- Do use a special slow-release bulb fertilizer at planting time. Then mark your bulbs somehow (I often use inconspicuous stakes at the edges of bulb beds, or even a squirt or two of spray paint) so that you can spread the same fertilizer (one is called Bulb Booster) over the bed each fall. This gives your bulbs the nutrients they need, when they need them. (You may also use 5-10-10 fertilizer in fall, but then you'll need to use it again when the bulbs have come up about an inch.)

- Don't fertilize when spring-flowering bulbs are in bloom or right after. Bulbs can take up food only when they're growing, and they grow from fall until just before blooming. Feeding when bulbs have finished flowering has been shown to cause them to rot.

- Don't use bonemeal. For one thing, it encourages dogs and other animals to dig up the bulbs. Also, while bonemeal once contained the nutrients the bulbs require, the way it's made has changed, and it no longer provides the ample food that bulbs need.

- Do fertilize summer bulbs with a slow-release plant food for flowering plants when foliage appears, then use a water-soluble fertilizer once a month until the plants bloom.

The Planting Rule of Thumb

When should you plant your bulbs? Plant Lilies and other summer-flowering bulbs as soon as you buy or receive them. With Caladiums, wait until the soil is warm (sometime in May). The general rule with spring-flowering bulbs is that the smaller they are, the earlier they are planted. So Crocuses can go in the ground in September (continuing until November); Daffodils from October through December; and Tulips beginning the first of November and continuing until the ground freezes. Because Tulips need a chilling period, store them where the temperature is 50 degrees Fahrenheit or lower. Keeping them in a refrigerator is fine, as long as you don't store them near apples or pears, which give off a gas that can harm Tulip bulbs.

The question I am asked most often about spring-flowering bulbs (from November until after Christmas) is, "Is it too late to plant my bulbs?" The answer is no. As long as the ground is not frozen, you can still plant bulbs—even if it's January. Later than that, and they may or may not flower that spring. But if they're still in good condition, they should bloom the next year.

Protecting Your Investment

If squirrels, chipmunks, and other vermin are a problem in your yard, you have several choices. Stick with Daffodils, which rodents leave alone because they're poisonous to them; or plant bulbs in "baskets" of chicken wire; or use a bulb protectant, available at garden centers and nurseries. Soak bulbs in the protectant solution before planting, then spray plant leaves with the product in spring to guard against deer damage.

More on Irises

There's so much that can be said about Irises. If you have the opportunity to visit the collection at the Memphis Botanic Garden, do so. You'll come away inspired.

Dutch Irises are true bulbs and are available in bulb catalogs and in nurseries in autumn. I enjoy the shape and color of their blossoms, but their nicest trait is that they put up thin, grasslike foliage in fall—which stays looking nice all winter—then they bloom in spring. Plant them in early fall. If you want something different in Bearded Irises, look to specialty growers for reblooming kinds. They flower in spring and again in late summer or fall. Never overwater or overfertilize Bearded Irises; that can harm them. You'll probably need to dig up and divide them every four years or when they begin to bloom less, cutting out the old woody portion of the rhizome (which no longer blooms), letting the rhizomes dry several hours, and then replanting. Siberian Irises are among the most trouble-free of the group. They have grassy leaves and don't mind light shade. They also tolerate wet soil. Don't separate plantings until they're so crowded that they no longer bloom well.

If you have wet soil, look to Louisiana Irises, which—despite what you might infer from their name—are hardy throughout Tennessee.

A Great Beginning

For beginning gardeners—those who aren't yet sure of their abilities—bulbs are a grand place to start because success is almost assured. More experienced gardeners know that lots of bulbs in a yard help you quickly build a reputation as a green thumb—and you don't have to tell anyone how easy it was!

Arum
Arum italicum

Available from practically every mail-order bulb catalog, Arum italicum grows in shade and provides three-season interest in the garden. So, why aren't you growing it? Because, like practically everyone else, you never knew it existed. Arum doesn't behave like a Tulip or Daffodil. Shortly after you plant the tuber, silver-veined leaves appear and generally persist through the winter. Then, in spring, a greenish-white flower spathe (like Jack-in-the-Pulpit's) pops up. That's followed by colorful spikes of red-orange berries. Who could resist such an interesting plant? Certainly not me.

Bloom Period and Color
White flowers in spring; berries in summer or early fall.

Mature Height × Spread
12 to 20 inches × 12 to 24 inches

When, Where, and How to Plant
In autumn, several weeks before the first hard frost, plant tubers 5 inches deep and 12 inches apart in well-drained, moisture-retentive soil. If necessary, amend clay or rocky soils with compost or fine pine bark to improve them. Arum prefers a shady or mostly shady location. Work a granular bulb fertilizer into the soil at planting.

Growing Tips
Mulch lightly after the arrow-shaped leaves appear to conserve moisture. Water regularly beginning when the flowers appear and continuing, if conditions are dry, until the berries develop. Early each fall, apply a bulb fertilizer according to package directions.

Care
Maintain a light mulch to hold moisture in the soil. Once established, Arum takes little care for several years. It multiplies by increasing its tubers within the clump and by seeding new ones from the red-orange berries that appear after the leaves. No pruning or pinching is necessary, but when flowering decreases, it's time to divide. Arum root clumps can be more than a foot deep when mature, so dig carefully when dividing. The plant is subject to few if any pests.

Companion Planting and Design
Plant along the edges of shady perennial borders, where its mottled leaves, Calla-shaped flowers, and berries provide three-season interest. Pair with Hostas and wildflowers.

My Personal Favorite
'Pictum' has narrower leaves (less arrow-shaped and more spear-shaped) and creamy white veins.

Caladium

Caladium bicolor

When, Where, and How to Plant

Large leaves are the hallmark of Caladiums, and they will reach their potential in a shady spot with average garden soil amended with compost or equally rich potting soil. Tubers will rot in cold, wet, or heavy soils. Plant tubers indoors in April; bottom heat encourages faster sprouting. In May and June, after the soil is warm, plant more tubers and nursery-grown plants directly in beds and pots. Space plants 12 to 16 inches apart. Work a pelleted, slow-release fertilizer into the soil at planting time.

Growing Tips

Water regularly to prevent drought stress. Apply a water-soluble fertilizer, such as 20-20-20, every other week to plants in containers, monthly to those in beds.

Care

Slugs and snails may seek tender new leaves as they emerge; ask at a nursery about barriers to deter them and wait until plants are up and growing to mulch with organic matter, then surround each clump. Caladiums are troubled by few other pests. Flowers are interesting but deplete the tubers; cut them off as soon as they appear. When the leaves die down in fall, dig up tubers and store in a dark, warm place in dry peat moss over winter.

Companion Planting and Design

Excellent alone or in shady beds, or with Ferns, Hostas, and white Impatiens. Use in a container with trailing Verbena along the edges.

My Personal Favorites

'White Christmas' has substantial white leaves boldly veined and edged in green. 'Carolyn Wharton' has crimson patterned leaves with green edges.

If you're a bit tired of Impatiens and want a plant that will shine in the shade, you can't do better than Caladium. With big, bold leaves in red, green, white, and pink—often complemented by contrasting veining and splotches—this plant is something special. Caladiums are at home in containers and even as houseplants, as well as being stars of the woodland garden. Most of the tubers sold in the United States are grown in Florida, so you can be sure they'll take the most torrid summer in stride.

Bloom Period and Color

Summer until frost; grown for heart-shaped leaves in green, red, white, and pink.

Mature Height × Spread

1 to 2 1/2 feet × 1 to 2 feet

Canna

Canna species and hybrids

Wow, will you look at what plant breeders have done to Cannas! They took a stodgy, old-fashioned plant and made it glamorous. No longer are Canna leaves simply green. The dramatic striped foliage of many new hybrids practically glows in the dark, making the plants beautiful even after the flowers fade. One leaf may feature red, pink, yellow, and gold, which sounds gaudy but somehow isn't. There's also a nice selection of dwarf Cannas now. One thing hasn't changed, though: Butterflies and hummingbirds like Cannas as much as people do.

Bloom Period and Color
Summer in red, yellow, salmon, and pink.

Mature Height × Spread
20 inches to 6 feet × 12 inches to 3 feet

When, Where, and How to Plant
You may start rhizomes indoors in April in peat pots filled with potting soil; water just enough to keep moist but not soggy. After the soil warms outdoors, plant these starts or purchased plants in a sunny spot with average garden soil amended with compost, or in large containers filled with rich potting soil. Fertilize with root stimulator at planting time; mulch.

Growing Tips
Keep soil evenly moist until plants are established, then let it dry out slightly between waterings. Occasionally apply a water-soluble fertilizer made for flowering plants. Overfertilization with nitrogen will produce leaves but no flowers.

Care
Canna leaf roller, slugs, and snails can be pests. Leaf rollers pupate inside newly emerging leaves and distort them. Cut the leaves off and sprinkle diatomaceous earth or insecticidal dust labeled to control these pests into the cut leaf area. In Zone 7, Cannas will survive most winters, if mulched well. But to be safe, and in Zone 6, cut down clumps at the end of the season, dig up the rhizomes and let them dry until the dirt falls off (do not wash or scrape). Store where temperatures are above freezing in dry peat moss.

Companion Planting and Design
A combination of Canna cultivars makes a bold bed. Choose companions that can stand up to their drama—Fountain Grass, annual Sunflower, and Cleome.

My Personal Favorite
'Pink Sunburst' has red, green, and yellow leaves topped by pink flowers that may remind you of Gladiolus.

Crocus

Crocus species and hybrids

When, Where, and How to Plant

In fall, plant spring-blooming Crocus 3 to 5 inches deep and 3 inches apart in a sunny location. Plant fall bloomers the same way when they become available. Shallow planting produces floppy flowers. Any average garden soil that drains well will sustain them. Add granular bulb fertilizer at planting time and mulch with shredded leaves.

Growing Tips

Each fall, spread a bulb fertilizer over the soil where Crocus is planted and water in. Root growth begins in the fall, so it's important to water during dry spells from September until the ground freezes hard. Maintain a 1- to 2-inch mulch to keep the soil cool in the summer and to prevent heaving the corms out of the ground in winter when soil alternately freezes and thaws.

Care

Little maintenance is needed. When flowers are few, plan to dig and divide the clumps during the next dormant season. Replant immediately. Hungry rodents may dig up corms, but few other pests trouble Crocus. Planting bulbs in a home-made chicken-wire basket or applying a repellent to them can deter field mice.

Companion Planting and Design

Plant Crocus in groups in shrub and flower beds or in drifts across the lawn. Use a dozen or more of each color for best effect and place them where you can see them from inside the house or will go by them each day.

My Personal Favorite

Among the fall-blooming true Crocuses (different from *Colchicum*, which is called Autumn Crocus), I like *Crocus speciosus*, which has pretty violet blooms.

Winter weather in the Volunteer State doesn't begin to compare to the snows and blows of, say, Chicago or Minneapolis. But that doesn't mean that around the end of January or the first of February, Tennesseans aren't ready for a sign that spring is on its way. Just in time—even if snow is on the ground—tiny cup-shaped Crocuses in white, as well as shades of purple and yellow, pop up to relay that welcome message. Since they're small and easy to plant, you may want to buy a bunch.

Bloom Period and Color

Late winter into spring in white, purple, yellow, and bicolors.

Mature Height × Spread

4 to 6 inches × 1 to 3 inches

Daffodil
Narcissus species and hybrids

Nothing lifts my spirits more in late winter and early spring than having a host of Daffodils blooming in various spots around my yard. The cheery yellow flowers make me smile and convince me that warm weather is truly on its way. Every fall, I plant early, midseason, and late-blooming cultivars, making sure I have white, pink-cupped, and fragrant ones, as well as a variety of yellows. Then I enjoy an array of delightful Daffodils for a couple of months outside and also indoors, where they are nice in arrangements.

Bloom Period and Color
From February through April, you can have Daffodils in yellow, white, orange, pink, or a combination of colors.

Mature Height × Spread
4 inches to 2 feet × 2 to 6 inches

When, Where, and How to Plant
Plant small bulbs 6 inches deep and large bulbs 9 to 12 inches deep, and both 2 to 6 inches apart beginning in October and continuing until January, if the ground isn't frozen. Just about any soil is suitable (as long as it's mostly in sun), but clay should be improved with organic matter. All bulbs need good drainage, or they'll rot. Mix a granular bulb fertilizer with the soil in the hole.

Growing Tips
Each September or October, spread granular bulb fertilizer on top of the soil where bulbs are planted. Never feed when the bulb is blooming or just afterward, as this can cause bulbs to rot. Water occasionally during autumn dry spells.

Care
After the flowers fade, snap off the stalk, but leave the foliage to dry naturally. As it browns over a period of about six weeks, it is producing and storing food in the bulb for next year. If you braid the foliage, you interfere with this process. When clumps have gotten crowded and have few blooms, divide and replant. Possible pests include bulb mites (which suck the sap), botrytis (a disease characterized by reddish-brown spots on the leaves), and fusarium wilt (which causes the plant to yellow and die). Call the Extension Service for advice.

Companion Planting and Design
Naturalize Daffodils in meadows and on the edge of woodlands. I often plant golden yellow cultivars near Forsythia and Kerria shrubs and intersperse them with Grape Hyacinths.

My Personal Favorite
Petite 'February Gold' is one of the earliest to bloom.

Dahlia

Dahlia species and hybrids

When, Where, and How to Plant

Dahlia tubers come in clumps; do not divide before planting. Create a rich garden soil with ample additions of organic matter to a depth of 10 inches. In a sunny spot, dig a hole 1 foot wide and 6 inches deep. Work a pelleted, slow-release fertilizer into both the soil you leave and that you dig out. Next, lay tubers in a hand shape (horizontally) in the hole. Cover with 3 inches of soil; as the stems grow, add more soil gradually. Plant large Dahlias 18 inches apart, and smaller varieties 8 to 10 inches apart. Mulch plants deeply.

Growing Tips

Dahlias demand moist soil to perform. Use soaker hoses or water by hand to irrigate roots deeply, and to keep flowers large. Fertilize with a water-soluble plant food for flowering plants every two weeks from planting until buds are set.

Care

Dahlias can sometimes be troubled by a host of insects and diseases: slugs, snails, aphids, borers, beetles, mites, and powdery mildew. Check with the Extension Service about recommended insecticides, fungicides, and organic remedies. After frost kills the plants, dig up the tubers, hose them off, and let them dry in the sun. Store in layers in peat moss in a cool, dark place.

Companion Planting and Design

Dahlia conditions may not suit other plants that can share their sunny sites. Group Dahlias together in the border or fill one bed with them.

My Personal Favorite

If you like your Dahlia flowers *big*, you'll love lavender 'Emory Paul'.

Move over Chrysanthemums—Dahlias are a challenger for the title of most colorful fall flower. Their virtues include a range of blossom sizes—from no bigger than a button to larger than a dinner plate. Dahlia blooms also come in a variety of intriguing shapes, resembling Waterlilies, Zinnias, Daisies, and Cactus flowers. And they last at least a week as cut flowers. Since they're grown from tubers, planting may be different from what you're used to. But if you've raised tomatoes, you'll be successful with Dahlias—they're grown the same way.

Bloom Period and Color

Summer to fall in white and shades of red, pink, yellow, and orange, as well as bicolors.

Mature Height × Spread

1 to 7 feet × 8 inches to 2 feet

Grape Hyacinth
Muscari species and hybrids

Although the flowers have a similar form, there's a world of difference between true Hyacinths—which are rather stiff and formal—and little Grape Hyacinths, whose delicate clusters of intricate flowers pair well with many spring-blooming plants. Try white ones with early red Tulips, blue cultivars with sunshiny Daffodils, and either color to edge beds of pink or red evergreen Azaleas. Because they perennialize (come back year after year, spreading wider and wider), Grape Hyacinths soon appear to have created a royal purple carpet wherever they grow.

Bloom Period and Color
Early to mid-spring in shades of blue, purple, and white.

Mature Height × Spread
6 to 8 inches × 4 inches

When, Where, and How to Plant
In fall, plant bulbs 5 inches deep and 1 to 3 inches apart in any well-drained soil. Drainage is essential for Grape Hyacinths; if soil is too wet, the bulbs will rot. Full sun is recommended, but they can tolerate light shade. Close planting gives maximum effect when the plants are grown *en masse*. Mix a granular bulb fertilizer with the soil at planting time and mulch.

Growing Tips
Because *Muscari* sprouts leaves in fall, blooms in spring, and produces seedlings and offsets during the summer, water regularly all year. Each fall—anytime from the first of September until the end of October—spread granular bulb fertilizer on the soil where Grape Hyacinths are planted.

Care
Wait until foliage turns brown before removing it in late spring or early summer. If the plants become too crowded, dig and divide the bulbs after flowers have faded. Remove old stalks and replant immediately. This bulb has few if any insects or diseases that trouble it.

Companion Planting and Design
Grape Hyacinths are perfect partners to Daffodils and early Tulips. They're also pretty massed along the edges of beds containing spring-flowering shrubs and Dogwood trees.

My Personal Favorites
Muscari armeniacum 'Blue Spike' has light blue, double flowers that give the plant a frilly appearance. *Muscari botryoides* 'Album' has white flowers. *Muscari latifolium* has two-toned blooms—sky blue on top and deep violet below.

Iris

Iris species and hybrids

When, Where, and How to Plant

Plant rhizomes in spring and bulbs in fall. Bearded Irises need alkaline soil; Japanese, Louisiana, Siberian, and Crested Irises prefer acidic. Dutch Iris isn't picky. Choose a sunny site for Bearded, Dutch, Louisiana, Siberian, and Japanese Iris; shade for Crested Iris. All except Bearded Iris will bloom in light shade. Plant Bearded Iris rhizomes almost on top of the soil, half-exposed to the sun; other rhizomatous Irises about 1 inch deep; Dutch Iris, 5 inches deep. Space by the mature size: 3 to 4 inches for Crested Iris to several feet for large Bearded Irises. Put Louisiana and Japanese Irises and Flags in bogs; Bearded, Dutch, and Crested Irises demand excellent drainage.

Growing Tips

Fertilize all but Dutch Iris each spring with a pelleted, slow-release fertilizer. Keep soil moist around Japanese and Louisiana Irises. For all others, water when less than an inch of rain falls weekly.

Care

Cut off faded flower stalks. Every three years, divide rhizomes in late summer. If Dutch Irises get crowded, divide and lift after blooming ends. The most common pest is the iris borer, which leaves tunnels in the leaves. Kill them by hand in the leaves. If they reach the rhizome, cut them out, discard the affected part, and replant the healthy section.

Companion Planting and Design

Siberian Irises fit well in perennial borders. Japanese and Louisiana Irises grow along the edges of water gardens. Bearded Irises look best by themselves.

My Personal Favorite

An old favorite is purple-flowered *Iris siberica* 'Caesar's Brother'.

There probably isn't a more useful—and attractive—group of flowers than the various kinds of Irises. No wonder it's Tennessee's official state flower. There are bulb-grown Irises (such as delicate Dutch Iris) and different species of rhizomatous Irises—from the familiar Bearded or German Irises to the low-growing native Iris cristata, which fits so nicely into woodland gardens. Siberian Irises, with blooms that resemble butterflies, have become so popular because they're easy to grow, but don't overlook the more dramatic Louisiana and Japanese Irises, which like moist soil.

Bloom Period and Color

Spring flowers in a rainbow of colors—all except true orange.

Mature Height × Spread

4 inches to 4 feet × 4 inches to 2 feet

Lily
Lilium species and hybrids

In the summertime, Lilies are almost as versatile as Irises are in the spring. They're especially notable as cut flowers, but don't overlook the elegance they bring to any flower bed. With a combination of Lilies, you can extend the flower season. First to bloom are the Asiatics, then Aurelian hybrids, followed by the late Orientals. Lily flowers are found in solids, stripes, dots, and bands, with and without fancy edges. Most grow face up, but some face out and others hang down. It's fun to have some of each.

Bloom Period and Color
Summer to fall in orange, red, pink, yellow, cream, and white.

Mature Height × Spread
2 to 8 feet × 1 to 3 feet

When, Where, and How to Plant
Lily bulbs are available in spring and fall, but fall is the preferred planting time, although you can set out potted Easter Lilies in spring after the chance of frost has passed. Pick a spot that's in sun for at least 6 hours daily and has well-drained soil. Amend clay and poor soils with organic matter and add a pelleted, slow-release fertilizer. Plant bulbs so that their tops are covered with 2 inches of soil (1 inch for Madonna Lilies) and they're 14 to 18 inches apart with a stake next to taller varieties. Never place Easter Lilies with other Lilies—they may transmit a virus that can kill the others.

Growing Tips
Lilies enjoy lots of moisture from early spring until late fall—drying out even during dormancy can damage Lily bulbs. Spread pelleted, slow-release fertilizer on the ground around the stems when leaves sprout. Mulch well to conserve moisture.

Care
Stake as needed. Deadhead flowers, removing as few leaves as possible. Dig and divide bulbs when stems are going dormant; cut stems down to two inches above ground in fall. Lily flowers last up to a week indoors; remove the anthers so the pollen won't stain whatever it touches. In the South, diseases are usually more of a problem than insects. Consult the Extension Service for remedies.

Companion Planting and Design
Try *Coreopsis* 'Moonbeam' with yellow Asiatic lilies; 'Stargazer' with Snow-on-the-Mountain and Coleus.

My Personal Favorites
'Pink Floyd' is an early bloomer in two shades of pink. 'Star Gazer'—rose with white edges—flowers later.

Lycoris
Lycoris species

When, Where, and How to Plant

Grow both species of *Lycoris* in rich, well-drained garden soil amended with compost. Choose a spot with full or partial sun. When bulbs become available, till soil or dig holes in planting area to 8 inches deep. Mix a slight handful of granular 10-10-10 with the soil at planting time. Plant bulbs 6 to 12 inches apart and 6 inches deep.

Growing Tips

Lycoris doesn't need a great deal of water, just enough to keep the plant from wilting. Let the soil dry out between waterings in summer. Fertilize with a pelleted, slow-release fertilizer when the leaves sprout.

Care

Mark the location of the bulbs with inconspicuous stakes so you don't accidentally dig them up when the foliage goes dormant. Do not mow or cut down the clumps of faded foliage until spring. Crowded clumps will continue to bloom for several seasons, then stop. Move or divide them while dormant in summer. Replant immediately. They don't like being moved, though, and may take a couple of years to begin blooming again. Few pests bother *Lycoris*, but bulbs will rot in wet soils.

Companion Planting and Design

Sprinkle *Lycoris* throughout perennial beds or plant them alone where they can amaze kids and neighbors.

My Personal Favorites

If you've tried the red- and pink-flowering *Lycoris*, go for something different: *L. albiflora* has cream-colored flowers, and *L. aurea* produces pale yellow blooms. They're fun, but not necessarily hardy—I dig mine every year.

As you might expect from its common names—Naked Ladies, Magic Lilies, Surprise Lilies—this is a plant with a difference. Actually, it's two plants that are different. The straplike leaves of Lycoris squamigera *appear in spring and grow until summer, then wither and disappear. A month later, sturdy leafless stems pop up, with pink flowers radiating from the top. Red-flowered* Lycoris radiata *(Zone 7 only) puts up its flower stalk in August or September, then leaves appear. Both are delightful—and fun—surprises in the garden.*

Bloom Period and Color

Late summer or early fall in red or pink.

Mature Height × Spread

12 to 36 inches × 6 to 12 inches

Zones

7 for *Lycoris radiata*; 6 and 7 for *Lycoris squamigera*

Spanish Bluebell
Hyacinthoides hispanica

I admit to being partial to blue flowers—not just because it's a pretty color, but because blue blooms combine so nicely with plants that have pink, red, yellow, and white blossoms. Still, that's not the only reason I'm enthusiastic about Spanish Bluebell, which produces loose spikes of attractive bell-shaped flowers in midspring. They're adaptable to soil and light conditions, they bloom nicely on the edges of my shady woods, and they're no trouble. They even make nice cut flowers. Every fall, I add a few more to the garden.

Bloom Period and Color
Spring in blue, pink, or white.

Mature Height × Spread
6 to 18 inches × 6 to 12 inches

When, Where, and How to Plant
Grow Spanish Bluebells in average garden soil. Locations with winter sun and summer shade under deciduous trees are ideal for naturalizing. Plant bulbs in fall, before the ground freezes. Space them 5 inches deep and at least 6 inches apart—clumps will be loose and stems sprawl attractively when not crowded. Mix a granular bulb fertilizer with the soil when planting.

Growing Tips
If possible, keep soil evenly moist during the growing season, but allow plantings to dry out when dormant in summer. Spread granular fertilizer made for bulbs annually in fall. Mulch lightly.

Care
Snap off flower stalks as they fade. Remove unsightly leaves after they turn yellow and then brown. Spanish Bluebell bulbs multiply rapidly and may need dividing every few years. Dig, divide, and replant clumps of bulbs after the leaves have begun turning brown. Seedlings and offsets can be left in place until large enough to transplant. Few pests trouble the plant, but bulbs can rot when weather is wet and drainage is poor. If there are insect or disease problems, consult the Extension Service for advice about controlling them.

Companion Planting and Design
They are excellent in woodland gardens with Vinca, Cast-Iron Plant, and dwarf evergreen shrubs. Combine with other bulbs, such as Crocus and Snowdrops, for flowers in earliest spring.

My Personal Favorites
'Danube' has dark blue blooms, and 'Rose Queen' is an appealing pink with a slightly different appearance.

Tulip

Tulipa species and hybrids

When, Where, and How to Plant

Tulips thrive and naturalize best in a sunny place that has deep, rich, well-drained soil amended with organic matter. Plant bulbs in mid- to late fall—as late as December if the ground isn't frozen. Keep bulbs refrigerated or in a cool place before planting. Space hybrid Tulips 6 inches apart and 6 to 12 inches deep. Plant species Tulips at a depth twice the height of the bulbs and a similar distance apart. Add bulb fertilizer and cover the bed with 2 inches of mulch.

Growing Tips

If fall rainfall is lacking, water Tulips if possible. Spread granular bulb fertilizer according to package directions on top of the soil of established bulb beds in September or October.

Care

Deeper planting and letting the leaves die down naturally help Tulips come back year after year. Species Tulips seldom have pests. Rodents and deer may dig up hybrids. To deter rodents, line the planting area with close mesh wire or spray bulbs with a repellent. The only sure control for deer is a very tall fence.

Companion Planting and Design

Plant Tulips in the garden and in containers to take advantage of the host of colors, flower forms, and heights. Use in masses of one color or type for best effect. Place Pansies or Violas in complementary colors in front.

My Personal Favorites

'Black Hero' is a very dark Tulip with double flowers that look like Peonies. 'Apeldoorn' is a red Darwin hybrid that returns well. Red and pink 'Ancilla' blooms early and its blooms resemble Waterlilies.

My husband and I have the same discussion every fall—I want to plant more Daffodils; he wants more Tulips. Since he's the hole-digger in the family, you can be sure our yard usually has plenty of Tulips. Actually, don't tell him, but I'm a Tulip fan, too. It's hard to match the drama of a lush, burgundy-colored Parrot Tulip with fringed flowers or the loveliness of lily-flowered Tulips. Besides, I've discovered a secret—plant Tulip bulbs one foot deep, and they'll return for at least five years.

Bloom Period and Color

Spring in every color except true blue.

Mature Height × Spread

6 to 18 inches × 4 to 6 inches

Grasses *for Tennessee*

Until recently, gardeners thought of grass and lawns as synonymous terms. But that's no longer true. Ornamental grasses—extremely popular in Victorian times—have once again entered the picture. Instead of planting another deciduous shrub, many gardeners are now adding a tall Miscanthus. Or instead of using a dwarf annual or perennial to edge a flower bed, they plant Carex or Japanese Blood Grass.

Ornamental grasses, which come in an array of sizes to fit any garden, add pizzazz to the landscape. The larger grasses have an imposing presence year-round; the smaller ones make nice accents. And I love the sound they make when they rustle in the breeze.

As Easy as 1, 2, 3

There's nothing difficult about growing ornamental grasses. The simple directions you need are given with each entry in this chapter. The only thing you may find difficult is that all ornamental grasses need to be cut back at the beginning of March each year.

With smaller grasses, such as Mondo and Monkey Grass, the process is simple. Using handpruners, loppers, hedge clippers, or a string trimmer (depending on how

large a stand of grass you need to cut back), cut off all old foliage (leave about 1 inch so you don't damage the plant's crown) and remove the brown foliage from the garden. Then, when the plants begin growing in a few weeks, you won't have any ugly mixture of brown and green straplike leaves.

But the task is somewhat more difficult with large ornamental grasses, simply because of their sizes. The first year or two, a string trimmer will do the job; although, most of the time, you'll need to leave a base of leaves 9 to 12 inches high. In following years, you may have to use a chainsaw.

But don't avoid this chore. It makes all the difference in the appearance of your grasses. And something that many people don't know is that the annual trimmings from ornamental grasses make wonderful—and free—mulches. I often pile the old foliage from large ornamental grasses in natural pathways through my woods, where it lasts a long time.

Dividing ornamental grasses is the same as dividing perennial plants. See the introduction to the "Perennials" chapter for directions.

Getting to the Root of a Good-Looking Lawn

A wide expanse of lush green lawn sets off a landscape as nothing else can. But many of us don't aspire to that perfect ideal. We want grass that will stand up to an impromptu game of touch football and the foot traffic generated by frequent backyard cookouts—but still be soft enough so that we can slip off our shoes and walk barefoot in it.

Tennessee is in a transition zone when it comes to lawn grasses. Both warm- and cool-season grasses grow here; unfortunately, neither does as well as it would farther north (cool-season species) or south (warm-season types). That just means that we have to work a little harder if we want good-looking grass.

Cool-season grasses—Fescues, Perennial Ryegrass, and Kentucky Bluegrass—grow best when temperatures range from 60 to 75 degrees Fahrenheit. Cool-season grasses do best in spring and fall and often grow some in mild spells during winter. In the hottest part of summer—especially if rainfall is lacking—they go dormant, greening up again when temperatures moderate and rain returns.

Warm-season grasses—mostly Bermuda and Zoysia in the Volunteer State—thrive at temperatures above 80 degrees Fahrenheit. That means they stay green despite the heat of a Tennessee summer, but they turn brown as soon as frost arrives in fall and don't green up again until temperatures are consistently warm again the next spring. Warm-season grasses are also not as winter-hardy as cool-season grasses, and they generally don't do well in shade. When temperatures fall below 15 degrees Fahrenheit—and especially zero and below—they may be killed. (Meyer or Z-52 Zoysia is considered the hardiest.) But warm-season grasses grow shorter and thicker than Fescue, making the thick "carpet" of grass that many people want.

Cool-season grasses are usually started inexpensively from seed, although more and more, gardeners are turning to Fescue sod for its ease of installation and instant effect. Warm-season grasses are sodded, although Zoysia may be started from small sprigs or plugs. Sprigging is less expensive than sod, but it may take a very long time to achieve coverage.

If you have a new home, choosing the grass you want is the first step. If you have an existing lawn, you'll probably want to stick with what's there. Tall Fescue and Zoysia are the most versatile grasses.

What you want to avoid is seed mixtures of different types of grasses. It's fine to grow a blend of three cultivars of Tall Fescue—because they all need the same conditions and care. But the same cannot be said of a mix that contains Creeping Fescue, Kentucky Bluegrass, and Tall Fescue. Each of those grasses has different watering, mowing, and fertilizing requirements. Eventually one of those grasses will "win out" and take over; and the survivor may not be the one that's best for your yard.

Usually the mixes of several species of grass seed are for shade. That's because there's not one outstanding grass for shade in our state. Creeping Fescue is a good shade grass, but it can't take the heat. Tall Fescue is usually the best bet in the shade, and even it may need to be overseeded (with half the recommended amount of seed for new grass) each fall. If Tall Fescue doesn't grow, your shade may be too deep for grass; consider trying a shade-tolerant groundcover instead.

First Things First

First, you need to have your soil tested. This will tell you if you need to lime your soil (something that's best done several months ahead, as lime takes some time to become effective).

The best and—if you really want to do it right—the *only* time to start a new Fescue lawn or renovate an old one is fall. It's okay to patch bare spots in a Fescue lawn in spring or install pieces of Fescue sod, but September is the month to start from seed.

On the other hand, you should wait until May—when temperatures have warmed up—to install or patch a Zoysia or Bermuda lawn.

Whether you're planting seed or sod, begin by getting rid of weeds. Don't use a selective herbicide (one that kills only the weed and not the grass) because that persists in the soil for some time and will prevent germination of new seed or harm roots in new sod. In a new lawn, water the bare soil daily for a week, and then kill the weeds (by hoeing or hand, or with a nonselective herbicide that doesn't persist in the soil). Then repeat the process. That gets rid of most of the weed seeds that would come up among your grass.

Decide if you want to sow seed or install sod. More cultivars of grass are available in seed than sod, and seed is much less expensive than sod. But seeding takes longer to establish a lawn than sod, which looks good almost instantly. High-quality sod is more weed-free than a lawn grown from seed, and it's easier to use on hills and slopes.

Prepare the soil by removing rocks and debris and tilling 2 to 4 inches deep, adding topsoil if your soil is extremely poor. Mix in a slow-release lawn fertilizer. Then rake the area, afterwards rolling it with a lawn roller (from an equipment rental store), if you're establishing an entire lawn.

Sowing Seed

Use a drop-type fertilizer spreader for large areas; a broadcast spreader for small ones. Follow the directions on the bag of seed for the amount to use. Rake to cover the seeded area with 1/8 to 1/4 inch of soil. Mulch *lightly* to help keep the soil from drying out. Most homeowners spread too much mulch—you should still be able to see the ground beneath the straw or other mulch.

Watering a newly seeded lawn is the critical part of the operation. Once the seeds have become wet, they can't be allowed to dry out or they won't germinate. This means at least daily watering (or twice daily in hot weather) until the new grass has grown to 2 inches tall; then water every other day until it has reached 4 inches tall. The water doesn't have to penetrate deeply, because there aren't any roots yet. So count on setting up the lawn sprinkler and turning it on each morning for seven to twelve days. Do the first mowing when the grass reaches 4 inches tall, cutting it to 3 inches high.

Installing Sod

The initial work of soil preparation is the same as with seeding. Calculate how much sod you'll need by multiplying the width of a strip of sod by its length. Arrange delivery of large amounts of sod so that it arrives just as you're ready to install it. If you plan to pick up a few strips of sod at a nursery, be sure you get it shortly after it has been delivered to the garden center; sod dries out quickly. Hose it down before you use it.

To start, lay the first piece of sod in a spot with a straight edge, such as along a driveway or sidewalk. After placing the first piece, unroll the second and put it as close

as possible to the first one—without overlapping, but avoiding gaps. Be sure that each piece is in close contact with the soil. Try to stagger the seams. It's not a bad idea to sprinkle each strip lightly with water after you get it in place, especially if you're working on a large area. Use a heavy-duty knife to cut apart strips so you can piece them into odd-shaped areas. Use a lawn roller on a large expanse of sod, then water deeply.

Just as you would a newly seeded lawn, stay off sod for at least two weeks. Walking on it when it's beginning to grow will harm it. Turn the sprinkler on and water daily for the first twelve to fourteen days, until the grass begins growing. Then you can cut back to twice-weekly watering and finally to once a week. Mow when Zoysia and Bermuda reach 2 to $2^1/2$ inches high and when Fescue reaches 4 inches high.

Important Lawn Care Tips

The most important thing you can do for a Fescue lawn is to never mow it shorter than 3 inches high. Taller grass shades out weeds and keeps the soil moist and cooler. Switching from "scalping" the lawn to letting it grow taller will make a world of difference in its appearance.

In spring, many gardeners like to use lawn fertilizer that contains a pre-emergent crabgrass control. But they don't always understand that it works by spreading a chemical that prevents seed germination. Not just crabgrass seed, but *any* seed. So you won't get any grass seed to grow for several months in areas that have been treated with pre-emergent crabgrass control. Never use a lawn fertilizer that contains weedkiller when you have trees and shrubs in or near the lawn. It can do unexpected damage.

Don't collect or rake up your grass clippings, unless the grass was so tall that the clippings are in big clumps. Regular glass clippings provide a mild fertilizing effect on your lawn—and it's free.

See page 232 for a chart on when to fertilize warm- and cool-season grasses, what type of fertilizer to use, and how much.

First we plant a lawn to frame the yard and provide a green background for all other plantings, and then we place graceful ornamental grasses throughout the landscape. That's twice as nice as staying with just one kind of grass.

Bermuda Grass

Cynodon dactylon

Bermuda is the grass world's Dr. Jekyll and Mr. Hyde. It's a dense, low-growing grass that can take heat, humidity, and even some drought. It feels wonderful when you walk on it and looks great all summer, as golfers know. On the other hand, it turns brown in winter unless over-seeded with Annual Rye (this works better on common Bermuda than the more popular hybrids). The aggressiveness that produces the thick carpet of deep green can also be a curse when it escapes into flower beds. And then there's the maintenance. Bermuda needs regular attention: mowing, fertilizing, and dethatching. But if you want the most beautiful lawn on the block—especially in warmer sections of the state—and you're willing to work at it, Bermuda is the way to go.

Optimum Mowed Height

1/2 to 1 1/2 inches

Zone

7

When, Where, and How to Plant

Only common Bermuda is available as seed. Hybrid Bermuda is planted from sod. Wait until temperatures are reliably warm both day and night—sometime in May—before installing sod or sowing seed. While it will grow in almost any Tennessee soil, this is a grass for full sun; it doesn't tolerate even partial shade. See pages 67 and 68 for tips on seeding and sodding a lawn.

Growing Tips

Bermuda Grass is known for its drought tolerance, but its appearance is much improved if it receives an inch of rainfall or water weekly. When Bermuda greens up in the spring, fertilize it with a slow-release lawn fertilizer. Water well. Repeat the application every six weeks until the end of August.

Care

Mow 1/2 to 1 1/2 inches high. Bermuda may need dethatching every year to look its best. Thatch is the buildup of decayed plant matter at the base of the grass. When it's more than 1/2 inch thick, you should rent a dethatching machine in spring to thin it. Brown streaks on the grass indicate mole crickets. Bermuda Grass mites cause clumps that interfere with the normal texture of the grass and eventually cause it to turn yellow and die. Consult the Extension Service for a recommended control. Overseed common Bermuda in fall with Annual Rye for a green lawn all winter.

My Personal Favorite

Floratex greens up sooner in spring and turns brown later in fall than most hybrid Bermudas. It may also require less maintenance, but does produce more seedheads.

Carex

Carex species and hybrids

When, Where, and How to Plant

Plant during spring in partial to full shade. Carex tolerates average soil, but prefers rich, moist soil. Amend clay and poor soil with organic matter. Space plants about a foot apart for massing. Mix pelleted, slow-release fertilizer into the planting hole at half the rate recommended on the label. Mulch with 2 inches of pine straw or fine pine bark.

Growing Tips

Water when rainfall is less than 1 inch weekly and temperatures are over 90 degrees Fahrenheit, or less than 1 inch every two weeks when temperatures are moderate. Fertilizer shouldn't be necessary. But if your plants don't look as good as they should, spray the leaves and the ground around the plant with a high-nitrogen, water-soluble fertilizer once every four weeks for two months.

Care

Carex isn't bothered much by pests. To keep the garden looking nice, you may want to trim back ratty-looking foliage in late winter or early spring. When plantings become crowded, dig up and divide plants in spring, replanting immediately.

Companion Planting and Design

Combine Black-Flowering Sedge (*Carex nigra*) with pale-pink Astilbes and the silver-leaved groundcover *Lamium*. Use *Carex morrowii* 'Aurea-variegata' to form a graceful, low-growing edge to a woodland flower border. *Carex elata* 'Bowles Golden' will be at home along the boggy edge of a water garden.

My Personal Favorite

Carex conica 'Variegata' is about 6 inches tall and has silver-edged leaves. It thrives in the dry shade of my backyard, a difficult spot for any plant.

Some plants seem to scream at onlookers, calling attention to themselves. Others are so quiet and unassuming that it's easy to overlook them. Carex falls into the latter category. But don't let the lack of glitz keep you from trying a few plants. When you're looking for a short, trouble-free plant for shade or partial shade, Carex is it. It's also a great choice if you need a low-growing edger; a groundcover with thin, gracefully arching leaves; or a grasslike plant to accent your more glamorous perennials. I wouldn't be without it.

Bloom Period and Color

Flowers are insignificant; grown for its leaves.

Mature Height × Spread

4 inches to 3 feet × 6 inches to 3 feet

Zone

A few cultivars are limited to Zone 7.

Feather Reed Grass

Calamagrostis × acutiflora

Sometimes it's hard to tell the various tall ornamental grasses apart without a scorecard. Feather Reed Grass makes it easy—instead of forming a fountain shape, it grows upright. And rather than developing plumes in late summer or early fall, its tall stalks spike up through the center of the grass in May or June. It's a plant that's suitable for any use you can think of for an ornamental grass—from anchoring the back of the perennial border to a stand-alone specimen plant near the driveway or mailbox.

Bloom Period and Color
Greenish-purple flowering stems appear in late spring or early summer; the airy plumes gradually turn golden yellow and become light tan by fall.

Mature Height × Spread
1¹/2 to 8 feet × 2 to 4 feet

When, Where, and How to Plant
Plant in spring in a sunny spot. *Calamagrostis* likes soil that stays slightly moist, if possible. (Avoid fall planting because it doesn't give the grass time to become established.) Gardeners with clay soil take note: Feather Reed Grass thrives in clay. Be sure to space plants so they have room to grow and won't be crowded. Mix pelleted, timed-release fertilizer in the planting hole. Water well and mulch lightly.

Growing Tips
Fertilizer will rarely be called for—too much encourages fast, weak growth. But if you think the grass isn't growing as well as it should, spread composted manure around the base of the plant. Keep the soil moist the first year after transplanting, or until the grass is established.

Care
Using handpruners, loppers, a string trimmer, or a saw, cut the plant back in early spring to 12 to 24 inches from the ground. If the plant needs dividing, dig it up in spring and cut it into several sections with an ax or saw. Replant immediately and keep the soil around the plants moist until they start to grow, then water regularly. You shouldn't encounter insect or disease problems.

Companion Planting and Design
I like the look of Feather Reed Grass surrounded by perennials with daisy-type flowers—Shasta Daisy, Black-eyed Susan, and *Gaillardia*—as well as Yarrow. It also looks nice with mounded shrubs such as 'Helleri' Holly and Barberry.

My Personal Favorite
'Karl Foerster' has very thin flower and seed stalks that turn from gold to silver as the season progresses.

Fountain Grass
Pennisetum species and hybrids

When, Where, and How to Plant
Well-drained soil is a must for almost all *Pennisetum* plants, so you'll need to amend clay with organic matter, such as rotted compost, peat moss, or fine bark. 'Rubrum' is more tolerant of clay and doesn't mind rocky soil, but it will grow better when its soil has been improved. In spring, choose a spot in full sun to plant container-grown grasses, or those that you've divided. A little afternoon shade won't hurt most kinds and is actually preferred by *Pennisetum alopecuroides* (Chinese Pennisetum), which produces reddish-purple plumes. Water with a trans- planting solution and mulch well.

Growing Tips
Water weekly until the plants have developed a good root system and are thriving, then water deeply whenever rainfall is less than normal. Fertilizer isn't usually necessary.

Care
You won't find many pest problems with *Pennisetum*. Its biggest fault is that it can self-sow, becoming a weed that has to be pulled out. (If that becomes a problem, clip off the flower heads.) Cut back perennial varieties in spring to about a foot tall and dig up and divide the plants, if crowded. At the same time, remove and replace annual cultivars.

Companion Planting and Design
Pennisetum looks nice paired with Black-eyed Susans and Daylilies of all colors. Plant 'Rubrum' with gray-foliaged Lambs Ear or Artemesia and in front of pink-flowered English Roses.

My Personal Favorite
'Little Bunny', which reaches no higher than 6 to 12 inches, thrives in my rocky soil on a hillside amid Creeping Phlox.

Clump-forming Fountain Grass is aptly named. Its graceful stems and fuzzy flower spikes arch outward, as though it were a fountain of grass. With a size more moderate than many ornamental grasses, Fountain Grass is a good choice for containers and small spaces. But beware: Several species—including the very popular 'Rubrum', which has eye-catching maroon foliage—are not perennial in Tennessee. Often people have lamented to me that they can't grow ornamental grasses, that they didn't come back, when the problem was that they had planted an annual Pennisetum.

Bloom Period and Color
Abundant white flower plumes appear in summer.

Mature Height × Spread
1 to 5 feet × 2 to 5 feet, depending on species

Japanese Blood Grass

Imperata cylindrica 'Rubra'

Red and green aren't just for Christmas; this pretty little ornamental grass brings those holiday colors to your yard from spring through the first frost of fall. It's an upright grower that produces stalks that are green on the bottom and red on top until they turn mostly red— a brilliant, clear red that will impress passersby—and finally "fade" to burgundy in fall. You'll enjoy Japanese Blood Grass as a striking accent or en masse as a colorful border. I've even used it to liven up container plantings.

Bloom Period and Color
Doesn't usually flower; grown for red foliage from summer to fall.

Mature Height × Spread
1 to 1¹/₂ feet × 1 foot

When, Where, and How to Plant

It's worth taking time to locate the perfect spot for Japanese Blood Grass: a site with full or partial sun, where the afternoon sun will shine though the back of this grass. When the sun hits the red blades, the plant seems to glow as if it were on fire. Set out container-grown plants from spring through summer in average, well-drained soil. Water with a transplanting solution at planting time and mulch with pine straw.

Growing Tips

Water regularly when rainfall is less than an inch per week. Fertilize each spring with a scant handful of granular 5-5-5 fertilizer spread in a circle around the base of the plant, and water well. If you can't find 5-5-5, use several tablespoons of 10-10-10 around each plant.

Care

In March, before the plants start growing, use a string trimmer or handpruners to cut Japanese Blood Grass back to a couple of inches high. If you notice in summer or fall that some of the blades have reverted to green, pull those plants up and remove from the garden. They won't ever turn red again. Insects and diseases aren't usually a problem.

Companion Planting and Design

Think of Japanese Blood Grass as an accent plant, adding a brilliant scarlet exclamation point to the flower border. Or use it to edge a west-facing flower bed or section of lawn.

My Personal Favorite

Usually sold as 'Red Baron', this plant always makes me smile because it reminds me of Snoopy in the *Peanuts* comic strip.

Miscanthus
Miscanthus sinensis

When, Where, and How to Plant
Although Miscanthus grows largest in soil enriched with organic matter, it tolerates just about any kind of soil. Give it as much sun as possible, since the grass becomes floppy in too much shade. Plant in spring, about 3 feet apart, using a transplant solution, and mulch.

Growing Tips
There's no need to fertilize unless the plant isn't growing well; then spread a handful of granular 5-5-5 in a circle around it and water in. The first year, water when rainfall is less than an inch weekly; in following years, additional moisture is rarely required. Slow growth the first year is normal.

Care
Cut the grass back at the beginning of March. In early years, it can be done with loppers, then you'll need a string trimmer, and finally you may have to get out the ax. But it's a job that must be done—new green growth popping up through old brown leaves is unsightly. But that's about your only chore since Miscanthus is troublefree—it's rarely bothered by pests.

Companion Planting and Design
Mass several Miscanthus plants as an informal hedge. Planted singly, as specimens, Miscanthus adds a sense of height beside a water garden and also serves as a background for colorful perennials, such as Black-eyed Susan, Purple Coneflower, and Daylilies.

My Personal Favorite
When I saw Miscanthus 'Morning Light' at the National Arboretum, it seemed to glow when the sunlight hit it. I had to buy one and was pleased to find it looks just as nice in my yard.

The Victorians were onto something when they made Miscanthus a popular part of their landscapes. Its slender foliage grows up and out, cascading like a silvery waterfall. In late summer, flower plumes arise, glistening like silk for weeks, then slowly—as cold weather approaches—turning from pink, bronze, or red to a fluffy beige fountain that lasts all winter. During cold weather, Miscanthus is a sort of outdoor dried flower arrangement. It's not hard to tell from that description that this is my favorite ornamental grass; it may become yours, too.

Bloom Period and Color
Showy plumes develop in late summer and early fall, fluffing out and lasting until cut off the next spring.

Mature Height × Spread
3 to 12 feet × 2 to 6 feet

Mondo Grass
Ophiopogon japonicus

People often confuse Mondo Grass with Liriope. It's true that the plants are similar— both are short grasses that thrive in shade, make good groundcovers, and bear lavender or white blooms. But Mondo Grass is shorter than Liriope and spreads by underground stems. Unfortunately, it isn't quite as cold hardy either—it may disappear in exceptionally cold winters. But when you need a tiny, grasslike plant—especially to go in a rock garden— Mondo is your plant. It's a perfect illustration of good things coming in small packages.

Bloom Period and Color
Lilac or white flowers in early summer, followed by blue seed stalks.

Mature Height × Spread
6 to 8 inches × 1 foot

Zone
7

When, Where, and How to Plant
Buy container plants and set out any time from mid-spring until early fall in a shady or mostly shady spot with average to good soil. Combine a pelleted, timed-release fertilizer with the soil in the planting hole. Mulch with a light organic material, such as pine needles or shredded leaves, to keep down weeds and retain soil moisture.

Growing Tips
Water weekly when rainfall is less than usual. Each spring, lightly sprinkle 20-20-20 pelleted fertilizer around established plants and water well.

Care
Cut back to a few inches high in March each year to keep the planting looking neat. Snails and slugs may nibble leaves, especially in shade and when the soil is moist and/or mulch is thick. You can remove them by hand and destroy; set out saucers of yeast water or beer; put barriers in place, such as copper edging; or ask at a garden center about new organic slug controls. The Extension Service can also offer advice on chemical control of these slimy pests.

Companion Planting and Design
Mondo Grass is used much like *Liriope*— as a groundcover and the border of a flower bed. But it also adds an arching, grasslike note to container plantings. And it looks nice with Astilbe, *Heuchera*, and other shade-loving flowers.

My Personal Favorite
Black Mondo Grass (*Ophiopogon planiscapus* 'Nigrescens') has black foliage and white (or pinkish) flowers and spreads very slowly. It's quite a conversation piece, and *the* choice for those who want something different.

Monkey Grass
Liriope species and hybrids

When, Where, and How to Plant

Plant in ordinary soil anytime from just after the last frost of spring until early autumn. Mix a pelleted, slow-release fertilizer with the soil in the planting hole. Mulch lightly with an inch or two of pine straw or fine pine bark. While most Monkey Grass prefers to live in light shade or partially shady areas, a few cultivars ('John Burch' and 'Silvery Sunproof', for instance) like full sun, so check the plant label to be sure.

Growing Tips

Water weekly if rainfall is below normal; this is particularly important if the plants receive half a day or more of sun. If plants haven't been growing as fast or robustly as you would like, spread 1/4 cup of 5-5-5 granular fertilizer in a circle around the base of the plants after pruning them. If you can't find 5-5-5, substitute several tablespoons of 10-10-10. Water in and replace the mulch.

Care

With a string trimmer or pruners, cut foliage back to 3 inches high in March each year before new growth starts. Pests are rarely a problem.

Companion Planting and Design

While the most common uses of *Liriope* are as a groundcover and around the edges of a border, consider placing individual plants (especially showy cultivars) in rock gardens, at the base of trees or shrubs, around ponds, or in containers.

My Personal Favorite

I like *Liriope spicata* 'Silver Dragon', which has green leaves streaked with silvery white, in my woodland garden near Hostas with white and green leaves.

Practically everyone recognizes Monkey Grass. It's a neat little plant with green or variegated grasslike leaves and attractive blooms followed by black fruits for the birds. Because of those virtues—plus the fact that it's foolproof— Monkey Grass has been overused in Tennessee landscapes, especially as an edging plant. But don't let that deter you, if you like the way it looks and need something easy to grow. And if you'd like something different, but still simple enough for a beginner, look for unusual cultivars such as Liriope muscari 'Silvery Sunproof'.

Bloom Period and Color

Violet, purple, or white flowers in early summer, followed by stalks of black fruits.

Mature Height × Spread

8 to 18 inches × 12 to 18 inches

Pampas Grass
Cortaderia selloana

The South has adopted Argentina's giant Pampas Grass. It grows well in the heat and can shoot up to 8 feet tall its first season, and to 20 feet in subsequent years. It's obviously not a plant for small yards, but many gardeners love its old-fashioned appearance, especially the plumes, which someone has described as looking like cotton candy. Female plants are showier than males, so buy one when it's in bloom to be sure of sex. Avoid Cortaderia jubata, *which is sometimes sold as Pampas Grass; it's weedy.*

Bloom Period and Color
Feathery white or pink plumes from midsummer on.

Mature Height × Spread
20 feet × 15 to 20 feet

Zone
7 (6 and 7 for 'Andes Silver')

When, Where, and How to Plant
Don't be as concerned about the type of soil in which to place Pampas Grass as with finding a spot with enough room for the grass to spread out. Plant from late spring until midsummer in full sun. Because this is such a fast-growing plant, don't bother with fertilizing it at planting time.

Growing Tips
You'll want to water enough so that newly planted Pampas Grass doesn't wilt; continue watering weekly during dry spells until the plant is growing nicely. After that, watering is no longer necessary. Since fertilizer is also unneeded, the gardener has very little to do during the growing season except stand back and watch this plant take off.

Care
In early spring, cut Pampas Grass back to 3 feet tall (or as short as you can, if the growth is too thick to get it to 3 feet). Remove all the foliage from the area (it makes a long-lasting mulch, by the way). Occasionally, Pampas Grass will reseed; dig up the volunteer plants and give them to friends or dispose of them. It has few insect or disease problems.

Companion Planting and Design
Pampas Grass looks best against dark evergreen backgrounds, such as in front of Canadian Hemlock, but it can make a good hedge or windbreak. I've grown 'Pumila', which gets to be 3 to 5 feet tall, in large tubs on the patio (but it's not hardy in Zone 6).

My Personal Favorite
'Silver Comet' has delicate, variegated leaves and grows about 6 to 8 feet tall.

Switch Grass

Panicum virgatum

When, Where, and How to Plant

You probably don't have an area in your yard that isn't acceptable to Switch Grass; it's one of the most adaptable plants around. Give it at least half a day of sun, and it won't mind what the soil is like—be it wet or dry, clay or sandy. Mix pelleted, slow-release fertilizer with the soil and mulch the ground around the base of the grass after you've finished planting. Space according to mature size.

Growing Tips

Water weekly the first year; after that, water during dry spells. Fertilize in spring by spreading a handful of granular 5-5-5 in a circle around the base of the plant; water in. If you can't find 5-5-5, use ¹/₄ cup of 10-10-10.

Care

Cut Switch Grass back in spring before new growth begins, and dispose of old foliage. If the grass self-sows or spreads where you don't want it, the extra plants are easy to remove. Rarely will you see pests on this plant.

Companion Planting and Design

There are many ways to use the various cultivars of Switch Grass. It's right at home with perennials of all types—from Creeping Phlox in spring to Mexican Sunflower (*Tithonia rotundifolia*) in summer and Asters in fall. It's a good grass to use as a screen or *en masse*. It also looks nice with other grasses.

My Personal Favorites

'Rotstrahlbusch' has red foliage and reaches about 4 feet high. 'Heavy Metal' grows 3 to 5 feet and has metallic blue foliage.

Gardeners are always looking for plants that will grow well in either dry or wet spots in the yard. Here's a native plant that's unusual because it's right at home in either situation, both of which are common in Tennessee. Switch Grass has a more erect form than some other grasses. What makes it stand out is its long-lasting fall color, which may be yellow, gold, or orange. The foliage of 'Haense Herms' reliably turns orange-red in autumn, then fades to maroon. 'Heavy Metal' turns yellow in autumn.

Bloom Period and Color
Purplish-pink blossoms in midsummer fade to white, then tan.

Mature Height × Spread
3 to 8 feet × 2 to 4 feet

Tall Fescue

Festuca arundinacea

Tall Fescue is the standard, all-purpose grass in Tennessee. It's a cool-season grass that stays green in winter and copes with summer drought by going dormant, then reviving when rain returns. It tolerates more shade than Bermuda or Zoysia, doesn't require as much mainte-nance, and is cheaper to establish than either of those if you grow it from seed. Newer hybrids are bred to be more disease resistant than Kentucky 31. Whether I plant Kentucky 31 or another hybrid, Tall Fescue is my choice for a low-maintenance lawn.

Optimum Mowed Height
3 inches

When, Where, and How to Plant
Tall Fescue may be grown from seed or sod. While seeding is cheaper, sod gives you an instant lawn. The best time to plant Tall Fescue is fall (preferably by September 30 in Zone 7 and by September 15 in Zone 6). This is a cool-season grass that needs to get established before hot weather arrives. You can patch bare spots in spring—but you'll need to water regularly all summer. Tall Fescue grows in any soil, from full sun to partial shade; like most grasses, it won't do well in full shade. Also see pages 65 to 69.

Growing Tips
Fertilize three or four times a year with a slow-release lawn fertilizer—in early spring (if you like), in late spring, and in early fall. Also spread 6-12-12 fertilizer over the lawn in October to build good roots. Have the soil tested to determine if lime is needed; apply in fall according to test recommendations. Tall Fescue looks best when it receives an inch of water weekly.

Care
Mow Tall Fescue 3 inches high to con-serve moisture and choke out weeds. Leave the clippings to enrich the soil. Overseed in fall, if needed, to thicken. (Follow package directions for the amount of seed to use.) Turf insects and diseases aren't common, but if they do appear, consult the Extension Service for recommendations.

My Personal Favorite
Turf specialists are constantly improving this all-purpose grass, and I try every new cultivar. All are improvements over Kentucky 31. My current favorite is Rebel II.

Zoysia

Zoysia species

When, Where, and How to Plant

The best time to plant is late spring until mid-August, in average soil. Establish a Zoysia lawn by inserting sprigs or plugs (little pieces of grass and roots) into an existing lawn or by laying sod. (Sprigging is cheaper, but may take several years for complete coverage, as Zoysia spreads slowly. Also, for an extended period, you'll have two kinds of grass with differing needs.) Zoysia is for mostly sunny spots. Also see pages 65 to 69.

Growing Tips

Fertilize with a slow-release lawn fertilizer when the grass turns green in spring and again every six weeks until the end of summer. Although Zoysia tolerates some drought, it will look better if it's given an inch of water weekly.

Care

Many experts recommend using a reel mower for Zoysia. Keep the grass mowed between 1 and 2 inches tall. Occasionally cut a plug from the lawn and measure the build-up of thatch (decaying plant matter that collects at the base of the grass blades). When it builds up to $1/2$ inch thick, rent a dethatching machine in early summer and get rid of the thatch layer, which can prevent water and nutrients reaching the grass's roots. For a green lawn during winter, overseed with Annual Rye in early fall. Insects and diseases are numerous, but not common. In case of problems, ask the Extension Service for advice.

My Personal Favorite

Often homeowners have to go with those cultivars that are available, but if you can find it, El Toro is a good choice that has better color in the cool months.

Zoysia is the Mercedes of the lawn grasses that are adapted to our climate. It produces a beautiful, thick turf that feels soft underfoot and looks like a million dollars. It also tolerates dry weather and some light shade. When Zoysia is well maintained, weeds rarely get a foothold. It does turn tan in fall, but in case you'd rather be on the golf course than mowing grass, Zoysia grows very slowly. If your idea of the perfect lawn is a dense carpet of green, Zoysia will fulfill your dream.

Optimum Mowed Height
1 to 2 inches tall

Zone
7

Groundcovers *for Tennessee*

Groundcovers give your landscape a carpeted look. Many will grow in dense shade beneath trees where grass won't. But they're also useful for edging pathways, for unifying plantings of shrubs and trees, and for preventing erosion on slopes and hills that are too steep to mow. You may also want to think of groundcovers as "living mulch," keeping the soil moist and free of weeds.

Choosing the Ideal Groundcover

Select the groundcover that's ideal for any spot in your yard as you would any other plant—by matching the sun and soil conditions in the spot where you need the groundcover to the conditions preferred by various groundcovers. In addition, you may want to consider groundcovers with small leaves—Creeping Thyme or *Vinca minor*, for example—for small areas, and those with a more bold appearance for large areas, although this isn't a hard and fast rule.

One of the most puzzling things for the gardener installing a groundcover is how many plants will be needed. Here's a handy guide to help you figure how much ground 100 plants will eventually cover, according to how they're spaced. As you'll see, if you place Creeping Thyme 6 inches apart, 100 plants will cover 25 square feet. If you place them 12 inches apart, they'll cover 100 square feet, which will be a considerable cost savings to you, but complete coverage will be slower.

Space Covered by 100 Groundcover Plants

Planting Distance Apart (in inches)	Area Covered (in square feet)	Planting Distance Apart (in inches)	Area Covered (in square feet)
6	25	30	625
12	100	36	900
18	225	48	1,600
24	400	60	2,500

The Importance of Soil Preparation

Soil preparation is important before installing a groundcover because it will be a permanent planting. On steep slopes, you may not be able to do much soil amending; if so, it's important to match the type of soil in the spot with a groundcover that won't mind that type of soil.

Take a soil sample six weeks before planting and have the Agricultural Extension Service office in your county send it off to be tested. Till the soil about 8 inches deep. Spread 1 to 2 inches of organic matter (compost, peat moss, finely shredded bark, or rotted leaves) over the area and till it in. Mix in a pelleted, slow-release fertilizer in the individual planting holes. Or spread 10-10-10 over the entire area and till it in.

See "When, Where, and How to Plant" in each plant profile for the spacing needs of individual groundcovers. After planting, water well with a sprinkler and mulch with 2 inches of organic matter (use pine straw on hills and slopes). On hills you may need to cover the entire area with netting to keep the soil and plants from washing away in hard rains. You should be able to find this type of netting at a nursery or garden center.

One of your most important chores the first year or two after planting ground-covers will be weeding. If you keep a thick mulch in place, it will probably be just a matter of yanking up a few stray weeds here and there. But it's important to pull weeds out when they're young—once they've become established, it's much harder to kill them. Not only are weeds unsightly, they compete with your groundcover plants for moisture and nutrients.

Patience Pays Off

Everyone who plants a groundcover gets impatient after it goes in. We all want those little plants to instantly cover the space and look full and lush. That isn't going to happen. But I can tell you how to make your groundcover grow faster: Water and fertilize it frequently. Instead of watering weekly when rainfall has been less than an inch, water deeply twice a week with a sprinkler. I mix 20-20-20 water-soluble fertilizer in a hose-end sprayer and spray a new groundcover planting every Saturday morning until the middle of August. That really helps it to take off!

Bugleweed

Ajuga reptans

If you were to attribute human characteristics to Bugleweed, two might be boldness and impatience. Those aren't necessarily bad traits for a groundcover, especially when, as with Ajuga, they're combined with two more—beauty and an easygoing disposition. Bugleweed just wants to grow, and very little can stop it. If you have a small space to fill, you'll want to choose another groundcover that's more mild-mannered. But if you desire fast coverage by a plant with fabulous foliage—shades of metallic purple, bronze, green, and pink—look no further.

Bloom Period and Color
Blue, pink, or white flower spikes in late spring or early summer.

Mature Height
2 to 6 inches

When, Where, and How to Plant

Plant anytime from the last frost of spring through early fall. Bugleweed is so adaptable it will grow anywhere from full sun to shade. However, leaves become larger when the plant is placed in shade, and you'll have to water more in sun. Any well-drained soil is best, but I successfully grew *Ajuga* in clay for years. Space plants 6 to 12 inches apart, adding a pelleted, slow-release fertilizer to the soil in the hole.

Growing Tips

Water when rainfall is less than normal. Fertilizer isn't usually needed, but after a hard winter that has left Bugleweed's leaves bedraggled, mix a water-soluble 20-20-20 fertilizer in a hose-end sprayer and spray the plants. Repeat two weeks later, if needed.

Care

Because Bugleweed spreads by underground runners, it will invade the lawn unless restrained by metal or heavy plastic edging. I just mow it down; you may dig it out if you prefer. Nematodes may be a problem (for which there is no cure), but fungal diseases and root rot are more common where soil drainage or air circulation is poor. Check with the Extension Service for controls and move the plants to well-drained soil.

Companion Planting and Design

Ajuga's traditional roles are lining pathways and playing a supporting role to a variety of flowering perennials. But I also like it combined with spring bulbs.

My Personal Favorites

Create a carpet of color with the green, pink, and white leaves of 'Burgundy Glow'. 'Pink Elf' has bronze leaves.

Creeping Juniper
Juniperus species and hybrids

When, Where, and How to Plant

Creeping Juniper has three requirements for success: sun, well-drained soil, and plenty of space to spread. If Junipers are placed in too much shade, they will die, but it often takes several years, so homeowners are left wondering what went wrong. Space plants 5 to 6 feet apart in average, well-drained soil from spring until fall. Mix into the planting hole 1/2 cup of granular 10-10-10 fertilizer or a pelleted, slow-release fertilizer for shrubs. It's vital to mulch well between the Junipers to hold down weeds. If planting on a slope, use pine straw, which isn't as likely to wash away in heavy rains as bark chips are.

Growing Tips

For the first year or two, water weekly if rainfall is less than an inch. Fertilize with a pelleted, slow-release fertilizer in April or May.

Care

Add to the mulch as needed to keep it about 3 inches thick. Remove any weeds that pop up. Junipers are subject to a number of insects and diseases, including bagworms, which may be picked off by hand in the evening. For other problems, often indicated by tips or entire branches browning and dying, check with the Extension Service for help in deciding on the proper controls.

Companion Planting and Design

Creeping Junipers are usually planted alone. They're especially popular for difficult hillsides.

My Personal Favorites

Try 'Turquoise Spreader'; the turquoise-green color really stands out on a plant that grows about 6 inches high. 'Emerald Sea' has bright green needles.

Creeping Junipers may not be the most glamorous plants in your yard, but when you need a strong, shrubby presence and fast coverage on—for instance—a slope near a street, there's nothing better. If you want a very low-growing Juniper, it's possible to find cultivars that reach no higher than 4 or 5 inches. The needles of some prostrate Junipers, such as 'Bar Harbor', 'Prince of Wales', and Blue Rug (Juniperus honizontalis 'Wiltonii'), turn a brownish-plum color in fall; others stay green or bluish-green, so you have a choice.

Mature Height

4 inches to 3 feet

Creeping Phlox
Phlox species and hybrids

Throughout the South, the most common species of this plant (Phlox subulata) is referred to as Thrift. Most of the year, Creeping Phlox isn't very noticeable, but in mid-spring, it creates sheets of shocking pink on hillsides and banks across the state. It's impossible not to be impressed. If you like the look but not that shade of pink, pick plants with white or lavender-blue blooms. Or consider other spreading phloxes: P. divaricata (pale blue), P. nivalis (white and pink), and P. pilosa (blue, pink, or white). All are excellent performers.

Bloom Period and Color
Pink, white, blue, and lavender in spring.

Mature Height
4 to 16 inches

When, Where, and How to Plant
If possible, purchase plants in spring when in bloom to match the color to those of nearby plants, making sure they don't clash. You may plant from mid-spring through the end of summer. *Phlox subulata* prefer average, well-drained soil and a sunny to partially sunny location. *P. divaricata* wants to dwell in shady, well-drained soil that has been amended with organic matter. *P. stolonifera* likes a shady to partially shady location with average, well-drained soil. If the plants' roots stay wet over winter, they will probably die. Mix a pelleted, slow-release fertilizer with the soil when planting.

Growing Tips
In hot summer months, when weekly rain totals less than an inch, water plantings regularly so the soil doesn't dry out. Otherwise, Creeping Phlox manages nicely on average rainfall. Fertilizer may not be needed. If a stand looks thin, spray with a 20-20-20 water-soluble fertilizer in spring.

Care
Shear lightly after blooming to ensure better growth. Spider mites may be a problem in dry weather. They can be prevented by spraying the foliage with water occasionally, or ask the Extension Service about a control.

Companion Planting and Design
Combine shade-tolerant types with Spanish Bluebells, Columbine, and white-flowering evergreen Azaleas. Combine sun-loving cultivars with Daffodils and Tulips in complementary shades.

My Personal Favorite
Phlox pilosa 'Moody Blue' (often sold as 'Chattahoochee') has blue flowers that have a red eye.

Creeping Thyme

Thymus praecox

When, Where, and How to Plant

From spring through summer, plant Creeping Thyme in a sunny spot that has extremely well-drained soil. This isn't a plant for clay; if it gets too wet, it dies. Rocky or sandy soils are fine. In Zone 6, place Creeping Thyme in sun most of the day. In Zone 7, it welcomes 3 or 4 hours of afternoon shade in the hottest part of the summer. Mix a pelleted, slow-release fertilizer with the soil at planting time. Space 6 to 12 inches apart.

Growing Tips

The first six weeks, water enough to keep the plants growing. After they've become established, they usually manage on their own, although you may want to water in prolonged drought. Fertilize yearly in spring with a 20-20-20 water-soluble fertilizer.

Care

After plants flower, mow them lightly with the lawn mower blade on its highest setting, or shear with a hedge trimmer. This encourages new bushy growth. If Creeping Thyme "melts" (becomes thin and anemic-looking) in hot, humid summer weather, cut it back or shear lightly. If plants become woody, rejuvenate by cutting back to 1 or 2 inches tall and letting them regrow. Creeping Thyme has few pest problems.

Companion Planting and Design

Plant Creeping Thyme in rock gardens, along pathways, and on the top of a wall so it can cascade over. Or pair it with Lamb's Ear.

My Personal Favorites

'Coccineus' has brilliant scarlet blooms. 'Albus' is white-flowered. *Thymus serphyllum* 'Minor' stays less than an inch high and has lavender blooms.

What's a nice little herb like Thyme doing in the groundcover chapter? Showing off the fact that it can do double duty in the garden. Creeping Thyme forms an aromatic mat that's often covered with flowers. Its nicest quality is that you can walk on it—and when you do, it gives off that characteristic Thyme scent. Or maybe you'll find a cultivar that smells like lemons or oranges—sniff when you buy the plants. Then place them between steppingstones and along walkways to take advantage of the fragrance.

Bloom Period and Color

Red, pink, lavender, or white flowers in late spring or early summer.

Mature Height

2 to 4 inches

English Ivy
Hedera helix

Many gardeners have regretted planting English Ivy. Not because it isn't a wonderful evergreen groundcover, but because they put it in too small a space. Ivy rule number 1: Give it room. Let it cover slopes and fill big beds beneath trees where it's too shady for grass. Ivy rule number 2: Don't be impatient. It's a fast, vigorous grower—once it gets established—but it can take up to three years to get going. An old rhyme expresses it perfectly: First it sleeps, next it creeps, then it leaps.

Mature Height
3 to 8 inches

When, Where, and How to Plant
Ivy is an adaptable groundcover that will grow in full sun (if you keep it watered) to deep shade. It also isn't fussy about soil, but green-leafed cultivars will perform better in a rich organic soil that stays moist, but not soggy. On the other hand, poor soil stimulates the growth of Ivy with variegated foliage. The ideal pH is 6 to 7, slightly acidic to neutral. Mix into the soil 2 to 3 pounds of granular 10-10-10 fertilizer per 100 square feet. Set out plants 12 inches apart from spring through summer. Mulch between plants to conserve soil moisture and keep down weeds.

Growing Tips
About six weeks after planting English Ivy, sprinkle a 20-20-20 pelleted, slow-release fertilizer over the bed. In subsequent years, use a pelleted, slow-release fertilizer in mid-spring or a 20-20-20 water-soluble fertilizer two or three times a season. Water frequently enough to keep the soil slightly moist.

Care
After exceptionally cold winters, Ivy foliage may be damaged. Be patient; it will return. To help it along, water weekly and spray with a water-soluble fertilizer. Scale (brown bumps on the bottoms of the leaves) and spider mites can be problems. Check with the Extension Service about controls.

Companion Planting and Design
Don't overlook Ivy's climbing possibilities or its potential in a hanging basket.

My Personal Favorite
'Gold Heart' is an attractive, well-behaved Ivy, which has deep-green leaves with a bright gold center and grows slowly to moderately.

Foamflower
Tiarella species and hybrids

When, Where, and How to Plant

Set out plants in spring and continue until midsummer. While you can place *Tiarella* in dappled or partial shade, it grows nicely in deep shade where many plants won't. Its main requirement is moist, but well-drained, acidic soil. If soil is dry, it will turn scrawny. And if it's where water stands over winter, it will rot. Mix a 20-20-20 pelleted fertilizer with the soil when planting. *Tiarella cordifolia* spreads by stolons; space plants 12 to 15 inches apart. Wherry's Foamflower (*Tiarella cordifolia* var. *collina*) is slower growing and develops into clumps; space plants 1 foot apart.

Growing Tips

To keep *Tiarella* thick and spreading, water when rainfall is less than normal. At the end of March, April, and May, fertilize by spraying the plants and the ground around them with a water-soluble fertilizer made for acid-loving plants.

Care

First thing in spring, and after thunderstorms, remove any tree debris that has fallen on the groundcover. If the planting isn't too large, and you'd like to keep it looking neat, cut down flower stalks after they fade. Foamflower pests are few. If the plant dies over winter, the cause is usually poor drainage.

Companion Planting and Design

Let it wander in woodland flowerbeds among Lenten Roses, spring-flowering bulbs, Ferns, Solomon's Seal, evergreen Azaleas, and Rhododendrons.

My Personal Favorite

'Cygnet' has foliage shaped much like deeply lobed oak leaves, but veined with red and pink flower spikes that reach 18 inches tall.

Foamflower proves that you can't judge a groundcover's toughness by its looks. This native plant has velvety foliage, pink buds, and airy white flowers. It's the picture of daintiness. But underneath that pretty exterior is a rugged plant that's evergreen all year—with reddish or yellow coloration in the fall. Nicest of all, it's a plant that thrives in those deeply shaded spots in the woods where you haven't been able to get anything else to grow. Before you know it, you'll have a carefree carpet of Foamflowers.

Bloom Period and Color

White or pink blooms in spring.

Mature Height

6 to 18 inches

Pachysandra
Pachysandra species and hybrids

Many groundcovers fade into the background; they're just a sea of neutral green in the landscape. Not Pachysandra. When viewed close up, its swirls of foliage add elegant texture to the landscape. The most common species (Pachysandra terminalis) is Japanese, but there's also the native Allegheny Spurge (Pachysandra procumbens), which is a nice choice for a wildflower garden. Its leaves are wider—flat green and often mottled; it also spreads somewhat more slowly. Both are very hardy and ideal for growing under trees where it's too shady for grass.

Bloom Period and Color
White or pinkish flowers in spring.

Mature Height
6 to 12 inches

When, Where, and How to Plant
Plant after the chance of frost is past in spring (and until August) in a shady spot with slightly acidic soil. Pachysandra is at home in partial to deep shade; too much sun turns the leaves yellow. This dependable groundcover prefers loose, well-drained soil that's been amended with organic matter, such as sphagnum peat or fine bark. Place plants 4 to 12 inches apart (slower-growing cultivars and *Pachysandra procumbens* at the closer spacing, if you want faster coverage; *P. terminalis* farther apart). Mix a 20-20-20 pelleted, slow-release fertilizer with the soil when planting.

Growing Tips
Water when less than an inch of rainfall has fallen during a week; the soil shouldn't be allowed to dry out completely, especially during the plants' first two years. Fertilize annually. You may spread a pelleted, slow-release fertilizer over the bed in late spring, or spray leaves and ground with a 20-20-20 water-soluble fertilizer (or a liquid fertilizer made for acid-loving plants) at the end of March, April, and May.

Care
Other than keeping tree debris picked up from the bed, Pachysandra requires no grooming. Remove any weeds that appear. If leaves turn brown and die, that's due to leaf blight. Ask the Extension Service about a recommended fungicide.

Companion Planting and Design
Compatible companions include Bleeding Heart, Astilbe, and Caladium.

My Personal Favorite
'Silver Edge' has light green foliage edged in silvery white that complements Hostas with white- and green-variegated leaves.

Spotted Dead Nettle
Lamium maculatum

When, Where, and How to Plant
Plant anytime after spring's last frost into early summer in average, well-drained soil. Spotted Dead Nettle is a plant for shady areas; it makes itself at home in either dappled or full shade. Because its marbled, veined, and variegated leaves are so attractive, try to choose a spot where it can readily be seen. Space plants 12 inches apart. Mix a pelleted, slow-release fertilizer with the soil in the hole at planting time.

Growing Tips
Water weekly if rainfall totals less than an inch. Fertilize in spring just before leaves emerge with a pelleted, slow-release fertilizer spread on top of the ground. Or, after foliage has appeared, mix a water-soluble 20-20-20 fertilizer in a hose-end sprayer and spray the plants and ground thoroughly.

Care
One of the nice things about having *Lamium maculatum* in your yard is that it doesn't require much care and isn't subject to many insects or diseases. In fall, after foliage has been killed by frost, remove it from the garden and toss onto the compost pile.

Companion Planting and Design
In light shade, the silver foliage of *Lamium* contrasts strikingly with the reddish or purple leaves of Heuchera and with red-leafed Coleus and Caladiums. It also brightens the ground beneath Rhododendrons.

My Personal Favorites
The light pink blooms of 'Pink Pewter' complement the silver leaves edged in green. 'Chequers' has flower stalks that look like Salvia and grows taller than most other cultivars, up to a foot high.

Who in the world is going to grow a plant named Dead Nettle? Or even worse, Spotted Dead Nettle? Actually, anyone who sees this groundcover's silver-splashed foliage and has a shady spot they'd like to light up. Because of its trailing habit, I've also grown Lamium in hanging baskets. Its only fault is that— although it's perennial—it isn't evergreen; in winter it disappears. Even so, you won't want to miss the beauty that Spotted Dead Nettle's marbled, heart-shaped leaves will bring to the darkest corners of your garden.

Bloom Period and Color
White, violet, or pink flowers in spring.

Mature Height
6 to 12 inches

Strawberry 'Pink Panda'
Fragaria frel 'Pink Panda'

A groundcover that also produces Strawberries? Why not? Strawberry plants produce runners that cover the ground quickly. This cultivar, developed in England, isn't your typical Strawberry, though. Its stems are red, the leaves are semi-evergreen (evergreen in mild winters), and the plants are covered with large, pink flowers in spring and fall, as well as sporadically in summer. Don't count on much fruit, though—just a few berries for your cereal, if you beat the birds to them. Still, it's an unusual and interesting choice for edging the driveway or front walk.

Bloom Period and Color
Pink flowers in spring and fall.

Mature Height
4 to 6 inches

When, Where, and How to Plant
Plant early to mid-spring. If you can obtain plants, you may also set them out in fall. Till the soil, and enrich it as you would a vegetable garden. Place the plants about 16 inches apart in full or partial sun or semi-shade. (Flowering will be better in full sun.) Mix 1 tablespoon of granular 10-10-10 fertilizer into each planting hole, or work a 20-20-20 pelleted, slow-release fertilizer into the top 4 to 6 inches of the soil. Mulch lightly, if at all, so runners can root easily.

Growing Tips
Watering during summer, when the plants produce runners, is essential. Whenever less than an inch of rain falls in a week, water to keep the soil moist. Fertilize annually in spring with a pelleted, slow-release fertilizer.

Care
Once runners have rooted and created new plants, these may be dug up with a trowel and transplanted elsewhere. If disease or insects strike, check with the Extension Service for advice.

Companion Planting and Design
Grow on the sunny edge of a partially shaded bed containing pink or white Astilbe, Bleeding Heart, and Cardinal Flower. Or plant in sun with Petunia, Dianthus, and Pentas.

My Personal Favorite
For years I've ordered Alpine Strawberries (*Fraises des Bois* in French) from White Flower Farm in Connecticut. They have smaller leaves than 'Pink Panda' and fruits the size of wild Strawberries—but with intense flavor—in spring and fall. Instead of producing runners, they spread 8 to 10 inches.

Sweet Box

Sarcococca hookerana humilis

When, Where, and How to Plant

Set out plants from spring until early fall, spacing plants several feet apart and mulching well between them. Sweet Box grows best in shady spots where the soil has been amended with plenty of organic matter, is slightly acidic, and drains well. If the plant gets too much sun, the leaves won't be very green. Mix a pelleted, slow-release fertilizer with the soil in the planting hole.

Growing Tips

For the first two years, water weekly if rainfall is less than an inch. After Sweet Box is established, it is drought-tolerant. Each March, fertilize with a water-soluble fertilizer made for acid-loving plants.

Care

Keep tree debris removed from the planting to keep it looking neat. About the only pest problem Sweet Box experiences is occasional scale, which appears as brown dots on the stems and undersides of the leaves. Call the Extension Service about a control.

Companion Planting and Design

Sweet Box creates a wonderful foil to spring-flowering bulbs—Daffodils, Tulips, and Grape Hyacinths—growing beneath deciduous trees. It also goes well with Lycoris, which flowers in later summer or early fall, and Coleus.

My Personal Favorite

I've never found named cultivars of Sweet Box at nurseries, but I did see *Sarcococca hookerana digyna* 'Purple Stem' growing in a Georgia garden. It was about 2 feet high and had purplish new growth. I was impressed with it, but don't think it would be hardy in Tennessee's Zone 6 gardens.

I'm always puzzled by the blank looks I get when I recommend this neat little evergreen plant. It has dark green, lustrous foliage, as well as blue-black berrylike fruit for birds. It grows in partial to full shade, slowly spreading to 8 feet or more. You would think a plant like that would be snapped up by everyone with a shady yard, especially since Sweet Box is an easy plant to grow. But so far, it's a well-kept secret. Maybe, between us, we can change that.

Bloom Period and Color

White flowers in very early spring.

Mature Height

8 to 18 inches

Vinca

Vinca minor

I don't know of a more attractive, easier to grow groundcover than Vinca. The glossy evergreen foliage looks nice year-round and is accented by clear blue flowers in springtime. Vinca minor has smaller leaves and is more cold hardy than Vinca major, which is better for Zone 7 as a groundcover but is ideal for containers statewide. I like to plant Daffodils so that they poke up around the edges of beds of Vinca. Just be sure you don't get the annual flower sometimes called Vinca instead of this perennial groundcover.

Bloom Period and Color
Spring in blue, white, purple, or maroon.

Mature Height
4 to 8 inches

When, Where, and How to Plant
Plant in springtime, spacing plants about a foot apart. If a neighbor with Vinca gives you some rooted cuttings, place them 6 to 8 inches from each other and keep watered well until they start growing. It grows in average well-drained soil, but you'll want to add organic matter to clay soil before planting. Shade or partial shade is ideal, but Vinca can take some sun.

Growing Tips
In its first year or two, while Vinca is putting down roots, water whenever rainfall is less than an inch a week. But once it's established, it rarely needs extra moisture. Whenever growth isn't as thick as desired or leaves aren't deep green, fill a hose-end sprayer with a water-soluble fertilizer that contains iron and spray the entire bed.

Care
When the planting is young, remove weeds regularly; once weeds get a foothold, they're difficult to eradicate. To encourage denser growth, cut the stems of mature plants back to 4 inches long in early spring with a string trimmer. If plants grow out of bounds, snip off the wayward pieces and root them to make new plants.

Companion Planting and Design
Grow Vinca in drifts beneath shrubs or trees and interplant it with bulbs, such as Crocus, Snowflakes, and Daffodils. Let *Vinca major* trail over the edge of container plantings.

My Personal Favorites
The white-edged leaves of 'Argenteo-variegata' are very appealing. They remind me of my favorite green-and-white Hostas and show up well at night. 'Mrs. Jekyll' has nice white blooms.

Wild Ginger
Asarum species and hybrids

When, Where, and How to Plant

You can put Wild Ginger—so named for the gingery fragrance of its roots—in the garden almost anytime the ground isn't frozen, but spring to summer is best. Choose a spot with plenty of shade and moist soil that's been enriched with lots of organic matter. Mix a pelleted, slow-release fertilizer into the planting hole. Space plants 6 to 10 inches apart (12 inches for *Asarum canadense*, which spreads more quickly). Mulch with pine straw.

Growing Tips

Wild Ginger welcomes watering when weather is drier than normal. Aim to keep the soil moist. I have never fertilized my plants. Decaying mulch and an occasional dressing with compost (spread on top of the soil around the plant) have kept them growing well.

Care

When Wild Ginger is growing beneath deciduous trees, remove fall leaves so they don't completely cover the evergreen leaves of Wild Ginger and so kill them. Although this plant spreads, it isn't invasive or even aggressive. If it overgrows its bounds, just pull up the extra plants. Occasionally slugs—which may pollinate the inconspicuous little flowers—can eat holes in the leaves. If the damage becomes serious, set up saucers of beer or yeast mixed with water to trap them.

Companion Planting and Design

Wild Ginger sets off a host of blooming wildflowers as well as Ferns, Azaleas, Rhododendrons, and Dogwoods.

My Personal Favorite

Asarum shuttleworthii 'Callaway' has rounded evergreen leaves that are extensively mottled with silver.

As soon as I spied the glossy, heart-shaped leaves veined in silver, I fell in love with Wild Ginger. That was ten years ago and nothing that has happened since has changed my mind about this delightful native plant with its "little brown jug" blooms. In fact, I've added more to my wooded yard. For an extensive groundcover, you may want to stick with the evergreen species. But for an interesting accent in a shady wildflower garden, the deciduous Canadian Ginger (Asarum canadense) is fine. It's also the most hardy.

Bloom Period and Color

Reddish-brown in spring.

Mature Height

4 to 9 inches

Perennials *for Tennessee*

Perennials are my favorite plants. They offer such a tremendous variety of shapes, sizes, colors, types, and blooming times that I never tire of them. Spring-flowering Candytuft creeps along the edges of flowerbeds, white and pristine. At 6 feet tall, Joe-Pye Weed towers over the garden in fall. And in between, a succession of perennial flowers come into bloom.

Unlike annuals, which usually bloom from spring until fall, perennials are in flower for a shorter period of time, occasionally as little as two weeks. This timing varies from species to species and offers the gardener the opportunity to plan a progression of bloom.

Practice Makes Perfect

This process of having at least one group of perennials in flower throughout the growing season depends heavily on your learning bloom periods through reading, observation, and trial and error. On your first attempt, you may find that all your flowers have finished blooming by the end of June, then there's nothing of interest for the rest of the year. That's when you realize you need to extend your seasonal palette to include plants that flower in midsummer and those that bloom in fall. Especially valuable in this quest are rebloomers—many Daylilies flower in June and again later in the season—and repeat bloomers (Gaillardia, for instance, and also some Daylilies, such as 'Stella de Oro').

Often catalogs or books will say that a certain perennial "blooms from spring until frost." Take that with the proverbial grain of salt. It may flower that long in Minnesota or New England, but it's a fact of life in Tennessee gardens that very few perennials bloom all summer because of our heat and humidity.

A perennial is defined as a plant that returns to the garden year after year. "Perennial" doesn't necessarily mean "permanent," however.

Some perennial flowers live long lives (Peony comes to mind), while others, such as Gaillardia, may return for two to three years and then have to be replanted.

How to Be Successful Growing Perennials

Because perennials stay in the same place for at least several years, it's important to prepare the soil carefully before planting. Till or dig the soil at least 12 inches deep and mix it with organic matter—peat moss, well-rotted mushroom compost, fine bark, compost, and so forth. This will improve drainage, which is essential to almost all perennials.

The number one reason perennials don't return in spring is that soil drainage is poor and plant roots stood in too much water over winter. If you don't want to spend the time or energy to amend flower beds with drainage-improving organic matter, plant perennials in raised beds instead.

It's always a good idea to have your soil tested anytime you're planting a new bed. For a small fee, your local Agricultural Extension Service office will send samples off to be tested in a laboratory. The results will not only tell you the pH of your soil (whether it's acidic, alkaline, or somewhere in between), but they will also give fertilizer recommendations.

Perennials look best in groupings of uneven numbers, such as three or five. Except for massive plants, rarely should they be planted singly. For the best aesthetic effect, also vary flower and foliage forms. Although perennials with daisy-type blossoms are among the easiest to grow, an entire garden of round flowers is rather dull.

Occasionally, mail order companies will send bare-root perennials. These should be soaked in water (or in water mixed with a transplant solution) for several hours before planting.

Some perennials require staking for best appearance. Double-flowered Peonies, for example, often end up facedown in the mud when it rains while they're in bloom. Placing an inconspicuous support around the plant as soon as it begins growing in spring can prevent this. Look through catalogs and garden centers for a variety of long-lasting supports made for various kinds of perennials. These go way beyond the old green-stained bamboo sticks. But if staking is a chore you'd prefer to avoid, choose species and cultivars that don't need to be supported.

Sometimes perennials get floppy because they've been overfertilized, especially with too much nitrogen. I rarely feed my perennials. I use a pelleted, slow-release fertilizer around Hostas in spring and that's about it, unless a plant looks a bit peaked or isn't growing as well as it should. Then I may spray it once or twice with a water-soluble plant food. This regimen assumes that the soil has been improved before planting takes place and that organic mulches are allowed to rot and provide a gentle dose of nutrients. You'll probably find that in average soil, perennials need less fertilizer than most of the other plants in your garden.

Care of perennials is ongoing from spring until fall, as various kinds bloom at different times. Deadhead your perennials (clip off the faded flowers) . With many types, you may then get rebloom. And even if you don't, you'll prevent rampant reseeding and the garden will look neater. Plants, such as Black-eyed Susan and Coreopsis, which have seeds much favored by birds, are the exception. By leaving the old seedheads on the plants, you may sacrifice some reblooming but you will feed your feathered friends.

In fall, after a hard frost, cut down the stalks and stems and toss them onto the compost pile. (Be sure that you don't include any seeds, or you'll have new plants popping up everywhere you apply the compost the next year!)

Sharing the Rewards

Eventually, most perennials get crowded and stop blooming as profusely as they did in the past. That's a sign to the gardener that they need to be separated, or dug up, divided, and then replanted farther apart. To put this chore off for as long as possible, avoid crowding your perennials when you plant—space them so that they have elbow room. This is especially important with plants such as Hostas, which don't like to be divided and take a year or so to recover.

How you divide a perennial varies somewhat with the type of plant. But the basic procedure is to wait for a relatively cool, overcast day and carefully dig up the entire clump. Work the roots apart—discarding old sections that no longer bloom—then replant the newer sections. This is easier and faster if two people work together and if you—or rainfall—have soaked the soil first.

Division may be done in spring or fall. I prefer spring, but if you choose to wait until autumn, don't put it off too long. The new plants need to establish their roots before cold weather arrives; otherwise, the plants may be killed by low temperatures.

After you've dug up the clump, shake and wash the soil off so you can see what you're doing. If the plant's root system is large, tease it into sections using two spading forks (this is where a partner comes in handy). With smaller sections of roots, you may be able to do the separating with a sharp knife. The pieces along the outside of the root system are generally the youngest and most vigorous. Excessively woody sections in the middle may be discarded (this applies particularly to Chrysanthemums).

Place the new divisions in a pail of water to soak while you finish dividing other plants; then replant immediately. That's all there is to it. Once you're finished, you have a number of new plants for other spots in the garden or to share with friends and neighbors. It's a nice reward for all your labors!

Anemone

Anemone × hybrida

When you plan a perennial border in which you want to have something in flower from spring until fall, the most difficult plants to find are the late-season bloomers. Enter Anemone. There are three types, one of which is a spring-flowering bulb. But hybrid Anemone—often called Japanese Anemone—and Anemone tomentosa are perennials that bloom in autumn. And, unlike most fall-flowering perennials, Anemone has delicate, not bold, blossoms. The pink, white, or red flowers sway in the slightest breeze on slender stems, giving rise to the name Windflowers.

Bloom Period and Color
Late summer and fall in white, rose, and pink.

Mature Height × Spread
2 to 5 feet × 2 to 3 feet

Zones
6, 7a

When, Where, and How to Plant
Plant container-grown Anemones in early spring or early fall, preferably in a partially shady spot. You may need to experiment to find the ideal soil. It should be moist (or kept moist by watering), but very well drained. Standing water over winter will kill Anemones. Amend poor or average soil with organic matter to add humus and improve drainage. Space clumps 1 to 2 feet apart and keep mulched.

Growing Tips
Unfortunately, Anemones don't do as well in the warmest parts of Tennessee (Zone 7b) as they will in the cooler sections. The plants can't tolerate drought, so water enough to keep the soil evenly moist at all times. As with most perennials, Anemones require little if any fertilizer if growing in good soil. Too much nitrogen causes fast, floppy growth. Renew mulch as needed so that it stays about 2 inches thick.

Care
Anemones form large clumps that can be invasive, or at least aggressive, spreaders. Pull up runners if needed. Divide clumps every three years. Tall stems may need staking; do this early in the season so the plants aren't flattened by thunderstorms. You should encounter few insects or diseases.

Companion Planting and Design
In partial shade, grow with Hostas, Ferns, and Carex. Turtlehead (*Chelone*) has similar flower colors and blooms near the same time.

My Personal Favorite
'Honorine Jobert' is a very old plant that bears an abundant crop of white flowers filled with contrasting yellow stamens.

Artemisia

Artemisia 'Powis Castle'

When, Where, and How to Plant
In spring, set out purchased plants (or your own rooted cuttings taken the previous summer) in any garden soil that drains well. If soil isn't well drained, plants will turn black and die. Space plants 3 feet apart on all sides. Artemisias prefer full sun, but won't object to an hour or two—no more—of afternoon shade. Don't fertilize at planting time—this causes overly rampant growth and floppy stems. Also, to avoid keeping the soil too moist, don't mulch.

Growing Tips
Once 'Powis Castle' has started growing, it shouldn't need watering from then on. No fertilizer is necessary, either. Wouldn't it be wonderful if all plants demanded this little of a gardener?

Care
Prune 'Powis Castle' in spring, when needed. If the plants flop over in summer, cut them back to 2 inches tall. Pinching the tips of the stems throughout the season keeps Artemisia compact and provides cuttings, which root easily in a mixture of one part sand to one part packaged potting soil. If you notice yellow spots on the plants' lower leaves, this is a sign of rust, a fungal disease that can develop in humid conditions. Cut the plant back to the ground, removing all leaves from the garden and destroying them.

Companion Planting and Design
Artemisia is an excellent filler plant with Antique or English Roses, Asters, Purple Coneflowers, flowering shrubs, and perennials.

My Personal Favorite
Artemisia schmidtiana 'Silverado' is a mounded form that tends not to melt in our climate, either.

Plants with gray or silver foliage are useful in the garden because of their softening effect and the way they complement many colors of flowers. But it's an unfortunate fact of life that gray-leafed plants don't like the heat—and especially the humidity—of the South. Gardeners often call this typical midsummer decline "melting." But 'Powis Castle' is one Artemisia that won't melt in the dog days of August, and it also won't take over, as some aggressive species may. Like all Artemisias, it's drought-tolerant, too. All that plus it's good-looking.

Bloom Period and Color
Grown for lace-cut, silvery gray leaves from summer to fall.

Mature Height × Spread
3 feet × 3 feet

Baptisia

Baptisia species and hybrids

Baptisia is a plant with a past. A native, it was used in the 1700s as a substitute for Indigo—which wouldn't grow in the U.S.—to make dye for cloth. That's how it got its common name, False Indigo. There are two types gardeners will enjoy: Baptisia australis *(sometimes called Blue False Indigo) and* Baptisia alba *(White False Indigo). Both produce stalks of pea-like blooms. White Baptisia is shorter than Blue Baptisia and blooms a few weeks later. You'll probably want both; they make a fine combination.*

Bloom Period and Color
Spring in blue or white.

Mature Height × Spread
3 to 4 feet × 4 to 5 feet

When, Where, and How to Plant
For maximum growth, plant in rich organic soil that drains well, but Baptisia tolerates average soil. The blue form needs full sun, but the white type will do nicely in partial shade or sun. Set out plants in spring, or sow fresh seed in late summer. Space plants 3 feet apart where they are to grow; once established, transplanting is difficult. Mulch with organic matter to keep the soil cool.

Growing Tips
Water regularly—so that the plants don't wilt—until established, then Baptisia is drought-tolerant. Plants are slow to begin blooming—a few flowers the second year and then it can take some time (up to five years, for seed-grown plants) for Baptisia to reach its full glory. You can encourage the plants along by spreading a pelleted, slow-release fertilizer over the soil in spring. If leaves turn yellow prematurely during the summer, use a water-soluble fertilizer for flowering plants that contains iron.

Care
Young plants, or those grown in partial shade, may need staking. Keep faded flowers cut off to promote continuing bloom. You may let the last flowers go to seed, if you like—the graceful seedpods make rustling noises in the breeze; cut while they still rattle to dry for arrangements. Watch out for voles.

Companion Planting and Design
Grow Baptisia with Bearded Iris, Shasta Daisies, Black-eyed Susans, and Cleome, which appreciate similar conditions.

My Personal Favorites
Baptisia pendula 'Alba' has a slightly weeping habit and white flowers. 'Purple Smoke' is lavender-gray.

Black-Eyed Susan
Rudbeckia species and hybrids

When, Where, and How to Plant
In spring, plant Black-eyed Susan in any soil that drains well and is in full or partial sun. Space plants of *Rudbeckia fulgida* species and 'Goldsturm' 18 inches apart, Cutleaf Coneflower (*Rudbeckia laciniata*) 1 foot apart, and *Rudbeckia nitida* 2 feet apart. Mulch lightly.

Growing Tips
Water frequently to keep the root zone moist until the plants are established; mature plants are drought-tolerant. Fertilizer isn't usually necessary except in very poor soil; in that case, spread a pelleted, slow-release formula for flowers once in spring. Or use a water-soluble flower fertilizer monthly during the growing season. Leave the plants standing in fall to provide seeds for the birds. Or you may cut the seed heads when dry in fall and save the seeds to plant in flats in late winter for spring transplanting.

Care
Divide *Rudbeckia* every three years in spring or early fall, but lift offsets and new seedlings anytime during the growing season. Replant them immediately, or pot them up and place in the garden later. This isn't a demanding plant—no pinching or pruning and few pests. Spider mites may occur in very dry sites at midsummer; spray with water once a week to prevent. Mildew may appear in late fall but is inconsequential.

Companion Planting and Design
Compatible sun lovers are Butterfly Weed, red-leafed Coleus, and Ornamental Grasses.

My Personal Favorite
'Goldsturm' is one flower that should be in every perennial garden.

Hardy Rudbeckia *warms up every bed with its golden yellow-orange shades. The one most easily found in nurseries is* Rudbeckia *'Goldsturm', which grows about 2 feet high and is a blooming machine from summer until fall, if you keep faded flowers removed. Be careful when you buy plants, since some* Rudbeckia, *such as the impressive hybrids of* Rudbeckia hirta, *are annuals. And a few—usually called Coneflowers—may reach an impressive 5 to 7 feet tall. Nice if you have room, but 'Goldsturm' is the best all-around choice.*

Bloom Period and Color
Summer to fall in gold and yellow.

Mature Height × Spread
8 inches to 3 feet × 18 inches

Bleeding Heart
Dicentra spectabilis

Take dangling heart-shaped flowers, arch them over deeply cut leaves in shades of green, gray, and blue, and the lovely result is Bleeding Heart. If you've got a shade garden, you'll want to overlook the gory name (or call it Dicentra) and grow this plant, since it's a must for every yard in spring. You'll find several choices of species—I especially like the fernlike leaves of Fringed Bleeding Heart (Dicentra eximia), which is native. But also consider many of the new hybrids, which bloom into summer and fall.

Bloom Period and Color
Late spring (or sometimes summer and early fall) with pink, red, or white flowers.

Mature Height × Spread
8 to 24 inches × 12 to 18 inches

When, Where, and How to Plant
Prepare the soil for *Dicentra* by adding organic matter to produce a nutrient-rich soil that will drain quickly, but not dry out between waterings. Plant dormant roots or purchased plants in spring. Space plants or roots 18 inches to 2 feet apart in shade or part-shade. Mulch lightly.

Growing Tips
Water deeply in spring when rainfall is less than normal to keep the soil moist and cool. If plants wilt in spring, water more often and add mulch. Fertilize with a balanced, slow-release, pelleted fertilizer when leaves appear every year.

Care
Little ongoing care is needed and few pests trouble *Dicentra*. The leaves of common Bleeding Heart will turn yellow and disappear by early summer. It's normal for the plant to go dormant this way; don't think you've done anything wrong. It will return next year. Pull up plants that result from self-sown seed; their flowers won't look like the parent plant. Crowded clumps can be divided in spring or fall. Cut pieces of the rhizome with two to four buds (or eyes) each. But avoid dividing unless the plant is over-crowded; it takes several years for plants to recover.

Companion Planting and Design
This is an excellent woodland plant with Ferns, Hostas, and Foamflower. Use rose-colored Impatiens to mask clumps of Bleeding Heart leaves going dormant.

My Personal Favorites
'Pantaloons' has pure white blossoms that combine nicely with many more brightly colored spring flowers. 'Luxuriant' has fire-engine-red blooms and blue-green foliage.

Boltonia

Boltonia asteroides

When, Where, and How to Plant

Unless you don't mind plants that flop over—or you're prepared to stake—Boltonia has to be grown in full sun. Excellent drainage is another essential. The plant prefers fertile soil, but grows in poor to average soil—it will just be shorter (which you may not mind at all). Plant in spring. Set plants at least 2 to 3 feet apart, or more, on all sides. Use a root stimulator at planting time, or mix a pelleted, slow-release fertilizer into the soil. Mulch lightly.

Growing Tips

Apply 20-20-20 pelleted, slow-release fertilizer each spring. Established plants are drought tolerant, but plants and flowers will be smaller if plants aren't watered in dry spells.

Care

Boltonia can be pruned down to 2 feet in late June to create a denser clump that will be shorter and bloom a bit later with better-looking lower leaves. Few if any pests or diseases bother Boltonia. Leave the plants standing after they've been killed by frost to attract goldfinches to your yard.

Companion Planting and Design

Boltonia is essential for naturalized plantings and to add fine texture and light colors to bolder, fall-blooming perennial borders. Grow with Asters, Chrysanthemums, Sedum 'Autumn Joy', and Goldenrod.

My Personal Favorites

'Snowbank' is considered the best flowering and least lanky cultivar; it grows 3 to 4 feet tall and about as wide. 'Nana' is a "dwarf" cultivar (2 to 3 feet tall) with purple flowers; it never needs staking.

I love daisylike flowers in the garden. Some people dismiss them as "common," but I think they're cheerful. They also go nicely with other plants and are always easy to grow. Boltonia embodies each of those qualities and adds one more that makes it a must in the sunny garden: It's completely covered with flowers in late summer and early fall when few other perennials are putting on a performance. You'll find a pink cultivar, if you're not fond of white and yellow; there's even a native with purple flowers.

Bloom Period and Color

Late summer and early fall in white, violet, or pink.

Mature Height × Spread

4 to 6 feet × 4 feet

Butterfly Weed
Asclepias tuberosa

As its name implies, Butterfly Weed attracts the "winged jewels" by the dozens, especially the beautiful monarch butterflies. (It also provides nectar for moths at night.) But I'd grow this attractive native plant even if it didn't. I love the bright orange flower clusters sitting atop shiny green leaves. And it couldn't be simpler to grow: As long as you place it in sun, it's carefree. New hybrids feature red or yellow blooms, but in Tennessee, orange is likely to top the popularity poll for some years to come.

Bloom Period and Color
Summer in orange, red, pink, yellow, or white.

Mature Height × Spread
2 to 3 feet × 2 feet

When, Where, and How to Plant
Plant in spring in a sunny spot that has average, well-drained soil. Too little sun and the plants will flop over. Too much moisture—especially in winter—and they won't return. Choose the location carefully: Mature Butterfly Weed has a deep taproot that usually breaks apart fatally in transplanting. Space 10 to 12 inches apart, and use a root stimulator when planting. Mulch lightly, if at all.

Growing Tips
Established plants are drought-tolerant and rarely need watering. Unless plants aren't growing well, they won't need fertilizer.

Care
Remove faded flowers to encourage a longer blooming time. Few pests bother Butterfly Weed except for aphids. Dislodge them with a blast of water from a garden hose and spray with insecticidal soap. Caterpillars found munching the plants will be the larvae of the monarch butterfly; don't kill them. If they do too much damage, see if you can transfer them to Butterfly Weed or Milkweed plants in the wild. Instead of dividing clumps, cut back plants to rejuvenate. If you deadheaded the first flowers, leave the second ones on the stems so that the purple pods—great for dried arrangements—will open in late fall.

Companion Planting and Design
Ideal for a wildflower meadow, this plant looks nice paired with Shasta Daisy, Black-eyed Susan, and Red Hot Poker.

My Personal Favorites
'Hello Yellow' has flowers exactly the color you would expect. Swamp Milkweed (*Asclepias incarnata*) is ideal for those always-damp spots in your yard.

Candytuft

Iberis sempervirens

When, Where, and How to Plant

Well-drained soil is a necessity for Candytuft. Full sun is also recommended; flowering will be less in partial shade. If necessary, amend average soil with organic matter to improve drainage. Plant in spring, using a root stimulator or transplant solution. Space plants 8 inches apart and mulch well with pine straw or finely shredded bark.

Growing Tips

When rain is below normal, water deeply, then let soil dry out slightly before watering again. If you're growing varieties that flower in fall as well as spring, these need to be watered weekly during summer, particularly if temperatures are high. Fertilizer isn't usually necessary, but you may want to apply a 20-20-20 pelleted, slow-release fertilizer after you cut back the plants when they've finished blooming.

Care

Cut Candytuft back by half after flowering to rejuvenate the plant and promote flowering in late spring and sometimes in fall. If the plant dies out in the center, prune it to several inches tall in late spring. Never prune Candytuft in fall; you'll be removing the next spring's flowers. Insect and disease problems should be few. If plants rot, the drainage wasn't good enough. Try another spot.

Companion Planting and Design

Let Candytuft spill over the edges of a flower bed or rock wall. Use as edging around spring bulb plantings, or combine with Dianthus.

My Personal Favorites

'Snowflake' produces many 2-inch flowers on a plant that gets to be 10 inches high. 'Autumn Snow' is the best fall-blooming Candytuft that I've tried.

Gardeners who want their yards to look neat and tidy appreciate the pure white flowers and the glossy evergreen foliage of Candytuft, which spreads to form a compact mound. It seems to shine like glossy snow on sunny March days. If temperatures stay cool, Candytuft blooms a long time, accenting a variety of spring-flowering plants. Several cultivars flower in fall as well as spring—provided you keep them well watered over the summer and the weather isn't too hot. Be sure to get perennial Candytuft; there are annual forms, too.

Bloom Period and Color

Early spring in white.

Mature Height × Spread

4 to 12 inches tall × 6 to 18 inches

Cardinal Flower
Lobelia cardinalis

A list of Cardinal Flower's attributes makes it sound too good to be true. It grows in part sun or shade, blooms in late summer when few other perennials do, produces tall spikes of brilliant red flowers much loved by hummingbirds, and self-sows so you always have a group of Cardinal Flowers. As if that weren't enough, it also stays in flower for at least three weeks. And it's ideal for those places in your yard that always stay damp. There simply aren't any excuses for not growing Cardinal Flower.

Bloom Period and Color
Late summer in red or pink.

Mature Height × Spread
2 to 4 feet × 2 feet

When, Where, and How to Plant
Set out plants in spring in rich, organic soil that has been amended with compost or other organic material so it retains moisture. Space plants 18 to 24 inches apart in part shade or part sun. Mix a pelleted, slow-release fertilizer into the planting hole. Mulch well with organic matter.

Growing Tips
Watering often enough to keep the soil moist is the key; otherwise, flowers are fewer and plants don't return the next year. If you have a group of Cardinal Flowers in an area of dry soil, it's worthwhile installing a soaker hose to keep them gently watered. Fertilizer usually isn't needed, but if lower leaves turn yellow, spray with a water-soluble fertilizer made for flowering plants that contains iron.

Care
Pruning, pinching, and dividing are seldom needed. When growing in moist soil, it should have few insects or diseases. Aphids and spider mites may be a problem in dry sites. Ask the Extension Service about controls, and water more often. Cardinal Flower can be short-lived; to make sure you always have plants, pull back the mulch around plants after flowering to enable reseeding.

Companion Planting and Design
Plant Cardinal Flower with Flag Iris near a water garden, or use it in a shady corner near the house to bring hummingbirds into viewing range from a window.

My Personal Favorites
'Rose Beacon' has rosy-pink flowers on 40-inch stems. 'Shrimp Salad' is an unusual color for Cardinal Flowers—a soft, shrimp pink.

Chrysanthemum
Dendranthema × grandiflorum

When, Where, and How to Plant

Plant florist Mums outdoors anytime weather is frost-free. Set out bedding plants in a sunny spot in spring, watering with a transplant solution, and mixing a pelleted, slow-release fertilizer with the soil. Avoid areas with dusk-to-dawn lights; Chrysanthemums won't bloom without nighttime darkness. Provide well-drained soil amended with organic matter. Because Mums have shallow roots, mulch is essential.

Growing Tips

Mums need regular watering to ensure that the soil doesn't dry out. Beginning in June, use a water-soluble fertilizer for flowering plants every other week until buds form. Don't fertilize after buds open.

Care

From late spring to July 15, occasionally pinch 2 inches off the tips of the stems. If you don't, they'll bloom in summer, not fall, when you really need the color. Pinching will also cause the plant to form a more compact shape and be less likely to require staking. If aphids or spider mites appear, ask the Extension Service about a control. After plants are killed by frost, wait until spring to cut them back. Every other spring, dig up and divide the plant, discarding the woody center portion.

Companion Planting and Design

Garden Mums make a show *en masse* in drifts where annuals might otherwise be used—between the sidewalk and driveway or street. Use them in perennial beds near other fall bloomers, such as Asters.

My Personal Favorite

Dendranthema zawadskii (*Chrysanthemum rubellum*) 'Clara Curtis' is easy to grow and has deep pink, daisylike blooms on a 2-foot plant.

It simply wouldn't feel like fall without colorful Chrysanthemums. Most of us buy them then, already in bloom. Or, hating to throw them away, we place pots of florist Mums we've bought or received as gifts in the garden once the weather has warmed up. But it's also enjoyable to buy Mums as small plants in spring and grow them to blooming size in fall. It's like the difference in buying a cake at a bakery and making one from scratch; you get a nice feeling of satisfaction from it.

Bloom Period and Color

Fall in white, yellow, pink, and shades of red, orange, and purple.

Mature Height × Spread

10 to 48 inches × 10 to 30 inches

Columbine

Aquilegia species and hybrids

I can't imagine a wildflower garden without Columbine in it. Practically everyone knows the plant, even if they don't know its name, because of the distinctive—often two-toned—nodding flowers and fan-shaped leaves that are Columbine's trademarks. Not only are they essential for wildflower plantings, they're also musts for attracting butterflies and humming-birds. But grow them also for their sheer beauty. If you haven't seen Columbine recently, you'll be surprised at the new flower colors and appealing variegated leaves. If breeders improve disease-resistance, it could become the almost perfect plant.

Bloom Period and Color
Spring in red, yellow, white, blue, purple, or pink.

Mature Height × Spread
9 inches to 3 feet × 1 foot

When, Where, and How to Plant
Plant Columbine in sun or shade any-time during the growing season they're available. Mid-spring and partial shade are preferred, but the plant is adaptable. Add organic matter to create a rich soil that holds moisture but drains rapidly. Space plants about 1 foot apart. Mulch to cool soil and increase moisture-holding capacity, but do not bury the crown, especially in winter.

Growing Tips
Water as needed so that the soil stays just moist. Fertilizer is rarely required; the breakdown of the mulch is usually suffi-cient to gently feed the plant. Renew the mulch each spring. Columbines rarely live more than a few years, so if the plants don't return one spring, it's probably not something you did.

Care
If you don't want the plants to reseed, remove the flowers as they fade. Or you may want to deadhead the first flowers to encourage more blooms, then allow the second blooms to reseed. Columbine is subject to a large number of insects, from caterpillars (which devour leaves) to leaf miners (which leave little "trails" in the foliage). Check with the Extension Service about controls.

Companion Planting and Design
Plant Columbines at the front of a border or along a walk where their delicate nature can be appreciated. Interplant with peren-nials that flower later in the year—Asters in sun, Ferns and Hostas in shade.

My Personal Favorites
'Crimson Star' has eye-catching red and white blooms. 'Lime Frost' has beautiful yellow-and-green variegated leaves on a plant that grows 18 to 20 inches tall.

Coreopsis
Coreopsis grandiflora

When, Where, and How to Plant
Set out Coreopsis plants in spring after the chance of frost has passed and continue until early September. Plant 12 to 18 inches apart in a sunny spot that has average, well-drained soil.

Growing Tips
Coreopsis is one of the easiest perennials to grow. It needs no fertilizer and, although you should water regularly while the plants are young, mature ones are generally drought-tolerant. Taller cultivars tend to get beaten down by thunderstorms and may need some support.

Care
The easiest way to deadhead Coreopsis is with handpruners or loppers. (If you have many plants, pinching them off by hand can be time-consuming.) Removing faded flowers encourages reblooming, prevents reseeding, and makes the flower bed look neater. But if you leave the seedpods on the plants, they entice large numbers of goldfinches. I wouldn't trade any amount of tidiness for the entertainment provided by these acrobatic birds standing on their heads to get at the seeds. Divide Coreopsis every three years to keep it blooming well. Knock aphids off with a stream of water or spray with insecticidal soap.

Companion Planting and Design
Coreopsis grandiflora is excellent for massing. Or add a few plants to a flower border near Shasta Daisy 'Becky' and Goldenrod. Place *Coreopsis verticillata* near annuals or perennials with pastel pink or blue flowers.

My Personal Favorites
'Early Sunrise' stays less than 2 feet tall and blooms the longest. 'Zagreb' is charming at the front of a border.

One spring I dug up all the shrubs along my front walkway and planted perennials instead. Into one section went six Coreopsis grandiflora. Two years later—thanks to the plant's habit of reseeding—I had a row 6 feet long and 3 feet wide. In mid-May, it became a sea of sunshiny yellow, putting on such a show that strangers would stop and ask what that plant was. Although it doesn't call as much attention to itself, Threadleaf Coreopsis (Coreopsis verticillata) has also earned a place in my garden.

Bloom Period and Color
Bright yellow to gold flowers in May and June.

Mature Height × Spread
1 to 3 feet × 6 to 18 inches

Daylily
Hemerocallis hybrids

There's much more to Daylilies than the gangly orange ones that bloom along roadsides or 'Stella de Oro'. 'Stella' has the wonderful trait of blooming numerous times through the season, but don't stop with it. Attend a Daylily show or visit a local grower (they're located throughout Tennessee), and you'll find spidery flowers in colors that appear to be dusted with gold or silver (or maybe fairy dust!). The curved and ruffled blossoms are what I love. Today's Daylilies are really something to look at—and they're as carefree as ever.

Bloom Period and Color
Late spring to fall in every color except true white and blue.

Mature Height × Spread
6 inches to 6 feet × 18 inches to 3 feet

When, Where, and How to Plant
Daylilies will survive in nearly any soil, but for optimum growth and flowering, amend soil with organic matter. Plant tuberous roots in spring after frosts have passed and purchased plants anytime from spring until late summer. Space them 1 to 2 feet apart in partial to full sun. Add a pelleted, slow-release fertilizer to the planting hole.

Growing Tips
Keep new plantings moist until growth appears. Then water when rainfall is below normal. To ensure a second crop of flowers, give rebloomers an inch of water weekly from the end of the first flowering period till new buds are formed. Daylilies are drought-tolerant once established, but will deliver fewer flowers when neglected. Fertilize with a slow-release plant food each spring after leaves appear or use a water-soluble fertilizer for flowering plants every other week during the growing season.

Care
Keep faded flowers picked off and don't allow seedpods to form. Cut down the stalks completely after flowering, but allow leaves to stand until killed by a freeze. Divide crowded clumps in spring. Daylilies experience few pests.

Companion Planting and Design
Daylilies can fill a bed on their own or are nice paired with Daffodils and perennials that bloom through the rest of the year.

My Personal Favorites
'Happy Returns' is a good repeat-bloomer. 'Winning Ways' is an old favorite in a beautiful yellow that never fails to look wonderful, no matter what the weather when it blooms.

When, Where, and How to Plant

Ferns demand a rich, organic soil to thrive and the more sunlight they receive, the more necessary constant moisture is to them. Shade or part shade is ideal for most, but read the plant's label to be sure. Plant from spring through summer, spacing plants 2 to 3 feet apart, depending on mature size. Mix a pelleted, slow-release fertilizer with the soil in the planting hole. Mulch with leaf mold or other organic matter.

Growing Tips

Consistent moisture is critical to success. The easiest way to keep the soil cool and moist is to use soaker hoses or sprinklers on timers. Spread a pelleted, slow-release fertilizer on top of the mulch each spring and water in.

Care

Ferns are excellent plants for low-maintenance landscapes. If you plant them in the shade and give them ample moisture, few pests should bother them. Gardeners also need do no pruning or pinching, just remove the occasional browned frond. Some Ferns have a habit that's known as self-shedding; their leaves will fall off in autumn. After they do, rake them up. But if the foliage withers in place, leave it over winter to protect the plant's crown; remove in early spring before new growth starts.

Companion Planting and Design

Enjoy Cinnamon Fern for excellent fall color, then trim off the bronze fronds and use in fall arrangements. Line a stream or water garden with Ferns, or sprinkle them throughout a woodland garden.

My Personal Favorite

Lady Fern (*Athyrium felix-femina*) is lacy and delicate.

There are so many Deciduous Ferns that it's hard to tell them apart without a scorecard. A few are distinctive: Cinnamon Fern (Osmunda cinnamomea) has impressive cinnamon-colored fronds that are nice in arrangements. Japanese Painted Fern (Athyrium nipponicum 'Pictum') has grayish leaves that sometimes take on a blue or red cast. Royal Fern (Osmunda regalis) grows 6 feet tall and 4 feet wide. But the plainer species are also valuable for their grace and charm. Be sure, when choosing, that you don't get one that spreads if you have little space.

Mature Height × Spread

1 to 6 feet × 1 to 4 feet

Dianthus species and hybrids

When, Where, and How to Plant

All Dianthus need full sun and any soil that's slightly alkaline and drains well. If your soil is acidic, you may need to lime it in fall before planting in spring. Space according to type: Sweet William at 10 to 12 inches apart, mat-forming Pinks at least 15 inches apart. Mulch Sweet William lightly, but not the ground-huggers.

Growing Tips

Avoid overwatering, which can lead to leaf diseases, but water will be needed during drought. If plants are growing in poor soil, fertilize in spring, before buds form, with a water-soluble fertilizer made for flowers. Sweet William may do better if fertilized monthly.

Care

Keep Dianthus deadheaded to promote reblooming and to keep the plants looking neat. Cut Sweet William's flower stalks to the ground after each flowering, but shear Pinks. Dianthus plants aren't long-lived and need to be divided every few years. Divide Sweet William every three years or so; cut stems will root easily in summer. Dig up spreading Pinks after the third year and cut into several chunks for replanting. You'll encounter few pest problems, except Sweet William is attractive to rabbits.

Companion Planting and Design

Grow low, spreading types at the front of a border or in rock gardens. Or combine with Candytuft and Tulips or Heuchera.

My Personal Favorites

'Laced Hero' has patterned burgundy-and-white blooms. 'Bath's Pink' is considered the best Southern performer.

The old-fashioned name for this group of plant is Pinks: Allwood Pinks (Dianthus × allwoodii), Cheddar Pinks (D. gratianopoli-tanus), Cottage Pinks (D. plumarius), and Maiden Pinks (D. deltoides). Even Sweet William (D. barbatus) can be considered part of the group—although officially a biennial, it acts like a perennial in Tennessee. All have flowers that are spicily fragrant and are long-lasting in arrangements. Foliage may be green or gray. It's the perfect plant for a cottage garden and, with so many to choose from, you'll want to grow several.

Bloom Period and Color

Late spring to early summer in pink, white, or red.

Mature Height × Spread

2 inches to 2 feet × 1 to 2 feet

Evergreen Ferns
Many genera, species, and varieties

When, Where, and How to Plant
All Ferns appreciate shade and moist soil that contains lots of organic matter, such as rotted leaves, compost, and sphagnum peat. They will generally grow all right—but won't reach their full potential—in more average soil. *Polystichum* plants are exceptions; they manage nicely in average, well-drained soil and are adaptable as to part sun and part shade, although the need for moisture increases as the amount of sun does. Plant Ferns when available from spring until late summer. Space 2 to 3 feet apart, according to mature size. Mulch well. Fertilize at planting time with a pelleted, slow-release formula.

Growing Tips
Provide consistent moisture all year, especially in dry weather. With organic-rich soil and a thick mulch, Ferns will probably get all the nutrients they need. But if leaves are pale, fertilize with 10-10-10 water-soluble fertilizer with iron.

Care
Although these Ferns are evergreen, that doesn't mean they never lose leaves. In fact, a few of the oldest leaves die each year. As with Deciduous Ferns, they may be self-shedding or wither in place. Groom as necessary to keep the plants looking neat. Add more mulch as it decomposes. You should experience few, if any, pests.

Companion Planting and Design
Ferns are great in naturalized landscapes and formal beds. Their stiff texture and evergreen quality add to both.

My Personal Favorites
Christmas Fern, a native, is the easiest to grow. *Polystichum setiferum* 'Divisilobum' has a very lacy appearance.

You know what Ferns look like and what an asset they are to the shady garden. What you may not know is that they don't have to die down in winter; some Ferns are evergreen, which adds another dimension to your woodland flower beds. Here are some to look for: Autumn Fern (Dryopteris erythrosora), Christmas Fern (Polystichum acrostichoides), Evergreen Wood Fern (Dryopteris intermedia), Hart's Tongue Fern (Phyllitis scolopendrium), Soft Shield Fern (Polystichum setiferum), and Korean Rock Fern (Polystichum tsussimense). In Zone 7, Japanese Holly Fern (Cyrtomium falcatum) is another choice.

Mature Height × Spread
18 inches to 2 feet × 2 feet to 2^1/$_2$ feet

Foxglove
Digitalis species and hybrids

Foxglove's stately spires of tubular flowers— some with contrasting dots inside—are romantic and beautiful. But when gardeners hunt for plants, they often get confused. Some Foxgloves are grown as annuals, and the most common kind (Digitalis purpurea) is a biennial, which grows one year and flowers the next. But there are also attractive perennial Foxgloves, such as Digitalis grandiflora and Digitalis × mertonensis. Whichever type you choose, once you've planted Foxglove in the right conditions, you should have plants from then on since they reseed prolifically.

Bloom Period and Color
Spring and summer in lavender, yellow, pink, and purple.

Mature Height × Spread
2 to 5 feet × 18 inches

When, Where, and How to Plant
The prime requirements for growing Foxgloves are partial shade and moist soil that's rich in organic matter. Set out plants in early spring. If growing from seed, start seeds in summer and transplant seedlings in early fall where you want them to grow. Space plants 12 inches apart. Add a pelleted, slow-release fertilizer to the soil and mulch well.

Growing Tips
Foxgloves require consistent moisture to flower, so water deeply and frequently. Fertilize annually with slow-release pellets in early spring. If leaves yellow, spray foliage with a water-soluble fertilizer for acid plants or a formula for flowering plants that contains iron.

Care
Stake individual stems if needed. Cut down the flower spikes right after blooming, and most plants will rebloom, although the new spikes will be shorter. Don't remove the second flowers, so they can reseed. (Foxglove is a short-lived perennial that dies out in about three years if not allowed to reseed.) If mulch is thick, pull it back to allow seeds to come into contact with the soil. Lift out crowded seedlings in very early spring and replant. Pests are few, except for slugs.

Companion Planting and Design
Foxgloves are perfect for adding height to shady borders and cottage gardens. They grow well with Ferns, Bleeding Heart, and Cardinal Flower.

My Personal Favorite
Digitalis × mertonensis is called the Strawberry Foxglove because its blooms are a delicious shade of salmon pink that will remind you of crushed strawberries.

Gaillardia

Gaillardia grandiflora

When, Where, and How to Plant

Gaillardia may be set out anytime from spring until summer. Place plants 12 to 16 inches apart in a sunny spot with average soil that drains well. Use a root stimulator or transplant solution at planting time. Mulch isn't needed, but a light mulch to deter weeds is fine.

Growing Tips

Keep soil moist until young plants begin growing, then water only to keep plants alive during prolonged dry spells. Fertilizer isn't usually necessary, but if blooming has slowed in midsummer and you feel the plants need a boost, use a water-soluble plant food formulated for flowers.

Care

Deadhead fading flowers to promote a long blooming season in hottest weather. Because individual plants rarely last more than three years, you may want to root stem cuttings in a mixture of sand and potting soil. Or you can divide a few plants each spring to prolong the planting. Excellent drainage is essential—root rot, crown rot, and mildews can be troublesome in wet or heavy soils. Gaillardia experiences few pests in appropriate sites. If leaves look mottled, suspect leafhoppers. Shear off the affected leaves and remove them from the garden; spray plants with insecticidal soap.

Companion Planting and Design

Plant *en masse* alone or with Sunflowers and other bold textured, brightly colored flowers, such as Coreopsis, Black-eyed Susan, and Goldenrod.

My Personal Favorites

'Goblin', which can't be beat, has red flowers edged in yellow. 'Baby Cole' has yellow blooms banded with red.

Plants with daisylike flowers are always the easiest to grow, and Gaillardia—also called Blanketflower—is among the easiest of the easy. If you're just getting started with perennials, it should be among your first choices. I've planted these heat- and drought-tolerant plants in all sorts of situations from dry soil to hillsides and, as long as they were in full sun, they bloomed for months. The blossoms have dark red centers and two-toned red and yellow petals that butterflies find appealing; so will you.

Bloom Period and Color

Summer to fall in red and yellow.

Mature Height × Spread

6 inches to 2 feet × 1 to 2 feet

Goldenrod
Solidago species and hybrids

You may still be thinking of Goldenrod as a "weed" that grows too tall, spreads like crazy, and causes hay fever. But plant breeders have once again taken a familiar native and made it a wonderful garden plant. They've developed cultivars that are shorter than the species and more manageable, but still undemanding. Goldenrod is a reliable performer in almost any soil condition from soggy to bone-dry. And it was never guilty of bringing on sneezing and watery eyes—that's due to other plants that grew nearby in the wild.

Bloom Period and Color
Late summer to fall in shades of yellow.

Mature Height × Spread
1 to 5 feet × 1 to 3 feet

When, Where, and How to Plant
Think of this as a tough plant that will grow well in sun and average to poor soil that's well drained. (*Solidago canadensis* thrives even in wet places.) So if you're tired of amending your soil with organic matter each time you plant, this is the flower for you. In fact, very rich soils can cause rampant growth and floppy stems. Set out plants from spring until fall, spacing them 12 to 18 inches apart.

Growing Tips
Once established, Goldenrod is drought-tolerant. The first two years, fertilize once in early spring with a pelleted, slow-release formula used at half the label recommendation. Mature stands shouldn't need fertilizing. If the center of the clump dies out, dig it up and divide it in spring, discarding the center.

Care
Clip off spent flowers to promote repeat flowering and prevent reseeding of hybrids; offspring will not come true. If new plants pop up, dig them up if they're in the wrong spot and replant elsewhere. If powdery mildew appears, thin stands to increase air circulation.

Companion Planting and Design
This is the perfect plant to naturalize in meadows. Goldenrod looks nice with Asters, Boltonia, Ornamental Grasses, and Chrysanthemums, all of which will be flowering at the same time. It also looks great with Black-eyed Susan, Purple Coneflower, and Coreopsis, which flower earlier but like the same conditions.

My Personal Favorites
'Golden Dwarf', 'Peter Pan', and 'Golden Baby' are delightful dwarf cultivars. 'Golden Wings' grows 5 feet tall and will knock your socks off.

Hardy Begonia

Begonia grandis

When, Where, and How to Plant

Prepare a rich garden soil that drains well by adding compost, sphagnum peat, and/or finely shredded bark to average soil. Any shady spot is fine—from dappled light to deep shade. Plant in mid- to late spring, after the chance of frost has past. Space them 18 inches apart at least. Be careful not to bury the crown. Plant shallowly, and cover soil with shredded leaves or other organic mulch.

Growing Tips

Hardy Begonias require consistent moisture to thrive, but cannot tolerate wet feet. Fertilize when new growth emerges in spring with a pelleted, slow-release formula or cover soil with half an inch of compost in very fertile soils. Use a water-soluble fertilizer for flowering plants any time during the growing season if lower leaves turn yellow. Keep mulch renewed year-round.

Care

Pinch off stem tips anytime during the growing season if plants are leggy. Remove flowers, and root those cuttings in water to increase the stand. Look for little bulbils in the leaf axils; these drop to the ground and create new plants. Or you may cut them off and set them in a flat of rich potting soil to root. Cut stalks down after first frost, and replenish mulch for winter protection; this is especially important in Zone 6. There are no serious insect or disease problems.

Companion Planting and Design

Grow in woodland gardens with Lenten Roses, Ferns, Hostas, and Columbine.

My Personal Favorite

Begonia sinensis grows about half as tall as the typical Hardy Begonia and has all-green foliage.

We all know what useful plants Begonias are in shady spots, but those are annuals, strictly for summer use or houseplants. But here's a perennial Begonia with leaves shaped like those of Angel-Wing Begonia—with attractive red veining on the undersides—and the Begonia blooms you've come to know and like. Best of all, for anyone with lots of trees in the yard, Hardy Begonia is carefree in light or deep shade. Plant it once, and it will expand to a nice clump that returns each year.

Bloom Period and Color

Summer to fall in pink or white.

Mature Height × Spread

10 inches × 2 feet

Heuchera

Heuchera species and hybrids

Anyone who thinks flowers are necessary for a plant to look fabulous hasn't been introduced to Heuchera. I've grown Heucheras that had green leaves with red veins and silver blotches, deep purple foliage with silver markings, and silver foliage with purple veins. All that and flowers, too. Of the two most common species, the one with the best blooms is Heuchera sanguinea and related hybrids—often called Coral Bells. Heuchera americana, a native referred to as Alumroot, has the most spectacular foliage. I like to plant both.

Bloom Period and Color
Spring in shades of white, pink, and red.

Mature Height × Spread
1 to 2 feet × 12 to 18 inches

When, Where, and How to Plant
Too much sun on purple-leafed Heucheras will "bleach" the foliage, so shade or partial shade is a must. Avoiding sun also helps keep the soil moist, another requirement for this group of plants, which produces new leaves throughout the growing season. But soil should also drain well; add compost or coarse sand, if necessary. The best time to set out Heucheras is spring, but you may plant them until late summer. Space 8 to 12 inches apart. Mulch well.

Growing Tips
Keep soil moist, but never saturated. Fertilize in early spring with half an inch of compost or with a pelleted, slow-release plant food at half the amount recommended on the label.

Care
Cut faded flowers with their stems to keep plants neat and encourage reblooming. Renew mulch each year. Divide clumps in early spring every third year and replant immediately. Take care when dividing—break apart; don't cut straight through the crown. Older plants may develop woody stems and sprawl over. Dig them up and replant a bit deeper. Heucheras have few insect or disease problems.

Companion Planting and Design
Plant cultivars with interesting foliage near the house or walkway, so they can easily be seen. Purple-leafed varieties shine near flagstone patios. Try planting Heuchera with Foamflower, Creeping Phlox, Bleeding Heart, Ferns, and Hosta.

My Personal Favorites
'Raspberry Regal' has tall flower spikes that make it ideal for cut flowers. For foliage, I like 'Pewter Veil'.

When, Where, and How to Plant

Plant in spring in a shady or partially shady flower bed with rich, organic soil that drains well. Since Hostas don't like to be moved, space them to accommodate mature spread, at least 1 to 3 feet apart. Overcrowding will also slow the plants' growth. Fertilize at planting time with a pelleted, slow-release fertilizer worked into each hole. Mulch well unless slugs are known to be a problem.

Growing Tips

Growth is optimized with consistent moisture, but Hostas will tolerate soil that dries out between waterings. Plan to water when rainfall is less than an inch per week. Apply a slow-release fertilizer around each plant when leaves appear in spring.

Care

Add mulch as needed. Cut down flower stalks as they fade so that seeds don't form and sap the plant's energy. Holes in leaves are usually caused by slugs. Look for telltale slime trails to be sure. If homemade traps (saucers of beer, yeast water, or an upturned grapefruit) don't work, ask at a garden center about controls. Try to avoid dividing Hostas, since it takes a year or two for them to recover.

Companion Planting and Design

Mass in shady beds, or use as accents with Ferns, Impatiens, and Caladiums.

My Personal Favorites

'Francee' is my all-time favorite for its deep-green leaves edged in crisp white. 'Patriot' is similar but with a wider white margin. 'Grand Tiara' has a bold gold edge. 'Tatoo' has green and gold foliage with the outline of a maple leaf in the center.

If I were to recommend only one plant for a shady yard, it would be Hosta. It has it all, starting with its great-looking leaves in shades of gold, green, cream, and yellow variegation—even blue (although many of the blue cultivars do better in the North). And don't overlook the blooms, which are butterfly favorites. Hostas are now being bred for interesting flowers, many with fragrance. Hostas also vary in size from miniature to 5 feet wide. Even if you plant dozens, you'll have plenty of variety.

Bloom Period and Color

Late spring to fall in white, lavender, and purple.

Mature Height × Spread

6 inches to 3 feet × 1 to 5 feet

e-Pye Weed
upatorium purpureum

Sometimes we tend to overlook plants that we're very familiar with, just thinking of them as part of the scenery. Joe-Pye Weed is a good example. You know that fall is on its way when you see the tall plants with their reddish flower clusters appear along roadsides. But the Brits noticed something in Joe-Pye that we Americans hadn't. They took it home, began breeding it, and are now selling wonderful new cultivars of this native plant back to us! Look for shorter varieties and ones with white flowers.

Bloom Period and Color
Late summer to fall in pink, shades of purple, and white.

Mature Height × Spread
3 to 7 feet × 2 to 4 feet

When, Where, and How to Plant
As its presence in wild plantings testifies, Joe-Pye is an adaptable plant. Although it will grow and bloom best in wet spots, it will tolerate almost any kind of soil. Full sun is also preferred, but the plant will manage with a couple of hours of daily shade. Plant it from spring until fall. This is a big plant, so space it $2^1/_2$ to 3 feet apart at the back of a border, meadow, or wildflower garden. Mulch, especially if moisture retention is a concern.

Growing Tips
Keep the soil moist at all times. Standing water is all right for short times, and boggy conditions are ideal. Use fertilizer sparingly. If Joe-Pye Weed isn't growing or blooming well, spread a slow-release fertilizer for flowering plants on the ground around it, or spray plants and soil with a water-soluble fertilizer.

Care
Control height by pinching Joe-Pye Weed once or twice after growth starts in spring and before May 15. Add to mulch as it thins. This is a plant that rarely suffers from insects or diseases. Cut it to the ground after flowering is finished.

Companion Planting and Design
Joe-Pye Weed is an ideal plant for a butterfly garden. Plant it with Shasta Daisies, Black-eyed Susans, Purple Coneflowers, and perennial Phlox. Use it also in wildflower meadows and with Water Cannas and Cattails in bog gardens.

My Personal Favorites
Spotted Joe-Pye Weed (*Eupatorium maculatum*) has stems with purple mottling. 'Alba' has white flowers. 'Gateway', which has wine-red stems, usually tops out at 5 feet.

Lenten Rose
Helleborus orientalis

When, Where, and How to Plant

Lenten Rose shines in shade, but be careful about placing it beneath deciduous trees because winter sun can burn the leaves and stunt the flowers. Dig average soil 12 inches deep and add compost, peat moss and finely shredded bark to create a deep, fertile planting area. Unfortunately for those with clay, Lenten Rose can't tolerate "wet feet" (water standing at the roots), especially in winter. Plant container-grown Hellebores in early spring. Transplant seedlings from around mature plants when they're 4 inches tall. Space plants 18 to 24 inches apart. Mulch with organic matter, such as pine straw.

Growing Tips

Although Lenten Roses prefer consistent moisture, they're surprisingly tolerant of dry weather—once they're established and if they're planted in moisture-retaining soil that's mulched. But you'll want to water enough to keep the soil moist when plants are young and during droughts. Use fertilizer sparingly, if at all; the decaying mulch will usually be sufficient to supply needed nutrients.

Care

Evergreen leaves can sometimes suffer winter damage. As flowers appear, clip torn leaves off so flowers can shine. The plant grows slowly, so it seldom needs dividing. Lenten Roses reseed enough to increase the stand if mulch is pulled away as the seeds mature. They aren't bothered by pests.

Companion Planting and Design

Place them where they can be seen in winter.

My Personal Favorite

'Royal Heritage' comes in a wide range of sumptuous colors.

Don't let anyone convince you that because it's winter, you can't have flowers blooming. Prove them wrong with Lenten Rose. This evergreen perennial is a standout in deep shade—or any other type of shade. The romantic-looking single flowers come in shades of green, cream, and pink and are often spotted inside. Once you've planted Lenten Rose, you'll have it in your garden forever because it reseeds (but not aggressively). Look for some of the new strains and hybrids hitting the market—they've been selected for intriguing colors.

Bloom Period and Color

Late winter to spring in white, lime, rose, and maroon.

Mature Height × Spread

14 to 18 inches × 12 to 18 inches

Peony
Paeonia lactiflora

There's no plant that evokes more memories than Peonies. Your grandmother probably grew them; so did your mother. And while this generation turns to "new and improved" perennials, we couldn't do without old-fashioned Peonies. Avoid having Peony flowers end up facedown in the mud after hard rains by choosing single flowers instead of doubles or by supporting the plants as soon as they begin to grow in spring. (I use a little wire cage.) Peonies take a while to get established, but once they are, they practically live forever.

Bloom Period and Color
May in pink, red, purple, yellow, and white.

Mature Height × Spread
12 to 30 inches × 12 to 30 inches

When, Where, and How to Plant
Till or dig soil 12 inches deep and work in organic matter. Soil preparation matters more with Peonies than most plants because they stay in one place for a long time. Full sun is recommended, but a couple of hours of afternoon shade are often welcomed. The best time to plant Peonies is in the fall; however, the plants are usually available only in spring. Do not plant too deep; set plants at the same level or slightly higher than they grew before. If you obtain dormant roots, plant them 1 to 2 inches deep. Do not crowd; plant Peonies 20 to 24 inches apart, depending on mature size. Mulch year-round.

Growing Tips
Consistent moisture is crucial; use soaker hoses for best results. Fertilize amply by placing 1/2 inch of compost on top of the soil in spring and summer and applying a pelleted, slow-release fertilizer in mid-spring.

Care
Use Peony supports as soon as the plants begin growing. Plants seldom need dividing and recover from it poorly. New Peonies may take two years to bloom well. If leaf diseases or insects strike, consult the Extension Service. Ants aren't a pest; they help the flowers.

Companion Planting and Design
Peonies tend to look best alone. Or place them on the sunny edge of a groundcover bed.

My Personal Favorite
Early and midseason cultivars, as well as those with single flowers, will do best in the warmer parts of the state. 'Festiva Maxima' is an old cultivar that still can't be beat.

Perennial Hibiscus
Hibiscus species and hybrids

When, Where, and How to Plant

Late spring and early summer are the best times to plant. The easiest way to tell the difference between tropical Hibiscus, which doesn't return, and Perennial Hibiscus, which does, is that the leaves of tropical Hibiscus are shiny and those of the perennial ones aren't. (*Hibiscus syriacus*, Rose of Sharon, is a shrub.) Sun is essential; so is moist, well-drained soil that's been enriched with organic matter. Water with a transplanting solution and mulch well.

Growing Tips

Water copiously throughout the growing season. Although Perennial Hibiscus doesn't require as much fertilizer as a tropical Hibiscus, it does like to be fed several times. Spread a pelleted, slow-release fertilizer around the base of the plant at the end of April. Follow up with a water-soluble fertilizer for flowering plants the beginning of July and the first of August.

Care

Plants reappear late in spring, after the soil has warmed up. Keep plants mulched to retain moisture in the soil. In Zone 6, add to the mulch in fall for winter protection. Japanese beetles will be a problem on all but *Hibiscus coccineus*. Leave seedpods on Swamp Hibiscus over winter to add interest to the yard.

Companion Planting and Design

For best effect, plant several Hibiscus plants together. Put the taller cultivars toward the back of a flower border.

My Personal Favorites

Grow 'Lady Baltimore' for its 6- to 9-inch ruffled blooms, which are deep pink with red "eyes" (centers). 'Disco Belle' (in red, pink, or white) is great for the patio.

When other plants in your garden are drooping in the dog days of August, Hibiscus is going strong, producing enormous flowers in clear, bold colors—and not just tropical Hibiscus, which is an annual. Less well known—and more valuable to those who want to plant once and enjoy flowers for years—are the Perennial Hibiscus. The 'Disco Belle' and 'Southern Belle' series of hybrids offer big blooms on compact plants. Swamp Hibiscus (Hibiscus coccineus; for Zone 7) is a native that likes wet soils and doesn't attract Japanese beetles.

Bloom Period and Color

Summer in red, pink, or white.

Mature Height × Spread

2 to 7 feet × 3 feet

Phlox

Phlox species and hybrids

Phloxes are such good garden plants that there is a confusing array of them. Several creeping types are listed in the "Groundcovers" chapter. But two other species provide outstanding selections that every gardener should try. Phlox paniculata (Garden Phlox or Summer Phlox) produces large, long-lasting flower clusters on 3- to 5-foot stalks. There is a nice variety of colors and many cultivars have a contrasting eyes. Phlox maculata—sometimes referred to as Carolina Phlox—has mildew-resistant foliage. Both stay in flower for a long time, impressing all who see them.

Bloom Period and Color
Summer in pink, red, white, and purple.

Mature Height × Spread
2 to 5 feet × 1 to 3 feet

When, Where, and How to Plant
In mid- to late-spring, set out plants in average soil that stays moist or can be kept watered. Add peat moss to rocky or sandy soils to improve their water-holding capacity. Full sun is fine for many cultivars, but all—especially those with deep-colored flowers—will appreciate a few hours of afternoon shade. (But only a few—partial shade leads to floppy stems that need staking.) Space plants 18 inches apart and mulch well.

Growing Tips
Water deeply if rainfall is less than an inch weekly. Fertilizer may not be necessary. If plants aren't growing or blooming well, use a water-soluble fertilizer for flowering plants.

Care
Deadhead flowers for a longer bloom period. Don't let Phlox go to seed; self-seeded plants will have magenta flowers and be so vigorous that they crowd out all other Phloxes. Mildew is Phlox's Achilles heel. Avoid the problem by buying mildew-resistant cultivars, spacing the plants farther apart so they have good air circulation, and not splashing water on the leaves. The Extension Service can recommend a fungicide to help prevent mildew, but you'll have to spray weekly, possibly more often in rainy weather. In dry weather, spider mites may also appear. Divide plants every three years.

Companion Planting and Design
Place Phlox at the back of a flower bed with other summer-flowering perennials in complementary colors.

My Personal Favorite
I can't imagine being without *Phlox maculata* 'Miss Lingard'. It has white blooms and has never mildewed in my yard.

Purple Coneflower
Echinacea purpurea

When, Where, and How to Plant
Every soil that drains well can sustain Purple Coneflowers. But they don't do nearly as well in rich organic soils as in average soil, so you needn't amend the soil before planting. Plant in a sunny spot from spring through summer. Space clumps 18 to 24 inches apart and do not bury the crown, then mulch up to but not over the crown.

Growing Tips
Water deeply but infrequently to encourage deep rooting and drought-tolerance. Do not fertilize except for a light dressing of compost in spring. Too much fertilizer, especially when the plant is grown in partial sun, will lead to tall stems and fewer flowers when crowded. Divide in spring or fall and replant immediately.

Care
Keep early faded flowers picked off to encourage more blooms, but leave the last ones intact. They will reseed and last over winter with attractive seedheads that will attract hungry birds. Japanese beetles can be a problem; pick off a small infestation and drop into a jar of water or oil to drown them. Remove and discard mulch around affected plants. The plant attracts many butterflies and thus their larvae; pick caterpillars off also. Control with insecticidal soap only if plants are being stripped.

Companion Planting and Design
Grow in meadows or naturalized landscapes as well as butterfly gardens with ornamental grasses, Gaillardia, Black-eyed Susan, and Yarrow.

My Personal Favorites
My favorite pink is 'Bright Star', which blooms abundantly.

Since it's obvious the blooms of this delightful plant aren't purple, my sons would always ask, "Why isn't it called Pink Coneflower?" But this name business gets even more confusing: There are also white cultivars—do we refer to them as White Purple Coneflowers? The best thing is not to worry about it. Just buy as many cultivars of this fabulous plant as you can find and have sunny spaces for. It has so many virtues that I can't name them all and no faults that I can think of.

Bloom Period and Color
Summer to fall in dusty pink or white.

Mature Height × Spread
2 to 4 feet × 1 to 2 feet

Red Valerian
Centranthus ruber

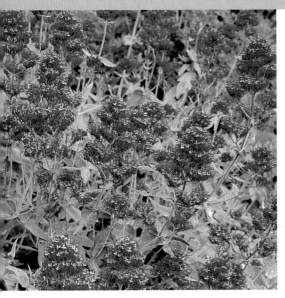

Once I ordered Red Valerian (or Jupiter's Beard) because I thought it looked interesting. Later I gave them little thought except to note that the airy reddish blooms looked nice in late spring. Then I was appointed to my church's flower committee, and I suddenly discovered that anytime from late spring until frost I could always find a couple of Red Valerian flower spikes for arrangements. What a joy! Be careful when you shop for this plant—there's another one named simply Valerian, and the two plants aren't anything alike.

Bloom Period and Color
Late spring in red, pink, and white.

Mature Height × Spread
1 to 3 feet × 2 to 3 feet

When, Where, and How to Plant
Red Valerian will grow in almost any soil, but prefers one that's well drained and has a pH of about 7.0 or slightly higher. If planted in a soil that contains lots of organic matter, Red Valerian's stems will flop over. (And in slightly acidic soil, it won't reseed as freely, which is probably good.) Plant 2^1/$_2$ to 3 feet apart in full sun, although a few hours of afternoon shade are tolerated. Use a transplanting solution at planting time, then mulch.

Growing Tips
Water regularly until the plant is established—then it will seldom need watering except in prolonged droughts. In very poor soil, fertilize once a year in spring with a water-soluble fertilizer. Too much fertilizer causes the Red Valerian to get leggy and flop over instead of growing straight and tall.

Care
Deadhead flowers to encourage reblooming. Cut back to 6 inches tall if plants get leggy or to encourage a large crop of fall flowers. Red Valerian reseeds freely, but the flowers won't necessarily be the color of the original plants; pull up those that you don't like. Divide after three or four years in spring or early fall; replant immediately. You should experience few if any pests.

Companion Planting and Design
Red Valerian is excellent for tough, dry sites. Combine it with other sun lovers, such as Purple Coneflower, blue Salvia, Verbena, and white Zinnias or Madagascar Periwinkle.

My Personal Favorite
Cultivars aren't usually available. Buy when they're in bloom to get the flower color you prefer.

Salvia

Salvia species and hybrids

When, Where, and How to Plant
Salvias thrive in sunshine and average soils that drain well. Amend heavy soils with organic matter to improve drainage. (Wet soil in winter causes the plants to rot.) Plant Salvias anytime after the last frost of spring through summer. Space 10 inches to 2 feet apart, depending on type. Mix a pelleted, slow-release fertilizer with the soil. Mulch well.

Growing Tips
Salvia is relatively drought-tolerant once it has become established in your yard, but blooms better when it receives regular moisture. If possible, water if rainfall is less than an inch a week. In containers, fertilize monthly with a water-soluble plant food made for flowers. Plants in the garden probably won't need fertilizer.

Care
Pinch Salvias each spring when they grow to be 4 inches tall and again at 8 inches to promote bushy new growth and more flowers. Keep faded flowers cut off to encourage reblooming and to prevent seeds from forming. Or wait and cut all flower stalks off after flowering is finished; you may find that they will rebloom several times. (The easiest way to do this is with loppers or a string trimmer.) Salvias may become woody at their crown and need dividing every four years or so. There should be few pest problems.

Companion Planting and Design
Use in beds and borders with Russian Sage, Dusty Miller, *Artemisia* 'Powis Castle', and pink-flowered Daylilies.

My Personal Favorites
The blooms of 'Blue Hill' are truly blue. 'East Friesland' has purple flowers on an 18-inch plant. 'Rose Queen' is probably the best pink.

Perennial Salvia is often referred to as "Blue Salvia" but, in addition to true blue, blooms may also be purple and—less frequently—red, pink, or white. All have tubular flowers borne on spikes and are excellent butterfly-attracting plants that don't need much attention. There are many species of Salvia and that can get confusing since some are biennial, some are annuals, and some are grown as annuals because they're not always winter hardy. Be sure you the ones you choose are perennial in your part of the state.

Bloom Period and Color
Late spring to fall in blue, purple, red, pink, or white.

Mature Height × Spread
1 to 2 feet × 1 to 3 feet

Sedum 'Autumn Joy'
Sedum × *telephium* 'Autumn Joy'

The common name Stonecrop tells you this is a plant for rock gardens. But it's valuable in many garden situations, because it's interesting throughout the growing season. The fleshy foliage is quite a contrast to most other perennials. 'Autumn Joy' (as well as related hybrids) offers large, dense flower heads that change color as they mature and attract hoards of butterflies. Plants that were grown from cuttings bloom in early fall, when it's hard to find flowers in the perennial garden. (If yours bloom earlier, they were grown from seed.)

Bloom Period and Color
Late summer to fall in pink or reddish shades.

Mature Height × Spread
18 inches to 2 feet × 18 inches to 2 feet

When, Where, and How to Plant
Amend heavy soils with organic matter to improve drainage. Excellent drainage is especially important in lightly shaded sites as plants will die in wet soils. Plant in a sunny, or mostly sunny, spot anytime from late spring until early fall. Fertilize with a water-soluble product for flowering plants. Mulch lightly, if at all.

Growing Tips
Water regularly but moderately if rainfall is less than an inch per week. Sedums prefer to dry out between waterings and have shallow root systems that cannot take huge amounts of water when small. Don't fertilize.

Care
Pinch Sedum 'Autumn Joy' once in late spring and again in early summer to encourage bushiness and to keep it compact. (These cuttings root easily if you'd like more plants.) If plants growing in part sun tend to flop over, cut them back by half toward the end of June. Few insects or diseases bother Sedum. If spaced correctly when planted, they won't need dividing for many years. When division is necessary, do it in spring.

Companion Planting and Design
Sedums are interesting massed in a bed where they can spread freely. But they also make a contribution to the perennial border when planted with Dusty Miller and *Artemisia* 'Powis Castle'.

My Personal Favorites
Everyone needs at least one plant of 'Autumn Joy'. But once you have that, go for these: 'Autropurpureum' has bronze leaves and reddish flowers; *Hylotelephium spectabile* 'Iceberg' has white flowers; 'Indian Chief's' blooms start out red and fade to pink.

Shasta Daisy

Leucanthemum × superbum

When, Where, and How to Plant

Shasta Daisies would rather grow in rich, moist soil, but will tolerate just about any soil as long as drainage is good. Amend clay with finely shredded bark or compost. Plant container-grown Shasta Daisies in spring or early summer in a spot that's in full sun or mostly sun. Space 18 to 24 inches apart, watering with a transplant solution. Mulch new plants, but do not cover the crowns.

Growing Tips

Although Shasta Daisies can tolerate some dry weather, they perform better and produce more blooms if watered regularly so that the soil stays moist but not saturated. Water deeply. You shouldn't have to fertilize in average soil; too much fertilizer causes tall, floppy stems.

Care

Keep flowers deadheaded or cut for arrangements. As flowers fade, cut down to the next visible bud to encourage reblooming. Clumps will die out unless you divide them. Every third year, divide and replant them right away. Do not remove volunteers unless they aren't true to the parent plants or they crowd the planting bed. Stake tall varieties with flower rings, if necessary. Insects and disease problems are few.

Companion Planting and Design

Fill a bed with Shasta Daisies, Bearded Iris, and Antique Roses for a cottage garden look.

My Personal Favorite

'Becky' is the best Shasta Daisy I've ever grown. It's more vigorous, blooms later than other cultivars, and produces large flowers for a long time.

"Daisy, Daisy, give me your answer true. I'm half crazy all for the love of you." When I was a kid and would go on rides in the country with my parents, my dad would always sing those words when spying a field of wild Daisies. While Shasta Daisies are hybrids, they're just as carefree as roadside plants. The main difference is their larger flowers. No wonder they're popular with seasoned gardeners as well as beginners. Another plus is that they're equally attractive in the garden and in arrangements.

Bloom Period and Color

Spring to summer in white and yellow.

Mature Height × Spread

1 to 3 feet × 18 to 24 inches

Sundrops

Oenothera fruticosa

There's something about plants with flowers the color of melted butter—they just seem to bring sunshine into the garden. Even on cloudy days, they look cheery. Sundrops certainly have that ability. It's a neat little plant—usually about 18 inches high and covered—from May into June—with 1- to 2-inch Buttercup-shaped flowers. For some reason, though, it's not well known, although it isn't difficult to locate plants. It's probably just been overshadowed by night-blooming Primrose, the best-known member of the Oenothera clan. Day-blooming Sundrops certainly deserve equal renown.

Bloom Period and Color
Late spring to early summer in yellow.

Mature Height × Spread
1 to 2 feet × 1 to 2 feet

When, Where, and How to Plant
Grow Sundrops in average soils that drain well; amend heavy soils with finely shredded bark to improve drainage. Wet conditions, especially in winter, cause Sundrops to rot. Full sun produces the best plants and most abundant blooms, although an hour or two of afternoon shade may be tolerated. Plant 18 inches to 2 feet apart in spring, watering with a transplant solution. Mulch very lightly to suppress weeds.

Growing Tips
After they've gotten established, Sundrops tolerate dry soil. You probably won't have to water except during prolonged droughts. Fertilizer is rarely required. In fact, while this plant doesn't spread as much as its relatives, too much fertilizer can cause quite a bit of spreading.

Care
Trim off leggy stems anytime during the summer. Cut Sundrops down after the first frost and pull up unwanted volunteers. Sundrops have few pests except spittlebugs, which leave gobs of foam on stems. Control them with a blast of water from the hose. Divide crowded clumps in spring or early fall. If plants fail to appear in spring, blame poor drainage.

Companion Planting and Design
Sundrops are perfect for informal beds with blue flowers, such as perennial Salvia, Stokesia, and Baptisia, as well as pink perennial Phlox. Because of their tolerance of less-than-ideal conditions, they're also perfect for sunny, dry beds around a mailbox or lamppost.

My Personal Favorites
'Summer Solstice' blooms about a month later than other cultivars. 'Fireworks' has red stems and large yellow flowers.

Verbena

Verbena species and hybrids

When, Where, and How to Plant

Grow Rose Verbena or *Verbena bonariensis* in any garden soil that drains well; amend clay soils with organic matter to improve drainage. These plants tolerate sandy soils and drought and keep blooming. Plant seeds or plants in spring; both will bloom the first year. Space plants 2 feet apart in a sunny spot. Mulch lightly.

Growing Tips

Keep soil moist until plants are established, then water infrequently but deeply to encourage drought-tolerance. Avoid fertilizer unless plants aren't growing well. Too much fertilizer causes excessive growth that will flop over and have to be pruned back.

Care

Pinch new plants when they are 6 inches tall and again at 10 inches to encourage branching that contributes to their airy effect. In mass plantings, cut back lightly after each flush of blooms. Deadhead flower clusters as they fade to promote reblooming. Verbena experiences few pests except powdery mildew, which may appear in late summer. This can't be "cured," although it can be prevented with regular use of a fungicide. While it doesn't look good, mildew doesn't seem to affect Verbena adversely.

Companion Planting and Design

Verbenas are excellent butterfly plants, attracting many species to seek its nectar all summer. Use a group with *Artemisia* 'Powis Castle', Coreopsis, Joe-Pye Weed, and Shasta Daisy.

My Personal Favorites

'Pink Sunrise' has pink flowers on stems that rarely get higher than 6 inches. 'Snowflurry' produces an abundance of white blooms.

Plants go in and out of fashion just as clothes do. At the moment, Verbena canadensis 'Homestead Purple' is a very popular plant. A vigorous grower covered in purple flower clusters, it's widely used in public gardens. Although officially rated for Zone 8, it returns for me in Zone 7 and seems perennial in Zone 6, too. But it reseeds prolifically, so plants won't die out. A nice result of 'Homestead Purple's' popularity is that other Rose Verbenas—in pink, reddish shades, white, and lavender—are getting new attention.

Bloom Period and Color

Spring to fall in purple, violet, white, and pink.

Mature Height × Spread

6 inches to 3 feet × 3 feet

Yarrow

Achillea species and hybrids

Gardeners in Tennessee face two kinds of diffi-cult situations. One is spots in the yard that stay constantly wet. The other is dry spots—maybe on a hill, possibly too far from a faucet—in full sun. We wonder, what in the world will grow and look good there without any attention from me? The answer for poor, sunny soils is Yarrow—some of which have gray leaves, some green—which blooms for a long time, makes an excellent cut flower, and may easily be dried for winter arrangements.

Bloom Period and Color
Summer to fall in yellow, white, and pink.

Mature Height × Spread
6 inches to 4 feet × 1 to 4 feet

When, Where, and How to Plant
As long as it has sun and well-drained soil, Yarrow is happy. If soil is too rich or moist, stems will be weak and flop over. Amend clay soil enough to improve drainage, but not so much that it becomes humus-rich. Plant Yarrow in spring, spacing plants 2 feet apart. Mulch isn't needed.

Growing Tips
Water sparingly until the plants are estab-lished, then only in prolonged droughts if they appear to be suffering. Avoid fertil-izer unless plants aren't growing well. Shade, too much soil moisture, and too much fertilizer cause stems to fall over instead of growing sturdy and tall. Fertilizer also causes rampant leaf growth at the expense of flowers.

Care
No pruning or pinching is needed except deadheading faded flowers. If desired, dig up small plants around established clumps in spring and summer and replant right away, watering with a trans-plant solution. Fungus diseases are occasional problems and are more preva-lent when plants aren't in full sun or dry soil. They include mildew, rust (spots on leaves), and rot. The first two are cos-metic; cut back the plants if they bother you. If clumps die out in the center, divide in spring or early fall.

Companion Planting and Design
Plant with blue- or purple-flowered annuals or perennials that don't mind dry soil. Or grow with Purple Cone-flower, Sunflower, Black-eyed Susan, and Boltonia.

My Personal Favorite
'Coronation Gold' never, ever flops over or needs staking. It's completely carefree.

Shrubs *for Tennessee*

Shrubs are the second most important plants in your yard (with trees being the first). But you'll have more shrubs than trees, and those shrubs will likely define your yard in a way that no other plant can. Banks of red, pink, and white Azaleas can transform your landscape into a springtime paradise. Hollies entice scores of birds to visit your property. Shrubs such as Camellia and Witch Hazel come into flower in the cold

winter months when the sight of flower blossoms is a rare and especially welcome treat. Hedges separate your land from your neighbor's, and shrubs planted as a screen ensure privacy or block an unsightly view.

Shrubs Are Versatile

In a word, shrubs are a most versatile group of plants. They come in many forms—from pyramidal to rounded to columnar—and have varied textures, which can be mixed and matched for a pleasing effect. Shrubs with little leaves have a neat appearance and seem to fit nicely in small spaces. Shrubs with large leaves are bolder looking and are ideal for larger areas, especially where they will be seen from a distance.

Shrubs can be colorful, too—and not just those that flower. If you like a large splash of color, look for shrubs with gold, purple, or red foliage or those with variegated leaves. But don't overdo it; use these shrubs as accents in a sea of green for the best effect.

Shrubs may be evergreen—either broadleafed, such as Boxwood, or needled, such as False Cypress. Or they may be deciduous and lose their leaves in fall. Usually, evergreens are placed in the most prominent spots for year-round effect and deciduous shrubs fade into the background except when they're flowering.

Whichever type you choose, always check the root system first to make sure it's in good shape. Don't buy a shrub that's rootbound—one whose roots wind round and round the ball of soil. It's difficult to get such a plant to grow well again.

Plan Ahead

One thing more than all others will make a difference in whether or not you're happy with your shrub selection—match the mature size of the plant to the spot where you want to put it. When you're planting a 1-gallon Azalea, it's hard to imagine that it might grow to be 4 feet tall and at least as wide. So you plant a half-dozen of them, spacing them maybe a foot apart—and then in a couple of years, you have to dig up every other one. And a few more years after that, you may need to do it again. It's much easier to plant a little shrub than it is to dig up a large one and transplant it. If those newly planted shrubs look too far apart, fill in between them with annual or perennial flowers until the shrubs reach their mature sizes.

Planting ABCs

Dig a hole that's twice as wide as the rootball and not quite as deep (this is to prevent the newly planted shrub from sinking into the hole and ending up lower than it was in its container, which can lead to root rot). Mix the soil removed from the hole with peat moss, fine bark, compost, or other organic matter. Carefully remove the well-watered shrub from the pot, and place it on firm soil at the bottom of the hole. Replace the amended soil firmly around the shrub's roots, leaving a shallow saucer or indented circle around the shrub on top of the soil—this is to hold water. Water slowly and thoroughly, and continue watering weekly if rainfall totals less than an inch. Spread mulch in the area around the shrub to hold moisture in the soil and to keep down weeds. Don't fertilize a shrub at planting time; wait until the next spring.

The shrubs on the next few pages will give you some excellent choices for flowering, berries, three-season interest, attracting birds and other small wildlife, screening, and just plain looking good in your yard. If you're looking for a new shrub, you're sure to find the perfect choice.

Aucuba

Aucuba japonica

Aucuba went through a period when it was considered hopelessly old-fashioned and much overplanted. That didn't deter me. I felt that a broad-leafed evergreen that brightened shady corners with gold and green variegated leaves was a keeper. Now Aucuba has been restored to horticultural good graces and is easy to find in nurseries. It may not be suitable for the colder parts of Zone 6, but if you like Aucuba's looks, I think it's worth taking a chance on. I'm now trying to see how many cultivars I can find.

Bloom Period and Color
Maroon to purple in early spring; red berries in fall and winter.

Mature Height × Spread
6 to 15 feet × 5 to 10 feet

When, Where, and How to Plant
To ensure a good crop of berries, a male and a female cultivar are needed. Place Aucuba where it will be in shade, or mostly shade, year-round. It likes moist, well-drained soil that contains plenty of organic matter. Add compost, peat moss, or finely shredded bark to the planting hole, if needed. Spring is best, but container-grown shrubs may be set out from May until the end of August if you water well during the summer. Use a transplanting solution at planting time and mulch with pine straw or fine bark.

Growing Tips
Adequate moisture is a must for Aucuba. Water to keep the soil slightly damp when the plant is young. After it becomes established, water deeply when weekly rainfall doesn't equal an inch per week. Spread a slow-release shrub fertilizer around the base at the end of April, if desired.

Care
If necessary, prune to keep Aucuba's shape neat and rounded. Don't do this with a hedge trimmer or shears; that will damage many of the leaves and the plant won't look good for some time. Instead, use handpruners to cut stems back to just above a bud. This shrub has few insect or disease problems.

Companion Planting and Design
Aucuba is excellent for foundation plantings on the north side of the house and beneath tall pines. It's also nice grouped with other shade-loving shrubs in woodland beds.

My Personal Favorites
'Variegata' is one of the hardier cultivars. 'Nana' grows 3 to 5 feet tall and produces abundant berries.

Beauty...

Callicarpa species and

When, Where, and How to Plant

Plant Beautyberry anytime from spring until fall. While it will grow nicely in part sun—especially in dappled shade—the production of berries is generally much greater when the shrub is placed in full sun. Beautyberry isn't particular about soil type and, in fact, probably does better in average soil than where soil is rich. Water with a transplanting solution, and mulch to keep down weeds.

Growing Tips

Ample watering leads to a plentiful supply of fruits, so if summer rainfall is deficient, soak the soil around the shrub weekly. Do not fertilize as that causes too much stem growth at the expense of berries.

Care

In late winter or early spring, cut out dead stems. Prune Japanese Beautyberry (*Callicarpa japonica*) back to 2 feet tall to encourage lots of new growth—and therefore an abundance of flowers and berries. Any overgrown Beautyberry may be cut back to 1 foot tall in early spring and allowed to regrow. In severe winters, if the top of the plant is killed, it will grow back from the roots. This shrub has no serious insects or diseases.

Companion Planting and Design

Naturalize native American Beautyberry under tall Pine trees that have been limbed up. All Beautyberries are stunning in fall when massed in groups.

My Personal Favorites

Purple Beautyberry (*Callicarpa dichotoma*) is very graceful and colorful; I like 'Early Amethyst', which reaches about 4 feet by 4 feet. *Callicarpa americana* is a native that naturalizes well.

I like to have a mixture of plants in my yard—some that are familiar old friends and some that are so different and such standouts that they make people stop and ask, "What in the world is that?" Although easy to grow, Beautyberry is in the latter group. Most of the year, this deciduous shrub doesn't call attention to itself. But when it becomes covered with lavender to purple berries in late summer or early fall, wow! And they last quite a long time—often into winter.

Bloom Period and Color

Pink or lavender in summer, followed by purplish or white fruits.

Mature Height × Spread

3 to 10 feet × 4 to 8 feet

oxwood
Buxus species and hybrids

Across Tennessee, we've grown up with Boxwoods. We've known them as useful foundation shrubs and as hedges. Visiting Colonial Williamsburg in Virginia and Andrew Jackson's home, the Hermitage, in Middle Tennessee, we've seen how enormous they can grow and how long they can live. Boxwoods are handsome, broad-leafed evergreens that have many uses—they're especially nice to add winter interest to a perennial border. If you want a rounded Boxwood, save yourself a lot of work: Read the label and choose a cultivar that grows that way naturally.

Mature Height × Spread
2 to 20 feet × 3 to 25 feet

When, Where, and How to Plant
In spring, plant Boxwoods in full to partial sun. Avoid placing the shrubs where they're subject to drying winds or in clay soil, which can contribute to root rot. Moist, well-drained soil is ideal; enrich it with an abundance of organic matter. Water with a transplanting solution, then mulch well.

Growing Tips
Water deeply once a week when rainfall is lacking. Fertilize each spring with a slow-release fertilizer for evergreen shrubs.

Care
Maintain a year-round mulch to protect shallow roots. Prune in early spring; winter damage can occur if Boxwood is pruned after July. Plants that are pruned with handpruners are better able to withstand snow and cold than those trimmed with hedge shears. Boxwood is subject to many insects and diseases. If foliage develops an off-color in spring or summer, the plant is usually suffering from root rot (the result of poor drainage). Nematodes will stunt roots. In both cases, the only cure (and it's not guaranteed) is to dig up and move the shrub. Try to keep male dogs from constantly wetting on the same spot, which damages the foliage.

Companion Planting and Design
Boxwoods are generally used as hedges and foundation plantings; they're perfect for formal or Colonial-style gardens. Dwarfs are nice to edge herb gardens.

My Personal Favorites
'Green Mountain' has proven to be extremely hardy and carefree for me in several parts of the state. The leaves of *Buxus sempervirens* 'Elegantissima' are edged in cream.

Buckeye
Aesculus species and hybrids

When, Where and How to Plant

Bottlebrush Buckeye will grow in any light from full sun to full shade; so will Red Buckeye, but it's less likely to lose its leaves early in fall if it's placed in part shade. Plant in moist, well-drained soil (preferably acid) to which you've added compost, finely shredded bark or peat moss. Be sure to give these Buckeyes plenty of room to grow—they spread considerably and produce suckers, so they shouldn't be crowded. Plant in early spring before growth starts. Water with a transplanting solution and mulch.

Growing Tips

Water young plants regularly to keep the soil moist. Then water deeply any week that rainfall is less than an inch. Fertilizer probably won't be needed, but if growth isn't fast enough, use a slow-release shrub fertilizer at the end of March.

Care

Most Buckeyes are troubled by leaf spots and diseases, but not Bottlebrush Buckeye. Occasionally, Red Buckeye will develop spots, but it's rarely serious. If given shade and the correct environmental conditions, these shrubs shouldn't be bothered by diseases or insects. Prune in winter if needed to keep them inbounds. Overgrown specimens may be cut back to ground level. Dig or pull up unwanted suckers any time of year.

Companion Planting and Design

Plant Buckeye shrubs beneath limbed-up tall trees or in a shrub border. They're also nice as specimen shrubs.

My Personal Favorite

'Rogers' has the largest flowers I've seen on a Bottlebrush Buckeye and it usually blooms a couple of weeks later than the native species.

Buckeye isn't just a tree; there are two native species that may be used as attractive flowering shrubs in Tennessee yards. One is Bottlebrush Buckeye (Aesculus parviflora), which has white flowers that look like the brushes you wash bottles with, only softer and larger. They're a foot tall and 2 to 4 inches around. It has leaves that turn yellow in fall. The other is Red Buckeye (Aesculus pavia), which, in mid- to late spring, has 6- to 8-inch red (or, occasionally, yellow) flower panicles that are very popular with hummingbirds.

Bloom period and color
White in midsummer (Bottlebrush Buckeye) or red in April or May (Red Buckeye).

Mature Height × Spread
8 to 20 feet × 8 to 25 feet

Burning Bush

Euonymus alatus

Fluorescent red, fire-engine red, brilliant scarlet—attempts to describe the fall color of Burning Bush simply don't do it justice. This deciduous shrub is one of the most reliable plants for spectacular fall foliage. When other shrubs may look fabulous some years and okay in some, Burning Bush always comes through. Although a true star in autumn, it's modest in its requirements, being adaptable to almost any growing situation except wet soil and extreme drought. You can even remove the lower limbs and grow it as a small tree.

Bloom Period and Color
Insignificant yellowish flowers bloom in late spring.

Mature Height × Spread
6 to 20 feet × 10 to 20 feet

When, Where, and How to Plant
Plant in early spring in any amount of sunlight (although leaf color is generally better in sun and part sun) and almost any average soil except those that stay wet. Add organic matter to dry soils and mulch with several inches of pine straw or fine pine bark.

Growing Tips
Although Burning Bush can tolerate occasional dryness, it does best when watered regularly, especially if rainfall is below normal. Because this shrub is a slow grower, you'll want to apply a slow-release fertilizer for shrubs in early spring before it leafs out each year. Follow package directions.

Care
Maintain mulch so that the soil doesn't dry out. Although scale is a serious problem on most Euonymus species, it's generally not on Burning Bush, which rarely has serious insect or disease problems. Provided the shrub has been given enough room to spread out, little pruning should be needed. However, it may be sheared regularly if grown as a hedge.

Companion Planting and Design
Burning Bush makes a colorful screen, or place it in front of evergreens where its glowing fall color will be much more noticeable.

My Personal Favorites
'Compactus' isn't quite as small as its name makes it sound—about 10 feet high, although it grows slowly. The shrub is a nice shape and has outstanding fall leaf color. 'Rudy Haag' attains about half the size of 'Compactus', making it great for small spaces. Its fall color tends to be more rosy than screaming red.

Butterfly Bush
Buddleia davidii

When, Where, and How to Plant
Plant Butterfly Bush in spring in a sunny spot. (Partial shade cuts down on the shrub's growth and the number of flowers it produces.) It tolerates just about any soil as long as it's well drained, but fertile, moist soil is ideal. Use a transplanting solution, and mulch well.

Growing Tips
Butterfly Bush will survive some dryness, but it won't produce lots of blooms all summer unless it receives ample moisture. That means watering when weather is dry. The usual rule is an inch of water per week—rainfall or that applied by the gardener. Spread a slow-release shrub fertilizer at the base of the shrub when you cut it back each spring or in April. A light application of lime every other fall can be beneficial.

Care
Because Butterfly Bush produces its flowers on new growth, it's important to cut the bush back to about a foot tall in early spring before leaves have begun to grow. Cut off the flower clusters as they fade so the shrub will also bloom more and much longer. Insects and diseases shouldn't be a problem. Avoid insecticides, as they can harm butterflies. The blossoms may be used in arrangements, but unfortunately they don't last long.

Companion Planting and Design
Make Butterfly Bush the centerpiece of the perennial flower border or mass several of the shrubs together.

My Personal Favorites
'Pink Delight' has large, fragrant, true pink flowers. The stems of 'Peace' arch over gracefully with fragrant blossoms that are white with an orange throat.

If you've ever complained that fewer and fewer butterflies are visiting your yard—or that many are present one summer and not many the next—you can quickly change the situation. Plant a Butterfly Bush—its flowers are like a magnet to these winged jewels. The grayish foliage is attractive, too, as is the shape of the shrub. Graceful plumes of fragrant flowers (8 to 10 inches long) are available in shades of purple and lavender, blue, magenta, pink, rose, and yellow to match any flower bed color scheme.

Bloom Period and Color
Purple, blue, pink, yellow, and white from midsummer to frost.

Mature Height × Spread
6 to 15 feet × 7 to 10 feet

Camellia

Camellia species and hybrids

There's wonderful news on the Camellia front—no longer are these beautiful flowering shrubs just for the warmest climates. A group of cold-hardy Camellias, developed by Dr. William Ackerman of the National Arboretum, has extended their range throughout all of Tennessee. If you enjoy Camellias and live in Chattanooga, Memphis, or an area with a similar climate, also try placing Camellia japonica in a protected place. It's hardier than Camellia sasanqua and, even if its top growth is killed back by an unusually cold winter, it will generally grow back from the roots.

Bloom Period and Color
Pink, white, red, or variegated, from fall through spring.

Mature Height × Spread
10 to 15 feet × 5 to 10 feet

When, Where, and How to Plant
I prefer to plant Camellias in spring. They can be planted in fall, but an extra cold winter may kill or severely damage them. These evergreen shrubs need moist, well-drained, acidic soil that's been amended with lots of fine pine bark or peat moss. Place on the west side of the house or where evergreens block the morning sun in winter, preventing it from "burning" frozen leaves.

Growing Tips
Camellias have shallow root systems and will need regular watering when rainfall hasn't reached an inch per week. Spread 1 pound of cottonseed meal per inch of trunk diameter around the base of the plants in March or April, or spray with a water-soluble fertilizer for acid-loving plants after blooming ends.

Care
During cold spells, don't cover plants with plastic—that causes foliage to burn when the sun shines through it; use a blanket, mattress pad, or quilt. Although flowers may be damaged by temperatures below 32 degrees Fahrenheit, unopened buds aren't harmed. To keep the plant in shape, remove two or three leaves at the base of a bloom when you cut off faded flowers. Do other pruning after blooming stops. Potential pest problems are legion, but I've never experienced any.

Companion Planting and Design
Plant beneath tall Pines whose lowest limbs are 20 feet high.

My Personal Favorites
Of the cold-hardy Camellias, I like white-flowered 'Polar Ice' and 'Winter's Beauty', which has double, pink blooms. *Camellia japonica* 'Debutante' is an old pink favorite that's relatively hardy.

Carolina All...

Calycanth...

When, Where, and How to Plant

Buy Carolina Allspice when it's in bloom to make sure the flowers are fragrant (seed-grown shrubs often have no odor). Plant in spring in any average soil, whether it's acidic or alkaline. Moist, well-drained soil that contains organic matter is ideal. This shrub will adapt to various types of light, from full sun to part shade. If you don't want it to grow too tall, put it in an area that's mostly sunny; it may get leggy or scraggly in too much shade. Water with a transplanting solution at planting time and spread an organic mulch around the base of the shrub, beginning an inch or so from the trunk.

Growing Tips

Keep the soil moist around young shrubs, then water when rainfall has been less than an inch in any week during the growing season. Fertilize with a slow-release shrub fertilizer, applied according to label directions in March or April.

Care

Little pruning is usually required. If it's needed, prune in very early spring or wait until just after flowering, as the shrub blooms on new growth as well as the previous year's wood. Carolina Allspice has no insect or disease problems.

Companion Planting and Design

Plant Carolina Allspice where its delightful aroma can be appreciated—next to a garden bench or chair, near a walkway, or beside the patio. It pairs nicely with other shrubs in a border.

My Personal Favorite

'Michael Lindsey' has superb fragrance, good-looking foliage, and nice yellow fall color.

If you were to see Carolina Allspice growing in my yard in August, you might wonder what was special about this deciduous shrub. But if you visited in April or May (or sometimes into July), you would know the answer the minute you walked by it. The fragrance of the reddish-maroon flowers produced by this native plant has been described as smelling like strawberries, pineapple, or banana—or all three. To me, the scent is like Pineapple Sage. But however you describe the aroma, I think it's heavenly.

Bloom Period and Color

Maroon in mid-spring into summer.

Mature Height × Spread

6 to 10 feet by 6 to 12 feet

rape Myrtle

Lagerstroemia species and hybrids

Plant breeders, particularly at the National Arboretum, have made huge strides forward with Crape Myrtles. They're more cold hardy than before and come in an array of sizes, rather than just extra-large. Another advance is that the newer cultivars of Crape Myrtle aren't subject to mildew. They also bloom for a much longer time than they did in the past—you can now have Crape Myrtles in flower from June through September, if you like. Look for the cultivars that have names of Indian tribes; they're among the best.

Bloom Period and Color
Red, white, pink, or lavender in summer.

Mature Height × Spread
2 to 30 feet × 2 to 25 feet

When, Where, and How to Plant
If you don't have full sun, forget about Crape Myrtle. It simply doesn't bloom well in partial shade. Plant in spring in moist, well-drained soil that has been amended with organic matter. Water with a transplanting solution and mulch well.

Growing Tips
Water deeply when less than an inch of rain has fallen during the week. Spread a slow-release fertilizer for flowering shrubs at the base of the plant when leaves appear. Or spray it with a water-soluble fertilizer in April and in May.

Care
Remove spent flowers to increase the length of blooming time. After an especially cold winter, wait until Crape Myrtle has leafed out before assessing damage and pruning. Don't be concerned when the shrubs produce leaves late—that's typical. When winter has been normal, prune in early spring. Crape Myrtles look best when lower branches are gradually removed to expose the beautiful bark. Although other pests are possible, Japanese beetles are the worst. Hand pick them off, or check with a garden center about the latest controls. Do not place traps nearby—they attract more beetles to your yard.

Companion Planting and Design
For maximum impact, place several Crape Myrtles together and underplant with *Vinca minor*.

My Personal Favorite
'Tuskegee' can eventually grow 20 feet tall and as wide, but it's cold hardy, has beautiful red blooms for more than three months, does not develop mildew, and has colorful fall foliage.

Deciduous Azalea
Rhododendron species and hybrids

When, Where, and How to Plant

While you can get by with growing Evergreen Azaleas in full shade, Deciduous Azaleas prefer more sun. Filtered light—beneath tall trees with high limbs—is ideal, but half a day of sun is okay for most. Except for Swamp Azalea, which grows in wet ground, Deciduous Azaleas appreciate the same soil as the evergreens—moist, acidic, and containing plenty of organic matter. Excellent drainage is important. Water with a transplanting solution and mulch, if desired, to keep down weeds.

Growing Tips

Water when rainfall is less than normal. Unlike Evergreen Azaleas, most deciduous species aren't sensitive to occasional dry soil—once they're mature. But growth and blooming will be better if you water regularly during dry spells. Watering is also important during the plant's first few years in your yard, while it's getting established. Fertilizer isn't necessary, but many gardeners do like to feed these shrubs. Use a mild organic fertilizer, according to directions, in mid-spring.

Care

Don't shear Deciduous Azalea. Instead, as soon as the plant has finished blooming, use handpruners to thin out wayward growth. Pest problems are few.

Companion Planting and Design

Mass groups of these native shrubs together at the edge of woodlands or beneath tall pines.

My Personal Favorite

I like Swamp Azalea (*Rhododendron viscosum*) because I can grow it in wet places in my yard; it's hardy to -25 degrees Fahrenheit. Flowers are white or pink.

Deciduous Azaleas—often called Wild Honeysuckle—aren't as widely known or planted as their evergreen cousins, but they've been gaining ground recently. Bushes are taller, flowers are intriguing and often highly fragrant, and leaves usually turn fiery in fall. There are more than a dozen natives for Tennessee gardeners to choose from, with names like Sweet Azalea, Pinkshell Azalea, and Swamp Azalea. Cumberland Azalea is often seen in the Smokies and on the Cumberland Plateau. It has yellow, orange, or red blooms and prefers higher elevations. All are very hardy.

Bloom Period and Color

Spring to late July, depending on species, in yellow, cream, white, red, orange, or violet.

Mature Height × Spread

3 to 20 feet × 4 to 15 feet

Deciduous Holly
Ilex species and hybrids

Since there are many Evergreen Hollies, why would you want to grow one that loses its leaves in winter? In a word: berries! Bare branches are completely covered with red or orange (occasionally yellow) berries all autumn. Another advantage is soft, non-spiny foliage. There are two native species—Winterberry (Ilex verticillata) and Possumhaw (Ilex decidua)—plus Japanese Winterberry (Ilex serrata) and a large group of hybrids from crosses between the native and Japanese Winterberries. All are very hardy, large shrubs that are excellent for a natural landscape.

Bloom Period and Color
Inconspicuous white blooms in spring, followed by red, orange, or yellow berries in fall.

Mature Height × Spread
2 to 18 feet × 4 to 10 feet

When, Where, and How to Plant
Plant from spring until early fall, making sure that each group of female cultivars has at least one male (such as 'Raritan Chief' or 'Jim Dandy') to pollinate it. Full sun is best, although most can tolerate a few hours of shade. Moist, acidic soil is preferred by Winterberry, which also doesn't mind wet soils. Possumhaw will grow in moderately alkaline soil. Be sure to give them plenty of room.

Growing Tips
Although mature plants can usually manage during dry weather, Winterberry and the Deciduous Holly hybrids produce greater crops of berries if they're watered whenever there's less than an inch of weekly rainfall. Fertilize with Holly-tone in March or April.

Care
Cut berry-covered branches in fall and take them indoors to a tall vase (no need to put water in the bottom); they'll last quite well. If Deciduous Hollies get too large, wait until early spring to cut one-third of the stems back to ground level each year for three years. No serious insect or disease problems affect them.

Companion Planting and Design
Excellent for massing and for attracting wildlife to your yard. Plant Deciduous Hollies against a background of needled evergreens to show off the red fruits.

My Personal Favorites
I never met a Deciduous Holly I didn't like. *Ilex verticillata* 'Red Sprite' is fun because it's small (no more than 5 feet tall). *Ilex decidua* 'Warren Red' has glossy green leaves and produces a heavy crop of berries that last a long time. 'Sparkleberry' has spectacular scarlet berries.

Evergreen Azalea
Rhododendron species and hybrids

When, Where, and How to Plant
Plant in spring in a partially shady spot that has rich, moist, well-drained soil that's been amended with lots of organic matter. Use a transplanting solution and mulch well.

Growing Tips
Don't allow Azaleas to dry out. Water when weekly rainfall hasn't totaled an inch. In hot, dry summers, it's important to keep the soil around Azaleas moist because that's when the plants are producing their flower buds for next spring. If they don't get enough water, blooms may be sparse. Spray plants with a water-soluble, acid fertilizer at the end of March, April, and May.

Care
Maintain a 3-inch mulch year-round to hold moisture in the soil and to protect roots from the cold. Prune right after plants stop blooming. Galls may be a problem in wet years and spider mites in dry ones. Pick off galls by hand and remove them from the garden.

Companion Planting and Design
Evergreen Azaleas pair beautifully with Dogwoods and make nice foundation shrubs if the house faces north. Surround them with wildflowers in a woodland garden. I like white Tulips near red Azaleas.

My Personal Favorites
The one that visitors go nuts over in my yard is 'Girard Hot Shot', which has orange-red blooms that glow. It blooms midseason, so the flowers—which almost completely cover the plant—rarely get nipped by frost. The foliage is fiery in fall. 'Glacier' is my favorite white; it produces 3-inch blooms on a 6-foot plant.

Every once in a while I read that Evergreen Azaleas have become a cliché across the South. Well, that's one way to look at it. But I prefer to believe that we have found a plant that loves our climate and transforms spring landscapes into a fairyland of red, white, pink, and lavender. I simply don't think there's a more beautiful or useful shrub. It's true that we sometimes lose Evergreen Azaleas during that extra cold winter that comes once every ten years or so, but the solution is to plant hardy types, such as Girard hybrids.

Bloom Period and Color
Spring in shades of red, pink, white, lavender, orange, and variegated.

Mature Height × Spread
1 to 10 feet × 3 to 10 feet

Evergreen Holly
Ilex species and hybrids

Evergreen Holly shrubs aren't just smaller versions of the American Holly tree. The smooth, round leaves of Japanese Holly (Ilex crenata) will remind you of Boxwood, but it's hardier and much more disease-resistant. Inkberry (Ilex glabra) is a similar native; both have inconspicuous black fruits. Chinese Holly (Ilex cornuta) is known for red berries and glossy leaves that are prickly. It may not make it through the worst of Zone 6 winters. And don't overlook some of the hybrids, such as 'Foster', which can be kept pruned to size.

Bloom Period and Color
Inconspicuous white blooms in spring, followed by red berries in fall.

Mature Height × Spread
1 to 8 feet × 4 to 15 feet

When, Where, and How to Plant
First, learn the eventual height and width of the plant you're buying. Then you won't have to spend hours pruning overgrown Hollies that cover up the view from the living room windows. In spring, plant in a sunny or mostly sunny spot in well-drained, slightly acidic soil that's been enriched with organic matter. *Ilex crenata* does fine in partial sun or even partial shade, although it won't grow very fast in shade.

Growing Tips
The main reason for the demise of *Ilex crenata* 'Helleri' is too little watering. It's a good example that you can't plant and forget any evergreen shrub. For the first two or three years, keep Hollies watered when rainfall is below normal. However, Chinese Holly can withstand drought and heat once it has become established. Fertilize yearly in spring with a slow-release shrub fertilizer or Holly-tone.

Care
Prune in December to take advantage of the shrub's usefulness for holiday decoration. Inkberry has few pests. Spider mites may trouble Japanese Holly. Chinese Holly may be bothered by scale.

Companion Planting and Design
Depending on the type, Evergreen Holly shrubs make excellent hedges and barriers, go along walkways, serve as foundation plantings, and even make fine topiaries.

My Personal Favorites
Ilex cornuta 'Carissa' has only a small spine on the ends of its leaves. *Ilex cornuta* 'September Gem' fruits very early. *Ilex crenata* 'Beehive' is a compact, mounded plant that's hardy. *Ilex glabra* 'Green Billow' makes a nice groundcover.

False Cypress
Chamaecyparis species and hybrids

When, Where, and How to Plant

Plant in spring or in early autumn in a sunny spot that has moist, well-drained soil. Enrich the soil in the planting hole with organic matter. Water with a transplanting solution and mulch well.

Growing Tips

Water when rainfall hasn't averaged an inch per week—especially when temperatures are high. Soak the soil thoroughly each time. Fertilize with a fertilizer for evergreens at the end of November or with a slow-release shrub fertilizer at the end of March.

Care

Shape *Chamaecyparis* regularly, because it's difficult to prune an overgrown needled evergreen shrub. If you cut back a branch to a spot where there are no needles, it will not grow back. In late winter, remove dead stems and needles in the interior of the shrubs. Pinch tips of branches in late spring or early summer. Insects and diseases should not be a problem.

Companion Planting and Design

Match the type of *Chamaecyparis* to the spot where you need an evergreen shrub—some dwarfs are ideal for rock gardens; taller cultivars make good screens or hedges. Many are excellent as foundation plantings or in shrub groupings. Those with an unusual appearance make nice specimen shrubs.

My Personal Favorites

Chamaecyparis pisifera 'Golden Mop' is a dwarf with a threadleaf form (corded branchlets) that can only be described as "cute" (and I don't usually like yellow shrubs). *Chamaecyparis obtusa* 'Nana' stays about 2 to 3 feet tall and as wide; it's a nice choice in rock gardens.

Why grow a shrub whose name you can't pronounce? Well, it increases your choice of needled evergreens. Then there's its interesting appearance. It almost seems as though no two Chamaecyparis *plants look the same—they may be upright or drooping, remain dwarf or grow to 50 feet, have green needles or gold. The main useful species are Hinoki False Cypress* (Chamaecyparis obtusa) *and Sawara False Cypress* (Chamaecyparis pisifera). *Just be sure to read the plant's label to understand the eventual size; some become enormous trees. Oh yes, and say Kam-uh-SIP-a-ris.*

Mature Height × Spread
4 to 20 feet × 6 to 8 feet

Flowering Quince
Chaenomeles species and hybrids

The earlier a plant blooms in spring, the more welcome it is. That's why Flowering Quince has been planted across the South for generations. For many, the fact that the bright red flowers don't last much longer than a week or two doesn't matter a bit. This is a plant that welcomes spring, promising that warm weather and glorious summer are on their way. Part of its popularity may also be due to the fact that this is an almost indestructible shrub, often found still blooming around abandoned homesteads.

Bloom Period and Color
Red, pink, white, or orange in early spring.

Mature Height × Spread
2 to 10 feet × 3 to 10 feet

When, Where, and How to Plant
Plant in spring in a sunny place that has well-drained, acidic soil (leaves turn yellow in alkaline soils). Add organic matter to poor soil. Water with a transplanting solution, and apply mulch.

Growing Tips
Water to keep the soil moist when the shrub is young. Once mature, it's almost indestructible. In early years, fertilize in early spring with a shrub fertilizer.

Care
Cut stems when they're in bloom to bring indoors. (Or cut them in bud and take inside the house where the flowers will open.) Otherwise, do any pruning after blooming has finished. Renew an overgrown shrub by cutting one-third of the stems back to the ground each year for three years. Wash aphids off with a blast of water and spray with insecticidal soap. If many leaves fall off, it's usually due to excess rainfall and humidity.

Companion Planting and Design
Flowering Quince draws plenty of admiring glances when it's in bloom, but it's rather a plain Jane the rest of the year, so place it where it can be seen in spring but recedes into the background in summer. It's a good choice for a deciduous hedge. Cultivars with thorns make good barriers.

My Personal Favorites
'Cameo' is a relatively low-growing cultivar (maybe 4 to 5 feet high) with double, apricot-pink blooms and no thorns. 'Texas Scarlet' has abundant red blooms on a spreading plant that gets to be no more than 3 to 3 1/2 feet high. 'Spitfire' has the most vivid red flowers I've seen. It grows upright rather than spreading.

Forsythia

Forsythia species and hybrids

When, Where, and How to Plant

Forsythia is an adaptable plant, although it blooms best in full sun or in a mostly sunny spot. Any average soil is fine, whether acidic or alkaline, but moist, well-drained soil that contains organic matter is preferred. Plant anytime from early spring until fall.

Growing Tips

Forsythia is a tough shrub, but it doesn't like to dry out. When the plant is young, water to keep soil moist. Once it's older, water when rain is less than an inch weekly. Spread a slow-release shrub fertilizer in spring.

Care

There's more poor pruning with Forsythia than almost any other shrub. It should not be trimmed into a round ball or given a haircut (top lopped off). The right way is to wait until flowering is finished, then cut one-third of the stems back to the ground each year for three years. That retains the natural, gently weeping habit of the shrub while reducing the size. Forsythia generally experiences few pest problems.

Companion Planting and Design

Plant where the flowers can be seen from the house and the street. Plant large-cupped, gold-flowered Daffodils nearby to echo the color of the blooms. It's a good choice for planting on banks.

My Personal Favorites

'Spectabilis' has large, very showy flowers that are impressive, although its 10-foot by 10-foot mature size may not be for everyone. 'Gold Tide' is a groundcover Forsythia that grows about 2 feet tall and 5 feet wide. 'Fiesta' has gold and green leaves on a plant that reaches only 2 to 3 feet high.

I'm not about to hide my enthusiasm for Forsythia, or Golden Bells. Almost the first thing I do after moving to a new house is plant one of these graceful shrubs with the arching stems. I love the bright yellow blooms and the fact that they appear very early in the season. People who don't like this beautiful plant have usually planted it in a place where it soon became crowded. Give it room to grow, prune it correctly, and you'll have a harbinger of spring of which to be proud.

Bloom Period and Color
Yellow in early spring.

Mature Height × Spread
2 to 10 feet × 4 to 12 feet

Fothergilla

Fothergilla species

The advice "Buy plants that are interesting in more than one season" has almost become a cliché, but following it saves time, money, and space. No need to plant and care for three shrubs when one gives you the same effect. Fothergilla, a Southeastern native, shines in three seasons: white, honey-scented flowers in spring (appearing before the leaves on the dwarf species Fothergilla gardenii *and with the foliage on* Fothergilla major*), nice green or bluish pest-resistant leaves in summer, and some of the most spectacular fall color around. Might as well buy two!*

Bloom Period and Color
White in April and May.

Mature Height × Spread
2 to 10 feet × 2 to 9 feet

When, Where, and How to Plant

Fothergilla likes moist, acidic, well-drained soil that contains organic matter. In poor to average soil, mix in peat moss, compost, or very fine bark before planting. Avoid alkaline and wet soils. Even though this shrub may be planted in a mostly sunny spot, it grows and blooms—and the leaves color up better in autumn—if it's given full sun. Plant in spring. Use a transplanting solution and mulch well.

Growing Tips

Fothergilla needs regular moisture all its life. Follow the usual rule: Water deeply whenever rainfall doesn't equal 1 inch per week. Fertilize in spring with a slow-release shrub fertilizer spread in a circle on the ground around the shrub, beginning an inch from the trunk and continuing a foot beyond the tips of the branches.

Care

Maintain the mulch to keep moisture in the soil. *Fothergilla gardenii* tends to sucker; remove unwanted suckers at any time. Pruning is rarely needed on either species, and insects or diseases are almost never a problem.

Companion Planting and Design

This is an excellent plant for a mixed shrub border. Place it along the sunny edges of a woodland flower garden with Azaleas and Rhododendrons as well as perennial flowers. Because *Fothergilla gardenii* generally stays less than 3 or 4 feet high, it's excellent for small spaces.

My Personal Favorite

Fothergilla major 'Mt. Airy' is very hardy and has blue-green foliage and spectacular yellow-orange-red fall foliage.

Hydrangea
Hydrangea species and hybrids

When, Where, and How to Plant
Hydrangeas aren't picky about light—although most prefer some afternoon shade in the heat of summer (Oakleaf will tolerate full shade). What they really need is moist, well-drained soil that's been enriched with organic matter and a location that can be reached by a hose. Plant in spring.

Growing Tips
Regular watering is essential for all Hydrangeas. And they let you know if they're thirsty by wilting. With most shrubs, wilting is fatal, but with Hydrangeas you can water them well after they've drooped and they usually perk right up. Keep an eye on the plants in the hot summer months; depending on the soil, you may need to water twice a week if rainfall isn't adequate. Fertilize in spring with an acid fertilizer if you want blue blooms; lime in fall for pink flowers. (This isn't always foolproof, however.)

Care
Prune most Hydrangeas right after they bloom, if they need it. Exceptions are Smooth Hydrangea and Peegee Hydrangea, which are pruned in late winter or very early spring. Any Hydrangea can be rejuvenated by cutting it back to a foot tall. Cut flower heads from the plant just after they've faded, then use indoors in dried arrangements. If the shrub did not bloom, it's usually because the buds were killed by a late spring cold snap. Insects and diseases aren't usually serious.

Companion Planting and Design
Surround pink-flowered Hydrangeas with perennials that have blue blooms.

My Personal Favorite
'Snowflake' is an Oakleaf Hydrangea with especially lovely flowers.

Everyone knows Bigleaf Hydrangea (Hydrangea macrophylla), which produces big pink or blue "balls" in early summer. But do you know Lacecap Hydrangea, which has more delicate blooms? Or Oakleaf Hydrangea (Hydrangea quercifola)? Its enormous cone-shaped, white blooms really put on a show in shade. Then there's Peegee Hydrangea (Hydrangea paniculata 'Grandiflora'), which is often grown as a small tree. 'Annabelle', a cultivar of Smooth Hydrangea (Hydrangea arborescens), has 1-foot blooms on a 4- to 6-foot-tall bush. Look them over and soon you'll think, "Why not have one of each?"

Bloom Period and Color
Pink, blue, red, or white in summer.

Mature Height × Spread
3 to 10 feet × 3 to 10 feet

155

Kerria

Kerria japonica

About the time Forsythia finishes its spring show, Kerria takes over. You'll find two flower forms. The one that's easiest to find ('Pleniflora') has small, double blooms in a bright gold color. They look like little gold balls. (I've heard gardeners call this plant Yellow Rose of Texas.) My favorite cultivars have single, clear yellow blossoms shaped like Buttercups. Whatever the flower type, the shrub's stems—which have a graceful arching habit in the species and some cultivars—are green in winter, adding an interesting touch to the landscape.

Bloom Period and Color
Yellow or gold in mid-spring.

Mature Height × Spread
3 to 8 feet × 6 to 10 feet

When, Where, and How to Plant
Kerria is a shrub that suckers freely (especially in loose or rich soil) and eventually forms large colonies, if you let it. If you have a woodland spot to let it go, that's ideal. But don't crowd it. Leaves will burn in afternoon sun, so shade or partial shade is recommended. Plant from late winter until August. Kerria adapts to almost any soil. Use a transplanting solution and mulch lightly.

Growing Tips
Keep the soil moist in early years, until the plant becomes established. Later, if you can water during dry spells, you'll find less stem dieback and better blooming. Occasional watering will probably be necessary in rocky soil. Don't fertilize; that encourages excessive growth.

Care
Kerria will need to be pruned each spring after flowering finishes to remove dead stems and tips of stems that have died back, as well as to control size. To rejuvenate an overgrown shrub, cut one-third of the stems back to the ground each year for three years. Dig or pull up unwanted suckers at any time of year. Insects and diseases are not usually a problem with Kerria.

Companion Planting and Design
I always put Kerria not too far from my front door so I can glimpse the green stems in winter and enjoy the flowers in spring. The single-flowering species is an excellent companion for woodland wildflowers.

My Personal Favorites
'Shannon' has been delightful and trouble-free in my garden. 'Superba' has also done nicely and has slightly larger flowers.

Leucothoe

Leucothoe species and hybrids

When, Where, and How to Plant

Plant from mid-spring until fall in moist, well-drained, acidic soil. If you're interested in plants that have reddish coloration on the new leaves, buy the shrub in spring to make sure you get one that has this characteristic. Leucothoe doesn't do well in rocky soils that dry out or where it can be whipped by the wind. Improve the soil with organic matter, if soil doesn't contain ample humus. Water with a transplanting solution and mulch well.

Growing Tips

This is a shrub that must be kept watered; it often develops problems if it's stressed. Water often enough to keep the soil moist. Fertilize in early spring with a slow-release fertilizer made for shrubs.

Care

Keep a 3-inch mulch year-round to hold moisture in the soil. Prune right after flowering. If the plant has become overgrown, it may be cut back to 18 inches high and allowed to regrow. Leaf spots, caused by fungi, are fairly prevalent. Check with a garden center about options in fungicides, which are preventative rather than curative. (An organic control is 1 tablespoon baking soda in a gallon of water.)

Companion Planting and Design

Plant Leucothoe with Rhododendrons, or put it on a hill where its drooping form is an advantage. I like to place it to hide the leggy base of Carolina Jessamine.

My Personal Favorites

Leucothoe axillaris 'Sarah's Choice' is about 3 feet tall and produces more flowers than any other Leucothoe I've grown. *Leucothoe fontanesiana* 'Girard's Rainbow' has pink-coppery new foliage.

The various species and cultivars of Leucothoe have in common broad, evergreen leaves on graceful arching branches. This almost weeping effect is especially welcome in a shrub. Leucothoe fontanesiana grows 3 to 6 feet tall and as wide, and it is good in Zones 6 and 7a. Leucothoe axillaris (for the entire state) stays about 2 to 4 feet high. Florida Leucothoe (Agarista populifolia; also sold as Leucothoe populifolia) may reach 15 feet tall, although it can be kept pruned much shorter. It's a good choice for Zone 7 gardens.

Bloom Period and Color

White in spring.

Mature Height × Spread

2 to 6 feet × 3 to 7 feet

Loropetalum
Loropetalum chinense

This is one of those "see-it-gotta-have-it" plants. Early one fall I picked up a couple of Loropetalums at a garden center, then stopped by to visit several people before I went home. In every case, those who spied the colorful shrubs in the back seat of my car wanted to know what they were and where they could get one. Although there are green-leaf forms, go for the cultivars that have deep red leaves all year. Growing on arching stems, they really liven up the landscape in any season.

Bloom Period and Color
Pink or white in spring (and sometimes later).

Mature Height × Spread
6 to 12 feet × 5 to 10 feet

Zone
7

When, Where, and How to Plant
Plant anytime from spring until early fall in moist, well-drained, acidic soil. (Alkaline soil causes yellowish leaves.) Enrich the planting hole with organic matter to hold moisture. Loropetalum tolerates many light intensities, but part sun and part shade seem to be best.

Growing Tips
Water to keep the soil moist around young plants. Older specimens can tolerate some dryness, but all grow and bloom better (and are best able to withstand extra cold winters) if regularly watered whenever an inch of rain hasn't fallen in a week. After a hard winter and following pruning, fertilize in March or April with a slow-release fertilizer made for shrubs.

Care
Damage may occur when temperatures reach 0 or 5 degrees Fahrenheit (although in protected places, my shrubs have survived unscathed so far). If that happens, wait to see if leaves and stems regrow, then prune as necessary. Try to maintain the graceful shape, rather than lopping off the top of the plant. Loropetalum doesn't suffer from insect or disease infestations. Maintain a year-round mulch to hold moisture in the soil.

Companion Planting and Design
Use as a screen or group several together for maximum impact.

My Personal Favorites
My favorite so far is 'Burgundy'. Its leaves truly live up to the name and are a wonderful foil for the hot-pink blooms that begin opening in spring and continue to appear sporadically until fall. It is a fast grower with an open habit. In colder parts of the region, look for 'Zhuzhou Fuchsia'.

Nandina

Nandina domestica

When, Where, and How to Plant

In spring, plant upright-growing Nandinas in a shady or partially shady spot with rich, moist, well-drained soil. They develop larger crops of berries if they're grouped than if they're planted singly. Dwarfs are fine in full sun, although they'll appreciate some afternoon shade. (More sun means brighter fall color.) In Zone 6, place Nandinas in a protected place. Water with transplanting solution and mulch well.

Growing Tips

Keep soil moist, if possible, although mature plants can take quite a bit of dryness if in shade. Spread a slow-release shrub fertilizer at half the recommended rate in April, if desired.

Care

Mounded types need little pruning; just snip off winter damage and maintain the round form. When upright Nandinas become crowded, cut one-third of the canes back to the ground each year for three years to rejuvenate them. Do this in early spring before flowers appear so you don't interfere with next year's berries. Plants may die back to the ground when temperatures fall below 0 degrees Fahrenheit, but they grow back from the roots. No serious pest problems.

Companion Planting and Design

Standard Nandinas may be used for screening and as a not-too-tall hedge. Dwarf, mounded Nandinas are often used for edging.

My Personal Favorites

In Zone 7, try 'Alba', which develops an abundance of white berries but may not be as hardy as other selections. 'Harbour Dwarf' is my favorite low-growing Nandina.

When talking about Nandina, it's almost as though you're speaking of two different shrubs. One is an old Southern favorite that, because of its slightly Oriental appearance, is called Heavenly Bamboo. It has delicate foliage and long clusters of berries on bamboolike stems that reach up to 6 feet tall and prefers to grow in the shade. The other is a small, round ball that can tolerate quite a bit of sun, doesn't bloom or produce berries, and has more brilliant fall color. One shrub—two types—lots of uses!

Bloom Period and Color

White flowers in late spring followed by long-lasting, red berries. (Most dwarf cultivars don't bloom or produce berries.)

Mature Height × Spread

1 to 8 feet × 2 to 4 feet

Redvein Enkianthus

Enkianthus campanulatus

There's something about delicate, bell-shaped flowers that's quite appealing. And when they're cream-colored and veined with red (or just intense red) and cover the shrub in spring—well, that's hard to resist. But that's not all Redvein Enkianthus has going for it. Leaves are bluish-green in summer, changing to brilliant shades of red, orange, and yellow in fall. Also, its branches are almost horizontal, giving the shrub an arresting appearance in winter. In addition, it grows (usually slowly) to a medium size that fits into just about yard. Very nice.

Bloom Period and Color
White, pink, red, cream, or light orange in late spring to early summer.

Mature Height × Spread
6 to 10 feet × 4 to 12 feet

When, Where, and How to Plant

Redvein Enkianthus thrives in the same conditions as Rhododendrons—moist, well-drained, acidic soil that contains lots of organic matter. Add peat moss, compost, or finely shredded bark to average soil to improve its humus content before planting. Plant anytime from spring until early autumn in a sunny spot or in an area that receives a few hours of afternoon shade. Mulch well.

Growing Tips

In hot summers, Redvein Enkianthus will suffer if the soil is allowed to dry out. Water deeply at least weekly whenever rainfall is less than an inch over a period of seven days. Each spring, spread a slow-release shrub fertilizer in a widening circle around the base of the shrub, beginning 1 to 2 inches from the trunk and continuing to 1 foot beyond the tips of the branches.

Care

Maintain a 2- to 3-inch mulch year-round to hold moisture in the soil. Do any necessary pruning right after blooming ceases. The shrub doesn't usually suffer from diseases or insects.

Companion Planting and Design

Grow near Rhododendrons and Deciduous Azaleas.

My Personal Favorites

'Rubrum' offers up intense red in two seasons—large scarlet flowers in spring and fiery foliage in fall. 'Red Bells' has two-toned red and cream flowers and outstanding fall color; the shrub is more upright than 'Rubrum' and a few feet taller. 'Sikokianus' has maroon buds opening to red bells streaked with shrimp pink. Mmmm!

Rhododendron
Rhododendron species and hybrids

When, Where, and How to Plant
Taking time to site Rhododendrons correctly is one of the keys to success. The first need is outstanding drainage. Too much water is almost always fatal. Second is acidic soil that's been amended with half organic matter. Rhododendrons are *not* full shade plants; they need half a day of sun in order to bloom well. Place them where morning sun won't "burn" frozen leaves in the winter. To increase drainage, those with clay soil may plant Rhododendrons in raised beds, but be aware that if you do, you'll need to water and fertilize frequently. Mulch well.

Growing Tips
Water weekly if rainfall hasn't totaled an inch. This is especially important if temperatures are high. Spray the leaves and ground with a plant food for acid-loving plants at the end of March, April, and May.

Care
Trim off winter damage in spring as new growth begins. Prune some each year, right after flowering, to keep the shrubs in shape; pruning an overgrown Rhododendron isn't easy or always successful. Many insects and diseases pose potential problems, but if the shrub is properly planted and cared for, few should materialize.

Companion Planting and Design
Make Rhododendrons the centerpiece of a woodland garden by planting Ferns, Evergreen Azaleas, and wildflowers around them.

My Personal Favorite
'Roseum' is absolutely foolproof in any garden, although it often takes several years to begin blooming; give it plenty of room.

Many of us admire Rhododendrons, but aren't sure if we can—or should—grow them in our yards. Gardeners who live in Zone 7 have heard they do best in colder climates. All of us wonder if they aren't just for the mountains. Put those doubts to rest. Rhododendrons can be grown anywhere in Tennessee, as long as the soil is acidic, contains plenty of organic matter, and has good drainage. Rhododendrons also need half a day of sun or good, bright light. Oh, the gorgeous flowers they'll produce!

Bloom Period and Color
Shades of white, pink, red, lavender, or yellow in late spring.

Mature Height × Spread
1 to 15 feet × 18 inches to 12 feet

Rose

Rosa species and hybrids

Is there anyone who doesn't like Roses? Not too long ago, our choices were limited mostly to Hybrid Tea Roses, along with a few Miniatures. Now the selection is wide-ranging: Shrub Roses, Old Garden Roses, English Roses, landscape (or groundcover) Roses, as well as Hybrid Teas and Miniatures. If there's a Rose society in your area, consult its members for advice. I like to stick with Roses that have won All-America Rose Selections awards in the past ten years because I've found that they rarely develop blackspot or mildew.

Bloom Period and Color
Shades of white, pink, red, yellow, and bicolors from late spring until a hard frost.

Mature Height × Spread
6 inches to 8 feet × 8 inches to 12 feet

When, Where, and How to Plant
Plant bare-root Roses in mid- to late March in Zone 7 and late March to mid-April in Zone 6. Dig a large hole in an area that gets six or more hours of sun, and enrich the soil with plenty of organic matter. Build a cone of soil in the center of the hole and spread the bare roots over it so that the bud union (the swelling above where the canes and roots join) is at ground level or an inch above. Holding the bush upright, replace the soil. Water with a transplanting solution and mulch. Set out container-grown Roses in early summer.

Growing Tips
Roses need plenty of water and fertilizer. This means at least an inch of moisture per week. (Keep water off the leaves.) Fertilize with a granular rose food after each flush of flowers fades. You may also use a water-soluble fertilizer for flowering plants every other week. Stop fertilizing by the end of August to avoid winter damage.

Care
See page 251 for directions on pruning Roses. This needs to be done each spring. When you remove Roses from the bush, cut them 1/4 inch above a five-leaf cluster that's pointing toward the outside of the bush. Roses are subject to many insects and diseases.

Companion Planting and Design
Silver-foliaged *Artemisia* 'Powis Castle' accents Roses.

My Personal Favorites
Two that have been carefree for me are 'Fuchsia Meidiland'—a groundcover Rose with deep pink, double flowers—and 'Carefree Delight', which grows about 3 feet tall and has single pink flowers.

Smoke Tree

Cotinus coggygria

When, Where, and How to Plant
Because Smoke Tree likes loose, fast-draining soil, it's ideal for gardeners with poor, rocky ground, but it grows well in almost any soil except those that stay wet. Plant from early spring until early fall in full sun.

Growing Tips
Smoke Tree leafs out late—don't be concerned that it has died over winter when other plants produce their leaves before this shrub does. This is a plant that requires quite a bit of watering when young, so keep the soil evenly moist. Once mature, it can tolerate drier soil but may need watering in hot, dry summers. Fertilizer isn't usually necessary, but you may want to feed purple-leafed cultivars to encourage new growth, which is usually the most colorful. If so, use a slow-release fertilizer for shrubs at the end of March or April.

Care
Little pruning is necessary or desirable. If the plant develops straggly stems, trim them in early spring. Smoke Tree has no serious insect or disease problems.

Companion Planting and Design
Smoke Tree is usually grown singly as a specimen shrub, placed where it can be admired. But it's also nice as the centerpiece of a flower border surrounded by plants with pink or purple flowers or silver foliage.

My Personal Favorites
The leaves of 'Velvet Cloak' retain their maroon-red coloration all summer and are brilliant red in fall. 'Pink Champagne' is more compact (about 7 feet tall) with green leaves and long-lasting, feathery flowers.

Smoke Tree, or Smoke Bush, has to be the only plant ever to be grown not for the appearance of its flowers when they're fresh and new, but for the spectacular show the fluffy flower clusters put on after they've faded. The big, billowing blooms remind me of cotton candy. If you prefer Smoke Trees that have reddish-purple foliage, buy plants in mid- to late summer, because some fade to green late in the season. Seed-grown Smoke Trees have variable leaf color; 'Royal Purple' and 'Velvet Cloak' retain their coloration.

Bloom Period and Color
Yellowish in late spring to early summer; pink to purple "smoke" in early summer.

Mature Height × Spread
8 to 25 feet × 10 to 20 feet

Spirea
Spiraea species and hybrids

Gardeners of a certain age will always associate the name Spirea with Bridal Wreath (Spiraea prunifolia 'Plena'), a 6-foot shrub with graceful arching stems that are lined with tiny white blooms in spring and colorful foliage in fall. But anyone who's had some landscaping done in the past five years probably thinks of a low, mounded plant (Spiraea × bumalda)—often with chartreuse foliage—that has pink blooms from summer into autumn. Both are excellent choices for Tennessee gardens, as are all the other Spireas that you'll find at a nursery.

Bloom Period and Color
White in spring, or pink from spring into fall.

Mature Height × Spread
18 inches to 9 feet × 4 to 8 feet

When, Where, and How to Plant
Plant anytime from spring until fall in a sunny or mostly sunny spot. Spirea tolerates any average soil, except those that stay wet and don't drain well. For best results, enrich the soil with organic matter before planting. Space according to eventual mature size. Water with a transplanting solution and mulch if desired.

Growing Tips
Most Spireas need a moderate amount of water, especially when young. Water whenever weekly rainfall is less than an inch. Bridal Wreath types can tolerate some dry soil once they've become established. Fertilize in spring with a slow-release shrub fertilizer.

Care
Prune *Spiraea × bumalda* and Japanese Spirea (including 'Goldmound') in late winter or early spring before growth starts. Prune Bridal Wreath types very soon after they finish flowering. Rejuvenate overgrown shrubs by cutting one-third of the old stems back to the ground each year for three years. Numerous insects and diseases have an affinity for Spirea, but few are fatal.

Companion Planting and Design
The mounded Spireas are often massed together. Bridal Wreath usually stands alone, but may be paired with spring-flowering shrubs. Try *Spiraea japonica* 'Shirobana' with *Hydrangea arborescens* 'Annabelle' and a host of colorful Daylilies.

My Personal Favorites
Spiraea × bumalda 'Anthony Waterer' has leaves that are bluish-green in summer and red in fall. 'Limemound' forms a ball about 2 feet tall by 3 feet wide. *Spiraea japonica* 'Shirobana' has pink and white blooms on the same plant.

When, Where, and How to Plant

Plant from spring until early autumn in part sun or part shade. Full sun is okay, but plants grow larger and bloom better with some relief from the hot afternoon sun. In the wild, *Clethra* grows in wet places, so it appreciates moist soil that's acidic and contains plenty of organic matter. Use a transplanting solution after planting and mulch well.

Growing Tips

Although Summersweet is relatively adaptable, it performs best and produces the most flowers when watered regularly. Don't let the soil dry out. Fertilize at the end of March or April with a slow-release fertilizer made for shrubs.

Care

This delightful shrub is rarely subject to any insects or diseases. It flowers on the current year's growth, so do any required pruning in late winter before new growth begins. Little pruning is usually needed, but if it has grown too large for the spot where it's planted, cut back one-fourth of the stems to the ground each year for four years. The plant spreads by rhizomes and suckers; remove unwanted plants at any time.

Companion Planting and Design

Grow with Virginia Sweetspire on the edge of a woodland.

My Personal Favorites

'Chattanooga' (found at the Tennessee Aquarium) has nice white flowers on a shrub that grows to about 7 feet tall. 'Hummingbird' has white blooms on a compact plant (about 3 feet high) with deep green leaves in summer and clear yellow foliage in fall. 'Pink Spires' has nonfading, pale pink blooms, while the blooms of 'Ruby Spice' are rosy pink.

Don't you love plants that have a sweet aroma? I think flowers should smell as good as they look. Summersweet's pink or white flower clusters certainly do—and are appreciated as much by bees as humans. But fragrance and pretty flowers aren't the only sterling attributes of this native shrub. It thrives in those wet places that so many plants won't tolerate. It adapts to almost any light—from partial shade to full sun—and has excellent fall foliage color. To top it all off, it's easy to grow.

Bloom Period and Color
White or pink in mid- to late summer.

Mature Height × Spread
4 by 10 feet × 4 by 8 feet

urnum

Viburnum species and hybrids

There are so many Viburnums—and they differ so much—that you could grow just this shrub and still have a tremendous amount of variety in your yard. One attribute that most Viburnums share is berries—much appreciated by birds. The size and shape of the flowers vary, as does time of bloom, but generally flowers are white or pink. Most are deciduous shrubs, but some are evergreen. Doublefile Viburnum (Viburnum plicatum tomentosum) is one of the loveliest. The Snowballs are extremely popular, but do look for others.

Bloom Period and Color
White or pink in spring to summer; varies by species.

Mature Height × Spread
2 to 30 feet × 4 to 15 feet

When, Where, and How to Plant
Because Viburnums vary so, it's important to read the plant label and talk with a knowledgeable person at the nursery to learn the specific soil and light requirements for each species and hybrid. In general, you can count on most Viburnums being happy in sections of the yard that have 6 or more hours of sun (evergreens especially appreciate some afternoon shade). You're probably also safe in choosing an area with slightly acidic, moist, well-drained soil that contains organic matter. Plant evergreen Viburnums in spring; deciduous types from spring until fall. Water with a transplanting solution and mulch well.

Growing Tips
Water whenever rainfall hasn't amounted to at least an inch a week. Fertilize in spring with a slow-release plant food for flowering shrubs.

Care
The list of *potential* pest problems on Viburnums is long, but fortunately you'll rarely have to do battle with them. Do any necessary pruning just after flowering. Remove water sprouts (vertical growth on stems) as they appear.

Companion Planting and Design
There's a Viburnum for just about any shrub use in the landscape—screening, specimen, mixed into a shrub or flower border, or hedge. Because of the berries, these shrubs are a must for anyone who wants to attract wildlife.

My Personal Favorites
I enjoy the pink buds and white, sweetly fragrant flowers of *Viburnum* × *burkwoodii*, which blooms in early spring. *Viburnum* × *pragense* is the evergreen that has grown best in my garden.

Virginia Sweetspire

Itea virginica

When, Where, and How to Plant

Although Virginia Sweetspire is known for its love of wet soils—great news for those who have clay—it nevertheless is relatively drought-tolerant once it's established. So if you don't have any damp or moist places in your yard, plant the shrub in any average soil. It grows largest in full sun, but doesn't mind partial shade, making it a nice understory shrub. (I prefer to plant Virginia Sweetspire in part shade and soil that's on the dry side so it will stay more compact and not spread as much.) Plant any time from spring until early autumn, watering with a transplant solution at planting time and mulching well with pine straw or other organic material.

Growing Tips

Water regularly the first two or three years, to keep the soil moist. Once the shrub is established, water deeply during dry spells. Fertilize in spring with a slow-release fertilizer made for shrubs.

Care

Keep the mulch about 3 inches thick year-round. Do any needed pruning just after flowering is finished. Insect and diseases rarely bother Virginia Sweetspire. If you notice spots on the leaves, they are generally harmless.

Companion Planting and Design

Grow with wildflowers and Ferns, or place beside a water garden or stream.

My Personal Favorites

'Henry's Garnet' is the best-known and most reliable cultivar. It thrives in summer heat and winter cold, and it has excellent flowers and fall color. 'Saturnalia' sometimes has more brilliant red fall foliage.

This is one of my favorite deciduous shrubs. Maybe that's because I'm a native of Virginia. Or because I have so many tall trees and it fits naturally into a woodland garden. Or possibly it's my appreciation of its brilliant fall foliage. It could be the fragrance of the flowers, or the way it blooms after all the spring shrubs have finished. Or the fact that, once Virginia Sweetspire is planted, it needs almost no attention from me. All I have to do is stand back and admire it.

Bloom Period and Color

White in late spring to early summer.

Mature Height × Spread

3 to 5 feet × 3 to 6 feet

Witch Hazel

Hamamelis species and hybrids

Imagine what it's like to look out the window in January or February and see a shrub covered with yellow, red, orange, maroon, or copper flowers. It's a sight that definitely lifts your spirits. And it often leads to planting more Witch Hazels since it's fun to have various colors. You might want to train some as small trees. But Witch Hazel isn't a one-season shrub; several species and cultivars have excellent fall color. And the new leaves of Hamamelis vernalis *are reddish purple, making it interesting in three seasons.*

Bloom Period and Color
Shades of yellow, red, and orange in winter.

Mature Height × Spread
6 to 30 feet × 10 to 25 feet

When, Where, and How to Plant
Plant from late winter until fall in moist soil and full to partial sun. Witch Hazel is a good choice for those who have clay soil. All Witch Hazels, except the native *Hamamelis virginiana*, can also tolerate alkaline soil. Be sure to read the label to find the mature size of the shrub, and then space it accordingly. Some can grow quite large. Water with a transplanting solution and mulch well.

Growing Tips
Water regularly to keep soil evenly moist. In periods of high temperatures and drought, check twice a week to see if soil is dry. Fertilize in spring with a slow-release plant food for flowering plants.

Care
Add to mulch as needed to keep it about 3 inches deep. Do any necessary pruning to control size in late spring or early summer. However, it's fine to cut budded branches in winter, bring them indoors, and place in a vase so they will soon bloom. Witch Hazel has few or no pest problems.

Companion Planting and Design
Witch Hazel is ideal near a water garden, but should always be placed where it can be seen—and admired—in winter, especially from indoors. Try surrounding yellow-flowered shrubs with 'February Gold' Daffodils and purple-flowered Crocus.

My Personal Favorites
Hamamelis vernalis 'Christmas Cheer' is the first Witch Hazel to flower in my yard. Among the excellent *Hamamelis × intermedia* hybrids, my favorites are 'Jelena', which has copper blooms and 'Arnold Promise', which is still the best yellow I've grown.

Trees *for Tennessee*

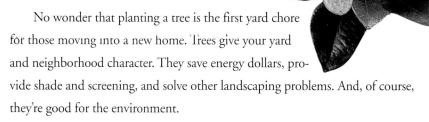

Try to imagine a world without trees—
without clouds of white Dogwoods in spring,
without the stately shade trees that sheltered you
and the games of your childhood, without
pecans or pine cones, without the brilliant
orange and scarlet and yellow foliage that
sends us into colder weather.

No wonder that planting a tree is the first yard chore
for those moving into a new home. Trees give your yard
and neighborhood character. They save energy dollars, pro-
vide shade and screening, and solve other landscaping problems. And, of course,
they're good for the environment.

Whatever a tree's use in the landscape, homeowners face a number of decisions
when selecting and planting one. To find the best tree for your yard, ask yourself a few
questions first.

Start with a Few Questions

What is your ultimate goal for this tree? What purpose will it serve in your landscape?
Do you want shade, flowers in spring, or a tree that will attract birds to your yard or
produce colorful fall foliage? Do you want one that will serve as a buffer between you,
your neighbors, and the outside world, or a tree that will be interesting to look at in
more than one season? Many trees have more than one attribute to recommend them.
Dogwoods, for instance, flower in spring and have leaves that turn fiery in fall, while
they also produce berries that are attractive to a host of feathered friends.

Do you want or need a deciduous tree (such as a Maple), a broadleaf evergreen
(Southern Magnolia, for instance), or a needled evergreen—sometimes called a conifer
(such as a Canadian Hemlock)?

Deciduous trees drop their leaves in autumn, which leads to raking. But it also
means that you can position a deciduous tree so that it blocks the sun from reaching

your house in summer, decreasing air conditioning costs, but letting sun through in winter to help warm the house and cut your heating bills.

Evergreens block the sun in summer and winter. Mostly they're used to add a green touch to the yard in cold weather, when everything else looks brown. They are also frequently used as a screen—to block views or foot traffic—year-round. As a group, evergreens tend to grow more slowly than deciduous trees. This may be helpful or not, depending upon your needs and goals. Although evergreens never lose all their leaves or needles, they do shed some of them each year. Sometimes homeowners think a Pine tree is dying when they see a bunch of interior needles turn brown and fall off. Not to worry; this is how the tree renews itself.

The Biggest Mistake Homeowners Make

How large will that small tree grow? Not learning the answer to that question—*before* buying and planting—is probably the biggest mistake homeowners make when choosing trees for their yard.

When you don't know the mature size of the tree you're planting, you're all too likely to place it too close to the house, sidewalk, or street. With one-story homes especially, keep perspective firmly in mind. Ask yourself: When this tree matures, how will its size and the size of the house compare? Also, look up: Are there power lines that may interfere with the tree when it reaches its eventual size?

A Big Investment

How hardy is that tree? That's an important question to ask when buying any plant for your yard. Often people assume that because a plant is for sale in their area, it will grow well there. That's not necessarily so. Always make sure that the tree is rated for your USDA winter hardiness zone (see page 248). But also pay attention to whether or not the tree can take the heat of a Tennessee August. A Fir, for example, is extremely winter hardy, but it languishes in heat and humidity. A tree is a big investment; no one wants one that won't live through a Zone 6 winter or Zone 7 summer.

Landscape Harmony

What shape or form will the tree develop as it grows? There are at least nine different shapes that various trees assume as they mature. These range from columnar (very narrow) to pyramid-shaped to weeping. Employees at a good nursery can tell you what the shape is for a tree you're considering. Or, often, the tree's tag will show a photo. Think of the effect that each form will have not only in and of itself, but also in relation to surrounding plantings and structures (house, garage, fence). While a weeping Ornamental Cherry is a delight in spring, you wouldn't want to fill your yard with all weeping trees; that would dilute the effect. Let the various forms of trees complement and harmonize with the entire yard.

The Search for the "Perfect" Tree

Does the tree develop any messy fruits, seeds, or droppings? A Sweet Gum is a pleasure in fall because of its scarlet leaves, but it's a nuisance in spring when the "balls" keep fouling up the lawn mower. And the hard, brown leaves of Southern Magnolia aren't a pretty sight.

But that doesn't mean you have to give up on these trees. Instead, site them so that their liability isn't a drawback. In the case of Magnolia, never prune off the lower limbs; they help hide the old leaves. Faded Magnolia leaves are also less of a liability when the tree is planted in a mulched bed instead of in the lawn. Or maybe you'll want to plant a Sweet Gum or other messy tree at the outer fringe of a some woods, so the fruits can fall harmlessly to the ground and not matter. Or try planting messy trees in the center of a groundcover bed.

It's easy to see why it's almost impossible to imagine a beautiful landscape without trees. Trees not only increase the value of your property, as studies have shown, but they add a sense of permanence and comfort. In the following pages, you'll find the perfect tree for any spot in your yard.

American Holly
Ilex opaca

Not all the trees you plant in your yard will be shade trees or flowering trees. Everyone needs at least one evergreen to add a touch of green to the landscape during the cold, dreary months of winter. And what better choice than a native American Holly? Just in time for Christmas— that season of red and green—it produces bright crimson berries, giving you a naturally decorated tree in the yard. And, happily, December is also the ideal time to cut Holly sprigs and branches to use indoors.

Bloom Period and Color
White blooms in spring; red berries in fall and winter.

Mature Height × Spread
15 to 40 feet × 8 to 30 feet

When, Where, and How to Plant
American Holly trees need moist, well-drained, acidic soil. In nature they may sometimes be found beneath trees whose lowest limbs start 20 feet off the ground, but that produces a very open habit that most people don't care for. Compact, pyramidal trees grow in full sun or mostly sunny sites. Avoid windy locations. For every three to six female Hollies (which produce berries), plant a male that blooms at the same time for pollination; they can be up to 100 feet apart. In spring, dig a hole as deep as the rootball and twice as wide. Place the tree in it and fill in with the soil dug from the hole. Mulch well.

Growing Tips
Water when rainfall is less than an inch weekly. In early years, fertilize with an organic fertilizer such as Holly-tone at the end of March or April.

Care
Prune anytime to maintain the pyramidal shape. The main pests are holly leaf miner (which leaves "trails" in the leaves), scale (which looks like tiny brown bumps on the stems and undersides of leaves), and spittlebug (recognized by the foam it leaves behind).

Companion Planting and Design
Place American Holly where it can be seen from the street and, especially, from indoors in winter. Use several for screening or a windbreak.

My Personal Favorites
'Jersey Princess' has lustrous dark-green leaves ('Jersey Knight' pollinates it). Don't overlook other evergreen Hollies, such as the many hybrids—'Foster', 'Nellie R. Stevens', and especially 'Emily Bruner' and 'James Swan', which were discovered in Knoxville.

Bald Cypress
Taxodium distichum

When, Where, and How to Plant

Plant in early fall or in spring in a sunny spot with acidic soil. This tree grows quickly and will become very large, so give it plenty of space. It's ideal for a boggy spot, but Bald Cypress tolerates almost any type of soil, as long as it isn't alkaline. Plant it in a hole the same depth as the rootball and twice as wide, replacing the soil dug from the hole. Mulch well, keeping the mulch 2 inches away from the trunk.

Growing Tips

Water weekly for the tree's first two years in your yard. After that it should be able to get by on rainfall. The first few years after planting, you may want to fertilize Bald Cypress to get it off to a good start. Fertilize each fall, after the "needles" have fallen, with a high-nitrogen fertilizer that's spread according to package directions.

Care

Yellowing "needles" probably mean the soil isn't acidic enough; spray with chelated iron and use a fertilizer for acid-loving plants. Pick off bagworms at dusk; spray the tree with waer if spider mites cause needles to turn brown anytime except fall. Prune dead branches any time. The knobby growths at the base are normal in wet sites; they're called *knees*.

Companion Planting and Design

Place the tree where its shedding bark can be admired. It's ideal for swamps and along lakes or streams, but I've even seen this impressive tree in a shopping center parking lot!

My Personal Favorite

'Apache Chief' is a handsome, wide-spreading specimen.

Most of us are used to thinking of trees that have needles as evergreen and trees that have leaves mostly as deciduous (losing their foliage in fall). Bald Cypress completely upsets those beliefs—it's a tree with needles, but they become a wonderful cinnamon color in autumn and fall off. There are several species of trees like this, and they're called deciduous conifers. Bald Cypress is especially valuable because it will thrive in those permanently wet spots in the yard, but it also does well in average soil.

Mature Height × Spread
50 to 85 feet × 18 to 65 feet

Canadian Hemlock

Tsuga canadensis

When I visit areas with cold climates, I admire the needled evergreens. Not just for their strong presence and deep color, but because I regret that we can grow so few of them in Tennessee. Sure, they're plenty winter-hardy, but they can't take the heat and humidity of a typical lowland Tennessee summer. An exception—despite the Canadian part of its name—is this stately tree, which has the added advantage of being right at home in shade gardens. Its outer branches weep slightly, giving the tree a graceful appearance.

Mature Height × **Spread**
40 to 90 feet × 25 to 35 feet

When, Where, and How to Plant

Hemlocks won't survive lack of water or too much moisture in the soil over winter, so their soil—preferably containing lots of organic matter—must be moist but well drained. They'll tolerate some sun, but will need more frequent watering in sunny spots; partial shade is ideal and full shade is okay. In early fall or spring, carefully remove burlap from roots and plant in a hole that's as deep as the rootball and twice as wide. Mulch well.

Growing Tips

Water regularly to keep the soil moist, especially when the tree is getting established and during dry spells. Canadian Hemlock is a fast grower; it rarely needs fertilizer.

Care

If using Canadian Hemlock as a hedge or screen, shear in spring or summer for a formal look, or thin branches for an informal appearance. While large numbers of pests are potential problems, most have little effect on well-maintained trees. In some areas, wooly adelgids have damaged or killed Canadian Hemlocks. Check with the Extension Service for the latest research and control recommendations.

Companion Planting and Design

Canadian Hemlock is often used as a tall hedge or screen. It grows nicely with shade-loving shrubs, such as Evergreen Azaleas, Rhododendrons, Mountain Laurel, and Oakleaf Hydrangea. It also does well with Ferns, Hostas, Cardinal Flower, and Astilbe.

My Personal Favorites

'Golden Splendor' is a yellow-needled cultivar. If you like weeping trees, 'Sargentii' grows no taller than 10 to 15 feet, but may be twice as wide.

Carolina Silverbell

Halesia tetraptera

When, Where, and How to Plant

Plant in early fall or in spring in the same type of spot you would plant a Dogwood—moist, acidic soil that drains well and contains lots of organic matter. Part shade is best, but Carolina Silverbell will also tolerate more sun. It's preferable to buy container-grown plants, rather than balled-and-burlapped ones. Dig a hole as deep as the rootball and twice as wide, place the tree in it, and fill in around the roots with the soil from the hole. Mulch well.

Growing Tips

Water the tree enough to keep the soil moist; don't let it dry out. Fertilizer probably won't be necessary, but if the tree isn't growing well, spread a high-nitrogen fertilizer for trees in a wide circle around the trunk after the leaves have fallen in autumn.

Care

Renew mulch as needed. Begin training this tree to a single trunk when young; otherwise, it will become a large shrub, which isn't as attractive as the tree shape. Prune—never removing more than one-fourth of the growth in one year—in spring, after flowering. This is a very insect- and disease-resistant tree.

Companion Planting and Design

Try to situate Carolina Silverbell on a hill or slope so that the flowers can be viewed from below. It's a nice understory tree with pines and looks attractive with Lily of the Valley, Evergreen Azalea, and Rhododendrons, as well as other spring-flowering trees.

My Personal Favorite

Trees sold as 'Rosea' will have pink flowers; the flowers on 'Arnold Pink' are larger than those on the species.

Tennesseans have a special fondness for spring-flowering trees, as witnessed by practically every neighborhood being filled with Dogwoods and Redbuds. Carolina Silverbell fits right into this trend. It's a charming native tree with graceful white or pink bell-shaped blooms hanging in delicate clusters along the branches in mid- to late spring before the leaves appear, and fruits that persist into winter. Experts recommend planting Carolina Silverbell where Dogwoods can't grow because of anthracnose. I concur, but suggest growing it even if you do have Dogwoods. They complement each other nicely.

Bloom Period and Color
White or pink in spring.

Mature Height × Spread
30 to 50 feet × 20 to 35 feet

Chaste Tree

Vitex agnus-castus

You may know Chaste Tree as a large shrub. Actually, it can be grown as a small tree or very large shrub, but I prefer it as a tree. Whichever way you want to train it, it belongs in your yard because of its easygoing disposition and its spectacular 6- to 18-inch fragrant, blue flower spikes at the end of summer and into fall. While not always winter-hardy in Zone 6, it thrives in hot summers. With the lower limbs trimmed off, it makes an airy shade tree.

Bloom Period and Color
Blue, lavender, white, or pink in late summer to early fall.

Mature Height × Spread
8 to 25 feet × 15 to 20 feet

Zone
7

When, Where, and How to Plant
Although tolerant of many situations, Chaste Tree prefers well-drained soil and full sun; flowers won't be as colorful in part shade. If you don't plan to prune the plant to a tree shape, place it 20 feet from other plants. In early spring, dig a hole as deep as the rootball and twice as wide, place the tree in it, and water with a transplanting solution to stimulate new root growth. Fill in around the roots with the soil from the hole; mulch well.

Growing Tips
During Chaste Tree's first two years in your yard, water whenever rainfall is less than an inch weekly. From then on, the tree can tolerate dry conditions—but it will grow best if watered regularly. Fertilizer isn't usually necessary; if needed to encourage growth, use 1 pound of 10-10-10 at the end of March or April.

Care
Remove lower limbs in very early spring to train to a tree shape. Do any other necessary pruning to remove winter damage at the same time. In very rainy weather, leaf spots may appear. While affecting the tree's appearance, they usually aren't serious. Other insect or disease problems should be few.

Companion Planting and Design
Chaste Tree's small size, interesting foliage, and late-season bloom make it a natural patio tree. It's often included as part of a shrub border.

My Personal Favorites
Vitex negundo may be a more reliable choice for Zone 6. 'Blushing Spires' has pink flower panicles and is a slow grower. 'Silver Spire' has white blossoms and is vigorous.

Dogwood

Cornus species and hybrids

When, Where, and How to Plant

Although Flowering Dogwood is known as an understory tree (growing beneath taller trees), it can take quite a bit of sun. If you have a choice, put it in partial shade. The ideal soil is acidic, moist, and well drained, containing plenty of organic matter. Avoid poorly drained soil. Plant in spring, in a hole twice as wide and the same depth as the rootball, refilling the hole with the dirt that was in the hole. Mulch well with pine straw.

Growing Tips

Dogwoods are shallow rooted and shouldn't be allowed to dry out; water when rainfall is less than normal—especially when temperatures are high. Fertilizer probably won't be necessary. To encourage growth in young trees, spread a granular high-nitrogen fertilizer for trees, according to label directions, in fall.

Care

Maintain mulch year-round. Prune after flowering, if necessary. Leave lower limbs on trees to protect the trunk from cold and damage. Dogwoods are susceptible to many diseases and insects. The most serious are borers (which often enter through holes in trunks caused by lawn mowers or string trimmers and kill the tree), leaf spots during wet springs (which can usually be ignored), and mildew (which looks like white powder on the foliage).

Companion Planting and Design

Underplant with Evergreen Azaleas and spring-flowering bulbs, such as Tulips and Daffodils.

My Personal Favorites

'Cherokee Princess' has large flowers, blooms early, and seems resistant to many fungal diseases. 'Big Apple' has extra-large berries and flowers.

Is there any tree that says spring more eloquently than Flowering Dogwood (Cornus florida)? Clouds of white (interspersed with occasional pink and red) define our Tennessee landscapes in April, and the tree's brilliant red leaves (and berries) enliven autumn. But in the high-elevation parts of the state, an anthracnose disease has killed most of our Flowering Dogwoods, causing us to turn to the Kousa Dogwood (Cornus kousa), which is relatively disease-resistant. It flowers up to a month later than native Dogwood and has a distinctive branching pattern that shows up well.

Bloom Period and Color
Spring in white, pink, and red.

Mature Height × Spread
20 to 30 feet × 20 to 25 feet

Flowering Cherry
Prunus species and hybrids

Thanks to cherry blossom festivals, different species of Flowering Cherry are gaining attention and becoming an increasing presence in the spring landscape. Yoshino (Prunus × yedoensis) has fragrant pink or white clusters of early blooms that appear before (or sometimes with) the leaves. Prunus serrulata 'Kwanzan' is known for large, double, rosy flowers and leaves that are reddish when new and bronze in fall. Prunus subhirtella 'Pendula' is a weeping tree with single pink blossoms. Rosy-flowered Sargent Cherry (Prunus sargentii) makes an excellent shade tree in Zone 6.

Bloom Period and Color
White or pink in spring.

Mature Height × Spread
6 to 40 feet × 8 to 30 feet

When, Where, and How to Plant
Plant in spring or early autumn in full sun and fast-draining soil. The trees will appreciate soil that contains organic matter. In clay, consider putting Flowering Cherries on mounds or in raised beds to avoid the possibility of root rot. Dig a hole as deep as the rootball and twice as wide, place the tree gently in the hole, water with a transplanting solution, and fill in around the roots with the soil that came from the hole. Water well and mulch lightly.

Growing Tips
Water when rainfall is less than an inch weekly, but be careful not to overwater in clay soil. Fertilize in late fall with a high-nitrogen fertilizer for trees, used according to label directions.

Care
You may cut branches while in bloom to use for arrangements. Do any necessary pruning as soon as flowers fade. Maintain a light mulch to prevent trunk damage from lawn equipment. Insects and diseases are troublesome with Flowering Cherry, which tend not to be long-lived trees. If problems appear, consult the Extension Service for causes and cures.

Companion Planting and Design
If you ever wanted a Japanese garden, these trees will give you the perfect start. Underplant with spring-flowering bulbs.

My Personal Favorites
Prunus × yedoensis 'Cascade Snow' has white flowers, dark green leaves in summer that turn orangish in fall, and fewer disease problems than most Flowering Cherries. 'Royal Burgundy' has foliage that is reddish-purple when new and reddish-orange in fall.

Fringe Tree
Chionanthus virginicus

When, Where, and How to Plant
Fringe Tree is quite adaptable as to light and soil requirements. But in the home landscape it will grow and bloom best in full sun and moist, well-drained, acidic soil that contains some organic matter. In early fall or early spring, dig a hole the depth of the rootball and twice as wide, and place the tree in it. Use a transplanting solution, and fill in the hole with the dirt that was removed; mulch.

Growing Tips
Water when rainfall is less than an inch per week. Spread compost or rotted leaves around the base of the tree each fall to feed it lightly.

Care
Fringe Tree leafs out late, so don't worry that something's wrong if foliage doesn't appear when it does on other trees. Possible pests include borers (which enter through the trunk; be sure to keep lawn equipment from nicking holes in the trunk) and scale (little brown "dots" on stems and underneath leaves). Rarely are they a big problem. To maintain the tree shape, train to one main trunk. Do needed pruning immediately after flowering.

Companion Planting and Design
Because Fringe Tree is quite tolerant of pollution and other urban conditions, it makes an excellent street tree. I like this tree next to a patio or placed where it can be admired by passersby, but it also looks nice near a water garden.

My Personal Favorite
Chinese Fringe Tree (*Chionanthus retusus*) has smaller flowers than Fringe Tree, but produces them several weeks earlier. It's often grown as a large shrub.

There are many wonderful small trees that flower in mid-spring. But why should the beautiful blooms depart your yard at the end of April? Fringe Tree, which produces large lacy clusters of white, fringelike flowers in May and June, is an excellent choice for extending the season. This attractive tree, also known as Grancy Graybeard, produces bluish berries in August, which are much appreciated by a variety of birds. It may be grown as a large shrub, but I think it's more useful and looks better as a small tree.

Bloom Period and Color
White blooms in late spring to early summer followed by bluish berries in late summer.

Mature Height × Spread
12 to 30 feet × 10 to 25 feet

179

Ginkgo
Ginkgo biloba

All it takes is one look—and you're hooked. One glance at the unusual fan-shaped leaves or the clear yellow foliage that covers the whole tree in fall, and you'll want a Ginkgo. It's reportedly 150 to 200 million years old and has an intriguing appearance that hints at its history. When young, it has a gangly appearance, like an adolescent who's all arms and legs. But as the "ugly duckling" ages, it grows wider and more graceful, becoming one of the most rewarding shade trees available.

Bloom Period and Color
Insignificant green blooms in mid-spring.

Mature Height × Spread
25 to 50 feet × 15 to 40 feet

When, Where, and How to Plant
Buy named cultivars of Gingko, as these will be male. (Female trees develop awful-smelling, messy fruits, which are to be avoided at all costs.) Plant in fall or spring. Soil may be alkaline or acidic, but it should be loose and well drained. Dig a hole that's the same depth as the rootball and twice as wide, place the tree in it, water with transplant solution, and replace the dirt. Mulch.

Growing Tips
Frequent watering after transplanting is important to get the tree off to a good start. Once it's established, water when rainfall totals less than an inch per week. Fertilize in early years, if you like, with 1 pound of 19-0-0 per inch of trunk diameter, in late fall after the leaves have been raked up.

Care
Young trees may need to be staked to hold them upright. Make sure stakes aren't attached to the tree too tightly and are removed in one year. Insects or diseases are rarely a problem. Prune in winter, if needed.

Companion Planting and Design
The most impressive Gingko trees I've seen are a pair placed just to the left of the entrance drive of the Baylor School in Chattanooga. Against a backdrop of tall pines, these two Ginkgoes seem to glow—they look as if they're made of gold leaf. If you have the room, plant two where they'll be noticed, and let them show off your good taste.

My Personal Favorites
'Shangri-La' has excellent golden yellow fall color. So does 'Autumn Gold', which is a wider-spreading tree.

Golden Rain Tree

Koelreuteria paniculata

When, Where, and How to Plant

In fall or spring, plant balled-and-burlapped or container-grown trees in full sun. Golden Rain Tree will adapt to almost any well-drained soil, whether it's acidic or alkaline. It also doesn't mind heat and wind, although the leaves on young trees may be nipped by late spring frosts, so a slightly protected spot would be welcome in the first years. If it isn't available, the tree will do fine anyway. Dig a hole twice as wide as the rootball and as deep. Carefully place the tree in it, removing any synthetic burlap and twine. Water well with a transplanting solution, and refill hole with the dirt that was taken from it. Water well and mulch lightly.

Growing Tips

Until the tree becomes established, water deeply in any week that rainfall totals less than an inch. After two years, it should be drought-tolerant. A medium- to fast-growing plant, Golden Rain Tree rarely needs fertilizer.

Care

As if to emphasize its carefree nature, Golden Rain Tree rarely needs pruning and has few serious insect or disease problems. Remove damaged limbs at any time; wait until winter to do any other pruning.

Companion Planting and Design

Plant this tree along the edge of a patio where you can sit under it and admire the sunshiny blooms. Underplant with yellow annuals or perennials.

My Personal Favorite

Bougainvillea Golden Rain Tree (*Koelreuteria bipinnata*) is a smaller tree that has yellow flowers in late summer and early autumn and more colorful seed capsules.

Golden Rain Tree is unusual: It blooms in early summer (when few other trees do) and, unlike most flowering trees, it does double duty as a shade tree. In summer, it develops clusters of copper-colored seedpods that hang on the tree decoratively until fall. But the real reason to grow this tree is its flowers—10- to 14-inch bright yellow clusters. Of course, it's nice that it tolerates just about any soil or climate conditions and, because of the tree's deep roots, it's easy to grow grass around it.

Bloom Period and Color

Yellow in summer.

Mature Height × Spread

30 to 40 feet × 25 to 35 feet

Japanese Cryptomeria
Cryptomeria japonica

The number of needled evergreens that stand up to the heat and humidity that are a natural part of the summer in most of Tennessee can be counted without running out of fingers. So if we want conical evergreens, sometimes we have to turn to trees whose names are hard to spell and pronounce. Call it Japanese Cedar, if you prefer, but plant this fast-growing conifer (which officially has "leaves" instead of needles, although you'd never guess it). Especially interesting for small spaces are the dwarf cultivars.

Mature Height × Spread
1 to 60 feet × 2 to 30 feet

When, Where, and How to Plant
While Japanese Cryptomeria is adaptable in most respects, it should be placed where it's sheltered from strong winds. Plant in a sunny or partly sunny spot in early fall or early spring in acidic soil that's rich and moist, but well drained. Dig a hole that's twice as wide as the rootball and exactly as deep. Place the tree carefully in the hole, water with a transplanting solution, and refill the hole with the soil that came out of it. Mulch with organic matter.

Growing Tips
This is a tree that needs ample moisture to do its best. Water when weekly rainfall doesn't total an inch. Fertilizer isn't usually needed, but a granular high-nitrogen tree fertilizer may be spread at the base of the tree in late fall (1 pound per inch of trunk diameter).

Care
Japanese Cryptomeria needs little pruning except to remove wayward growth. In early years, pinch the tips of the stems in early summer to encourage denser growth. Insect and disease problems should be few, but if the tips of stems or branches suffer dieback, consult the Extension Service for possible causes and cures.

Companion Planting and Design
Japanese Cryptomeria makes an excellent hedge or screen. It's also a fine specimen tree where an evergreen presence is needed in a prominent place in the yard and ideal for an Oriental garden.

My Personal Favorites
The "needles" of many cultivars turn plum or bronze in winter, but those of 'Gyokuryu' tend to remain deep green. The same is usually true of 'Benjamin Franklin'.

Japanese Maple

Acer palmatum

When, Where, and How to Plant

Seed-grown Japanese Maples will cost less than named cultivars, but you won't know what the eventual size or form will be. If you want a Japanese Maple whose leaves remain red in summer, buy one at that time. Plant from spring until early autumn in a partially shady spot—dappled shade beneath tall trees is ideal. (In full shade, the plants grow very slowly; in sun, the leaves are likely to fade color or burn.) Provide moist, well-drained soil that contains organic matter. The planting hole should be the same depth as the rootball and twice as wide. Water with a transplanting solution and mulch well.

Growing Tips

Never let a Japanese Maple dry out. It's especially important to keep the soil moist when the plant is young and during droughts. Spread a high-nitrogen tree fertilizer in late fall.

Care

Maintain the mulch year-round. Do not prune off lower limbs, which add grace and charm to the tree. There are few pest problems.

Companion Planting and Design

No longer just the *pièce de résistance* of Oriental gardens, elegant Japanese Maples have become the focal point of many partially shady yards. Those with cascading branches add appeal near a water garden.

My Personal Favorites

'Bloodgood' is the most tolerant Japanese Maple I've grown; it endures extreme heat and cold, sun and shade equally, while retaining a consistent red leaf color all year. 'Red Dragon', which has dissected leaves, also maintains its red color.

Wow! That's a common reaction to a beautiful, mature Japanese Maple. It may also be the reaction to the price of a 2-foot plant at a nursery. While the trees are often expensive, many gardeners believe they're well worth it, and their popularity is soaring with the increase in shade gardens. Due to a wide range of sizes (from a tiny mound to a tall tree), forms (upright or cascading), leaves (lobed or dissected), and seasonal colors, there's a Japanese Maple for every taste and place in the garden.

Bloom Period and Color

Insignificant purple blooms in late spring.

Mature Height × Spread

6 to 40 feet × 8 to 30 feet

Japanese Zelkova

Zelkova serrata

We Americans are impatient. When we plant a tree, we want it to be big as soon as possible. So when we buy a tree, the first (and sometimes only) question we ask is, "How quickly does it grow?" That leads to many bad choices, because fast-growing trees usually develop problems you want to avoid. That's not true of Japanese Zelkova, which may grow several feet a year when young. It's a well-mannered shade tree with Elmlike foliage and interesting bark (reddish when young, gray and mottled on mature specimens).

Bloom Period and Color
Insignificant blooms in spring.

Mature Height × Spread
50 to 90 feet × 40 to 60 feet

When, Where, and How to Plant
Plant anytime from spring through fall in full sun. Soil may be acidic or alkaline, but preferably it should be moist and well drained. Dig a hole as deep as the rootball and two times as wide. Carefully place the tree in the hole, removing synthetic burlap from balled-and-burlapped plants. Water well with a transplanting solution and pack the soil dug from the hole around the tree's roots. Mulch lightly with pine straw, shredded leaves, or fine pine bark.

Growing Tips
Water deeply but regularly in early years to establish a deep root system that can tolerate drought later. If placed in the proper growing conditions, Japanese Zelkova grows well without fertilizer. However, if young leaves are killed by late spring frost, you may want to fertilize in late fall with a high-nitrogen tree fertilizer, spread in a circle around the base of the tree according to package directions (or with 1 pound of granular 19-0-10 per inch of trunk diameter). Water in well.

Care
In exposed spots, spring frosts may damage the leaves of young trees. They will grow back. In winter, do any necessary pruning, including removing crowded branches. While the tree may occasionally suffer from disease or insects (especially beetles), these are usually not serious.

Companion Planting and Design
Japanese Zelkova is an ideal shade tree in urban areas and near highways, as it is quite pollution resistant.

My Personal Favorite
'Green Vase' grows especially fast and has more consistent fall color than many Zelkovas.

Lacebark Elm
Ulmus parvifolia

When, Where, and How to Plant
Plant in fall or spring in a spot that is in sunshine all day. Lacebark Elm will tolerate most well-drained soils and doesn't mind if it's acidic or alkaline. But the best results and fastest growth will be obtained in moist soil that contains organic matter. Remove any synthetic twine or burlap from around the roots and discard. Place the tree in a hole that's as deep as the rootball and twice as wide. Water with a transplanting solution, and refill the hole with the dirt that was originally in it. Mulch with 2 to 3 inches of organic matter.

Growing Tips
To get the tree off to a good start, water regularly when rainfall doesn't amount to an inch per week. In good growing conditions, fertilizer usually isn't necessary. As the mulch rots, it will gently feed the tree.

Care
Insects and diseases are not likely to be a problem, as Lacebark Elm is relatively disease-free and is subject to few insects. After the tree has grown to a moderate size, remove one or two of the lower limbs each winter for three or four years until the lowest limbs are at least 8 feet off the ground. This will enable the tree to show off its bark.

Companion Planting and Design
It's a good choice to plant near the street where the bark can be admired.

My Personal Favorites
'Golden Rey' has yellow leaves all season—clear yellow when they open and gold by fall. 'Dynasty' develops a nice rounded shape and has good orange-yellow fall leaf color.

Few people pay much attention to a tree's bark. We look for colorful flowers and interesting foliage instead. But once you've seen the shedding and mottled trunk of Lacebark Elm, you'll never think of bark as dull again. Eye-catching bark is especially important now that many of us want landscapes that have something of interest in all four seasons. This species is resistant to Dutch elm disease and Japanese beetles. Don't confuse this tree, which is sometimes called Chinese Elm, with Siberian Elm (Ulmus pumila), a fast-growing tree that's not recommended.

Mature Height × Spread
40 to 50 feet × 30 to 50 feet

185

Oak

Quercus species and hybrids

Oaks are the trees you plant for posterity. They seem to embody strength and majesty. In Tennessee we can grow a number of different Oaks in our yards. Southern Red Oak (Quercus falcata) tolerates poor soil. White Oak (Quercus alba) is slow growing and usually has good fall color. Neither is widely carried by nurseries; they're usually on your property when you move there. More readily available are Pin Oak (Quercus palustris), which will thrive in wet soil, and Willow Oak (Quercus phellos), whose leaves will remind you of a Weeping Willow.

Mature Height × Spread
40 to 80 feet × 25 to 60 feet

When, Where, and How to Plant

All Oaks should be planted in full sun and preferably in late winter, when they're dormant. White Oak and Willow Oak are tolerant of many situations, but they perform best when given moist, well-drained, acidic soil. Pin Oak will do fine in those wet spots in the yard, but will also thrive in moist, well-drained soil. Pin Oak must have acidic soil, though, as its leaves turn yellowish in alkaline soil. Remove synthetic twine and burlap before planting in a hole that's as deep as the rootball and twice as wide. Water with a transplanting solution, and put back the soil that came from the hole.

Growing Tips

Water deeply when trees are young and rainfall doesn't total an inch per week. Fertilize the second through fourth years with a high-nitrogen tree fertilizer applied in late fall.

Care

Gypsy moth may be a problem in some areas; oak wilt in others. Construction damage (when heavy equipment runs over the roots and knocks into the trunks) is often a delayed death knell to older Oaks, showing up three to five years later.

Companion Planting and Design

Because of their size, Oaks aren't for small yards. Place them on the edge of woods.

My Personal Favorites

Scarlet Oak (*Quercus coccinea*) has glossy green leaves in summer that turn a nice red in fall. The new growth of Nuttall Oak (*Quercus nuttallii*) is reddish-purple and leaves are red in fall. Its nicest quality, though, is that all the leaves fall off in autumn. (No having to rake in spring *and* fall!)

Ornamental Pear

Pyrus calleryana

When, Where, and How to Plant

Ornamental Pears will tolerate many types of soil, as long as they're well drained. Plant in late winter or early spring in a spot with full sun. Most people forget that these will grow to be very large trees—space them according to their mature height and spread. Dig a hole as deep as the rootball and twice as wide, place the tree in the hole and water with a transplanting solution. Pack the soil that was dug from the hole around the rootball, and water again. Mulch lightly to keep down weeds.

Growing Tips

Until the tree gets established, water it deeply when there's less than an inch of rain in any week. From then on, it should tolerate dry weather. No fertilizer is necessary.

Care

Insects are rarely a problem, but some cultivars of Ornamental Pear are subject to fireblight (leaves and stems look as though boiling water has been poured over them). Immediately prune back to nondiseased wood, disinfecting the saw or pruners between cuts. Do normal pruning in late winter.

Companion Planting and Design

This tree has a very stiff, formal appearance that looks out of place in informal or naturalistic landscapes. It's a good street tree and excellent for screening.

My Personal Favorites

Look for 'Chanticleer' (which isn't as large a tree as 'Bradford'), 'Edgewood' (which has silvery green foliage), and 'Fauriei' (which develops a pyramidal shape). 'Korean Sun' is good for small yards—it grows about 12 feet high and 15 feet wide.

Most people refer to this tree as Bradford Pear. That's the name of the first and most commonly planted cultivar, but there are many others that have the characteristic white flowers early in spring, glossy green leaves in summer, and excellent fall foliage color. All are better than 'Bradford', which has what experts call narrow crotch angles; these cause limbs to break, and often the tree splits in half. It's a serious problem, but doesn't mean giving up on Ornamental Pears. Instead, see some better choices under My Personal Favorites.

Bloom Period and Color
White in early spring.

Mature Height × Spread
30 to 50 feet × 16 to 35 feet

Paperbark Maple

Acer griseum

Imagine cinnamon-colored bark flaking naturally off a tree in thin sheets (horticulturists call this "exfoliating"). Then place this intriguing bark on a 25-foot tree that has a striking silhouette in winter, scarlet leaves in fall, and small flowers that develop into decorative winged seedpods. The result? Paperbark Maple, a tree that keeps your interest in every season. It has a delicate texture in summer and is the right size to fit into almost every yard. If you've been looking for something wonderfully different in a tree, Paperbark Maple is it.

Bloom Period and Color
Inconspicuous blooms in spring.

Mature Height × Spread
25 to 30 feet × 12 to 30 feet

When, Where, and How to Plant
Plant in spring in a sunny place. This tree is adaptable as to type of soil and pH, but it prefers moist, well-drained soil. Dig a hole twice as wide as the rootball and as deep, and place the tree in it. Use a transplanting solution, and refill the hole with the original soil. Mulch with pine straw.

Growing Tips
To do well, Paperbark Maple requires moisture—so don't let the soil dry out. Water regularly if the soil isn't naturally moist and rainfall is lacking. The tree is naturally slow growing (less than a foot a year), so you may want to fertilize in late fall with 1 pound of granular 19-0-0 per inch of trunk diameter, or with a high-nitrogen tree fertilizer applied according to label directions. Spread both in a widening circle around the tree, beginning 6 inches from the trunk.

Care
There are no serious pest problems with Paperbark Maple. It also rarely needs pruning. If any is required, do it in winter. Maintain a year-round mulch to keep moisture in the soil.

Companion Planting and Design
Plant Paperbark Maple as the focal point of a small yard or along the sunny edge of the woods on a larger property. It also fits nicely into a shrub border. Wherever you put it, this tree will garner lots of favorable comment.

My Personal Favorites
Few cultivars are available yet, but I imagine many will be hitting the market before long. Two I've seen are 'Gingerbread' and 'Cinnamon Flake'. Both are excellent.

Redbud

Cercis canadensis

When, Where, and How to Plant

Plant in spring or early fall in a sunny or partially sunny place. Redbuds adapt to acidic or alkaline soil and can grow in most average soils—except those that stay wet. They prefer moist, well-drained soil that contains organic matter. Dig a hole that's as deep as the rootball and twice as wide, and place the tree in it. Water with a transplanting solution, and refill the hole with the dirt that was removed from it. Apply mulch in a circle extending several feet from the trunk.

Growing Tips

Regular watering and fertilizing are the keys to success with Redbud. Water when rainfall is less than an inch in any week during the growing season. Fertilize in late fall, with 1 to 2 pounds of granular 19-0-0 per inch of trunk diameter, or with a high-nitrogen tree fertilizer applied according to label directions.

Care

Maintain a wide mulch around the trunk to prevent mechanical injury that leads to disease and insect damage. Control caterpillars organically with *Bacillus thuringiensis* (*B.t.*). Minimize pruning to lessen chance of disease. If pruning is necessary, do it in winter or after flowering.

Companion Planting and Design

Plant in the front yard so the early blossoms can be admired.

My Personal Favorites

'Forest Pansy' produces purple leaves. 'Royal White' has white flowers, and 'Tennessee Pink' has clear pink ones. Texas Redbud (*Cercis texensis*) has leaves that add interest to the landscape because they're leathery and glossy green; there are cultivars with magenta or white flowers.

Redbud is such a familiar tree that many of us tend to take it for granted. But if you enumerate its special traits—heart-shaped leaves, graceful branches, and an abundance of fuchsia-colored flowers before the leaves appear in early spring—you realize what a neat native tree this is. It also blooms before Dogwoods, so it extends the spring flowering season in your yard. As with Dogwoods, be careful to keep string trimmers and lawn mowers from damaging the trunk and allowing borers and disease to enter.

Bloom Period and Color
Pink or white in spring.

Mature Height × Spread
20 to 35 feet × 25 to 35 feet

Red Maple
Acer rubrum

Do you know why Red Maple got its name? It's not, as many suppose, because of the fall leaf color. Instead, "red" refers to the abundant flowers in early spring that give the tree a fiery glow. You can't count on unnamed Red Maples having excellent foliage color, so it's best to buy one of the numerous cultivars that are known for the outstanding show they put on in autumn. Red Maple is a relatively fast grower and tolerates wet soil—two more traits to endear it to homeowners.

Bloom Period and Color
Red in spring.

Mature Height × Spread
40 to 70 feet × 40 to 45 feet

When, Where, and How to Plant
Plant in late winter or early spring in a sunny spot. In the wild, Red Maples grow in low, wet areas, so they will certainly do the same in your yard if you have a difficult wet area. But if you don't, the tree is quite adaptable. The ideal soil is a moist, well-drained, slightly acidic soil, but average soil should also be fine as long as it isn't alkaline. Place the tree in a hole that's twice as wide as the rootball and as deep, water with a transplanting solution, and fill in with the soil dug from the hole. Mulch well.

Growing Tips
Red Maples need moisture from spring until fall. Water deeply if rainfall doesn't total 1 inch weekly. Fertilizer isn't usually necessary, especially if the tree is growing in the lawn and you fertilize the grass.

Care
Red Maples may occasionally be subject to disease, borers (which enter through the trunk), and leafhoppers (which cause the leaves to look mottled and bleached or browned and curled along the edges). Knock leafhoppers off with a strong stream of water, and spray young trees with insecticidal soap. Red Maples need little pruning.

Companion Planting and Design
Red Maple is a good choice wherever you need a shade tree that's attractive in three seasons. Place it where it can be seen in spring and fall from indoors or the street.

My Personal Favorites
'October Glory' and 'Red Sunset' are easy to find in nurseries and have fabulous fall foliage. Look also for 'Autumn Blaze', which is my current favorite.

River Birch

Betula nigra

When, Where, and How to Plant
Plant in fall or spring in a sunny or mostly sunny place with acidic soil. (Alkaline soil causes yellow leaves.) Moist soil is preferred, but River Birch adapts to any fertile soil, especially if watered. Place in a hole as deep as the rootball and twice as wide, water with a transplanting solution, and refill the hole with the soil that was dug from it. Mulch if soil is on the dry side.

Growing Tips
Keep soil moist during the growing season. Fertilizer probably won't be needed.

Care
In dry soils, maintain a 3-inch mulch. Prune River Birch in summer; its sap "bleeds" if a branch is cut in spring. While not harmful, it's messy and discolors the bark. Aphids, which suck the sap out of the leaves and leave a sticky substance behind, may appear on tender young growth. Hose them off with a hard blast of water, and spray with insecticidal soap. River Birch has few other insect or disease problems.

Companion Planting and Design
River Birch is right at home next to a pond or stream. Although it can be grown alone as a specimen tree, gardeners often like the look of a clump of three trees planted together in the same hole. You may be able to find some sold this way in nurseries.

My Personal Favorite
I've grown 'Heritage' River Birch at several locations in Tennessee and have always been pleased with its performance. It's terrific for clay soil and, unlike many River Birches, develops pleasingly yellow leaves in autumn.

When gardeners hear a name like River Birch, they naturally assume it's the answer to their search for a tree that doesn't mind clay soil, permanently wet spots, or areas that occasionally flood. And they're right. But that doesn't mean that folks who have average or drier soils should pass it by. This tree is so versatile—and so good-looking—that it belongs in every yard where there's room for it. It's cold hardy, heat tolerant, and has beautiful exfoliating (peeling) bark in shades of salmon and cream.

Mature Height × Spread
40 to 70 feet × 40 to 60 feet

Saucer Magnolia
Magnolia soulangiana

When you buy a small tree, it's tough knowing that you'll have to wait several years, while it grows, before you can enjoy its flowers. But there's not likely to be much delay before Saucer Magnolia begins flowering. It often is covered with full-size pink and white or purplish flowers when only 3 feet tall—and it only gets better as it grows older. Although it can be trained as a large shrub, I think it's more effective in the landscape as a tree. What a knockout in March!

Bloom Period and Color
Pink, purplish, or white in early spring.

Mature Height × Spread
10 to 30 feet × 15 to 20 feet

When, Where, and How to Plant
Saucer Magnolia is a tree with spreading branches, so be sure to give it plenty of room. Plant in spring in a sunny or mostly sunny spot with moist, well-drained, acidic soil that contains organic matter. Dig a hole as deep as the rootball and twice as wide. Place the tree in it and water with a transplanting solution. Refill the hole with the soil that came from the hole, and mulch with pine straw or fine bark.

Growing Tips
Water deeply whenever rainfall has been less than an inch in any week. Fertilizer generally isn't needed.

Care
Maintain a year-round mulch to keep moisture in the soil. Insects and diseases should not be much trouble. The most likely problem is one that's out of the gardener's control—unseasonably warm weather that encourages blooming, then a hard frost occurs, and the flowers are killed. Prune just after flowering, as needed, to develop a tree form (one trunk with four or five main branches starting a foot above ground level).

Companion Planting and Design
Give Saucer Magnolia a place of honor in the front yard. Or choose several, with varying flower colors, and place them in different areas of the yard.

My Personal Favorites
Two nice cultivars of Saucer Magnolia are 'Alba', which has white fragrant flowers, and 'Rustica Rubra', which has large reddish-purple blooms and red seedpods.

Serviceberry
Amelanchier species and hybrids

When, Where, and How to Plant

Plant container-grown or balled-and-burlapped trees in spring or fall. Although tolerant of many types of soil, Serviceberry prefers moist, acidic, well-drained soil and partial shade or sun. (My trees grow just along the edge of woodlands in rocky ground.) Pay attention to eventual spread if you decide to grow it as a multistemmed shrub instead of a tree, because it will take a lot of room. The planting hole should be as deep as the tree's rootball and twice as wide. Place the tree at the same depth it grew before, and refill the hole with the soil that was removed from it. Water well and mulch.

Growing Tips

In early years, water when nature doesn't deposit an inch of rain each week. Later, the tree should be able to cope with mild dry spells; water deeply during droughts. Serviceberry grows moderately fast and doesn't usually need fertilizer.

Care

Usually little pruning is needed, but if required, prune in spring after blooming has finished. Maintain the mulch year-round, especially in dry weather. Serviceberry has few insects or diseases.

Companion Planting and Design

This tree is essential if you're planting your yard to attract wildlife. The perfect spot for it is along the border of woods filled with spring wildflowers. Consider growing it with Shadbush (*Amelanchier canadensis*), a shrub form of Serviceberry that has excellent fall color.

My Personal Favorites

'Autumn Brilliance' has very red fall foliage and grows fast. 'Princess Diana' is also worth growing for its spectacular red leaves in autumn.

Like many native plants, Serviceberry has collected a number of common names. My mom always called it Sarvis tree. Other people call it Juneberry, for the dark little fruits in early summer (supposedly sweet and good for cooking; I wouldn't know, as the birds always get mine). Amelanchier arborea is the tree species most commonly available to gardeners, although Allegheny Serviceberry (Amelanchier laevis) is often found in the wild. Both have clusters of white flowers in early spring. They're fleeting, but to me, they're the sign that spring has truly sprung.

Bloom Period and Color

White in early spring.

Mature Height × Spread

15 to 30 feet × 20 to 30 feet

Sourwood

Oxydendrum arboreum

Sourwood has such an exotic appearance that it's easy to imagine it was discovered in some inaccessible place on the other side of the world. Instead, it's an easy-to-grow American native that most of us take for granted. At every season, Sourwood calls attention to its unusual beauty with its pyramidal shape and its 10-inch clusters of creamy bell-shaped flowers in summer followed in autumn by ivory seed capsules that hang down like splayed fingers from the tips of the branches—and the most brilliant scarlet foliage in the forest.

Bloom Period and Color
Cream in summer.

Mature Height × Spread
25 to 50 feet × 15 to 20 feet

When, Where, and How to Plant
In early fall or in spring, plant a balled-and-burlapped or container-grown tree in a prominent spot that has full or at least partial sun and acidic, well-drained soil. Although Sourwood tolerates some shade, it generally won't bloom as well or have fall foliage as colorful as it would in sun. Dig a hole as deep as the rootball and twice as wide; refill the hole with the soil that was removed from it. Water with a transplant solution, and mulch well with pine straw or shredded leaves—but don't let the mulch touch the trunk.

Growing Tips
When Sourwood is young, water regularly during dry spells. Once it's mature, it can tolerate some dryness, although you should water small and medium-sized trees during droughts. Fertilizer probably isn't going to be needed. However, if the tree isn't growing well, fertilize with a high-nitrogen tree fertilizer in autumn after the leaves have fallen off. Note, however, that slow growth is normal for Sourwood.

Care
Little pruning is needed, and the tree has few serious insect or disease problems.

Companion Planting and Design
Place Sourwood in a prominent location where it will show off its exotic looks and early autumn color. I have a small grove of Sourwoods at the edge of the woods just before my driveway, where they're the first thing visitors see.

My Personal Favorite
'Chameleon' is a kaleidoscope of fall color—leaves turn from green to yellow, red, and purple. Often you'll find all those colors on the tree at the same time.

Southern Magnolia
Magnolia grandiflora

When, Where, and How to Plant
Plant in early spring in a spot that's in full sun most of the day. Ideal soil conditions are rich, moist, acidic, and well drained. If possible, choose a site that's protected from winter winds. Place in a hole twice the diameter of the rootball and as deep, using the soil dug from the hole to refill the hole. Mulch with organic matter.

Growing Tips
Water deeply when rainfall is below normal. Fertilizer isn't necessary, but if you need faster growth, spread a high-nitrogen tree fertilizer beneath the limbs in late fall.

Care
Don't cut off the lower limbs of Southern Magnolia. That takes away its grace and means that falling plant debris (such as old leaves) has nowhere to hide. Do any needed pruning in very early spring. The white flowers look nice when cut and floated in a shallow bowl of water. The tree has few insect or disease problems.

Companion Planting and Design
This is a handsome specimen tree. I've also used a trio of Southern Magnolias for screening since they're attractive year-round and grow much faster than most people think they will, especially if watered and fertilized regularly.

My Personal Favorites
'Bracken's Brown Beauty' is a beautiful Southern Magnolia that is cold hardy in Zone 6. 'Edith Bogue' is also cold hardy and least likely to sustain snow damage. 'Little Gem' grows about 20 to 25 feet high and 10 to 15 feet wide. Its smaller leaves are nice in arrangements. 'Riegel' is also small, but has large flowers. 'Spring Hill' has a columnar habit.

No tree is more identified with the South than Southern Magnolia. So much so that most of us call this beautiful evergreen by the simple name of Magnolia. Don't let minor objections keep you from owning a true grand dame. There are dwarf cultivars for people who think the tree grows too big, and cold-hardy cultivars for those who live in the mountains. And the solution to the "messiness" of old leaves and seedpods is to plant in a mulched bed (not the lawn) and never remove the lower limbs.

Bloom Period and Color
White in late spring and early summer.

Mature Height × Spread
20 to 80 feet × 20 to 50 feet

Sweet Gum
Liquidambar styraciflua

Sweet Gum is beloved by kindergarten teachers and crafters and muttered over by those who mow the lawn. It's also admired by everyone for the shape of its deep green leaves and their impressive reddish-purple fall coloration. I avoid problems with the spiny balls by not planting it in the lawn or near a sidewalk, driveway, or street. By placing the tree on the sunny edge of woods or in an island bed, I steer clear of aggravation while enjoying some of the best and longest-lasting fall color.

Mature Height × Spread
60 to 75 feet × 30 to 45 feet

When, Where, and How to Plant
Sweet Gum, which likes sunny sites, grows fastest in moist or wet, acidic soils. (If soil is alkaline, leaves will turn yellow.) Plant in spring by placing in a hole as deep as the rootball and twice as wide. Refill the hole with the soil that was removed from it and mulch around the tree.

Growing Tips
Sweet Gum may take a year or two to get established. Keep the soil moist until it begins growing well. After that, water whenever the weekly total of rainfall is less than an inch. As with all trees, don't fertilize the first year after planting. But after that you may want to spread 1 pound of granular 19-0-0 per inch of trunk diameter in a wide circle beneath the tree's limbs in late autumn. Or use a high-nitrogen tree fertilizer according to label directions.

Care
Little pruning is needed for Sweet Gum, but winter is the time to do whatever pruning is required. Pests are most likely to be caterpillars (dust or spray with *Bacillus thuringiensis*) or scale (tiny dots on the undersides of leaves), which can be smothered with a light horticultural oil (sometimes called sun oil).

Companion Planting and Design
If one is a standout, two or three planted together as a small grove are dazzling. Remember, this is not a tree for lawns or small yards.

My Personal Favorites
'Cherokee' and 'Rotundiloba' generally do not produce the "balls" for which Sweet Gum is famous. 'Palo Alto' has reddish-orange fall color.

Tulip Poplar

Liriodendron tulipifera

When, Where, and How to Plant

Place Tulip Poplar in an area where it has plenty of room to grow (away from power lines and buildings). It prefers full sun and moist, well-drained soil that's slightly acidic. Moisture is essential; without it, leaves scorch and fall. In spring, plant in a hole as deep as the rootball and twice as wide. Refill the hole with the soil that was removed from it, and water with a transplanting solution. Mulch well with organic matter, such as shredded leaves or pine straw.

Growing Tips

Without adequate water, leaves often drop prematurely, making a mess. Keep soil moist at all times, but particularly when the tree is young and in dry weather. Avoid fertilizing unless the tree is not growing well.

Care

Potential insect and disease problems are numerous. Aphids are most common, producing a sweet secretion that is often followed by sooty mold (a brown-black fungus that covers the leaves and may cause them to turn yellow). Use a hose-end sprayer to try to wash off the mold, then spray the tree with insecticidal soap or a light horticultural oil to get rid of the aphids. Make sure the tree is well watered when it is suffering from insect or disease infestations; dryness will only make the problem worse.

Companion Planting and Design

Use as a specimen tree where it can be admired and has room to live up to its potential.

My Personal Favorites

Smaller cultivars include 'Ardis' and 'Compactum'.

Tulip Poplar is a beautiful tree, which certainly deserves its status as the official tree of Tennessee. It's tall and majestic, the flowers are mildly fragrant and the leaves turn yellow in autumn. But there's one problem—tiny Tulip Poplar tree seedlings are often given away to homeowners who have no idea how large they will grow. This is one of the largest of our native trees, suitable mostly for large properties. If it's a favorite of yours, look for some of the smaller cultivars now becoming available at nurseries.

Bloom Period and Color

Cream to yellow in late spring to early summer.

Mature Height × Spread

70 to 100 feet × 35 to 55 feet

Yellowwood

Cladrastis kentukea

You may not recognize the name of this tree, but if you drive Tennessee highways at all, you've probably admired its long clusters of creamy flowers and wondered what vine or tree they were growing on along the roadside. The flowers alone are reason enough to grow Yellowwood, but it brings many other fine qualities to the landscape—bright green leaves in summer that turn yellow in fall, smooth gray bark that adds winter interest to the yard, an ability to grow in alkaline soil, and extreme winter-hardiness.

Bloom Period and Color
White or pink in late spring.

Mature Height × Spread
30 to 60 feet × 40 to 50 feet

When, Where, and How to Plant
Plant Yellowwood in spring, placing it in well-drained acidic or alkaline soil and full sun. Dig its hole as deep as the root-ball and twice as wide. Water with a transplanting solution and refill the hole with the soil that came from it.

Growing Tips
If you want your tree to grow fast, regularly water and feed it. Keep soil moist when the tree is young; as it ages, you may want to water when rainfall hasn't totaled an inch per week, although established trees tolerate some dryness. Fertilize with 1 pound of granular 19-0-0 per inch of trunk diameter in late autumn. Or spread a high-nitrogen tree fertilizer, according to label directions, in a wide circle beneath the branches after the leaves have fallen.

Care
Pest problems are insignificant. The limbs and trunk of Yellowwood trees often join at a narrow angle, instead of at a wide angle. These narrow crotch angles become weak when bark in the crotch dies and can split or break in storms. Remove limbs with narrow crotches when the tree is young. Prune storm damage as soon as possible after it occurs, but do all other pruning in summer as this is a tree that "bleeds" sap (which is messy and disturbing to watch—although not harmful to the tree).

Companion Planting and Design
Grow it as a shade tree or lawn highlight.

My Personal Favorites
'Rosea' has fragrant, light pink flowers. Japanese Yellowwood (*Cladrastis platycarpa*) is a small tree that would be good for Zone 6 gardens.

Vines *for Tennessee*

Southerners have two opinions of vines: We love them *and* we hate them. We've experienced how quickly Japanese Honeysuckle can take over the corner of a lot and how Kudzu can devour everything in its path. And yet, that's still not enough to erase the nostalgic memories of sweetly scented Moonflower blossoms unfurling on warm summer evenings.

With the renewed popularity and availability of attractive pergolas, arches, and trellises, vines are growing in favor once again. Gardeners increasingly want Ivy-covered cottages, romantic Roses rambling over arbors, and vines such as Trumpet Creeper to lure acrobatic hummingbirds to our yards.

Vines Are Versatile

Not only are vines attractive, they're also living problem-solvers. They can quickly screen off an unsightly view, as well as have quite an impact on energy bills and outdoor comfort. A deciduous vine that shades the west or south side of a house cuts cooling costs considerably, and an evergreen vine can block cold winter winds. When you move into a new home with little landscaping, vines can be trained on a lattice frame to create cooling shade while you're waiting for young trees to grow. Vines also attract backyard wildlife, such as shelter-seeking birds.

Vines may be evergreen or deciduous, perennial or annual. Annual vines grow fastest and are inexpensive; often they're started from seed. Perennial vines take longer to get established, but are planted only once. Evergreen vines look good all year and are perfect for prominent spots in the yard. Deciduous vines are cold hardy; they block the heat of the sun in summer, but let warming rays shine through in winter.

How Vines Climb

Vines have four different methods of climbing. It's important to know which method a particular vine uses, because it determines the type of support on which you should place it.

Twining vines wrap themselves around a structure or object. They'll weave in and out of a chain-link fence or lattice, scurry to the top of a lamppost, and be right at home on a trellis. A good example of a twining vine is Moonflower.

Clinging vines cover large expanses of territory, such as blank walls or vacant hillsides. These vines produce aerial rootlets—called *holdfasts*—which are used to attach themselves to a structure. Think twice—maybe three times—before planting a vine that climbs this way to be sure that the spot you've chosen will be the plant's permanent home. Holdfasts are tough to remove and leave behind a residue that's almost impossible to scrape off. Examples are Ivy and Climbing Hydrangea.

Vines that produce *tendrils* reach out and cling to whatever's near—a chain-link fence, netting, lattice, shrubs, or a wire. An example is Passionflower.

Climbers aren't vines in the strictest sense, although we use them that way. They depend on the gardener to tie their arching canes to a support as they grow. Examples of climbers include climbing and rambling Roses.

Should Vines Be Grown on Houses or Trees?

Experts generally agree that vines shouldn't be grown on wood frame homes. That's because vines can cause moisture damage when placed directly on wood, and some vines can work themselves under siding or roof shingles. Then, too, there's the problem of what to do with the vine when the house needs painting. If you're interested in having vines on a wooden structure, consider training the vine on a hinged trellis that's placed six inches away from the house.

Vines generally do not harm masonry and brick that are in good condition. However, when a surface is completely covered by an evergreen vine, it's difficult to know when mortar is beginning to crumble or when cracks have developed. Vines often attach themselves to these cracks, making them larger. If you love the idea of an

Ivy-covered brick cottage, occasionally check the wall under the vine to make sure it's in good shape.

Do a little research before growing vines on trees. A strong vine (such as Wisteria) can eventually strangle a tree, but clinging types (such as English Ivy and Climbing Hydrangea) often beautify a bare trunk.

When selecting vines for any purpose, it's important to check the plant listings in this book and match the size and growth habit of the vine to the space where you want to put it. The majority of the time, when a homeowner becomes disenchanted with a vine, it's because the vine grows too large or too aggressively for its location.

Vines are more likely to require mainte-nance—usually regular pruning—than some other plants. But because of their benefits and beauty, I believe they're definitely worth the time and energy you put into them. I still plant Morning Glory, even though it spreads its seeds and I know I'll have to pull up volunteer vines next year. But I consider that a small price to pay for such a charming plant. Some of my fondest childhood memories are of the bright purple flowers on my grand-mother's Morning Glory, which scrambled up the fence around the dog run. I loved to get up early to see the big blossoms open as the sun hit them, and then watch as they faded in the heat of the afternoon. What fun it was on overcast days to see the flowers "fooled" to remain open.

With their combinations of beauty, utility, and intrigue, you are sure to find a perfect vine for every location.

Carolina Jessamine
Gelsemium sempervirens

Every February I attend a gardening conference on Sea Island, Georgia. On the drive down, I enjoy the yellow blooms of Carolina Jessamine as they scamper up telephone poles, climb fences, and decorate mailboxes. Finally, I bought three of these attractive evergreen vines for my back fence, and I love watching them flower in late winter. When temperatures dip into the low teens, the foliage becomes semi-evergreen, but the flowers are usually reliable. Carolina Jessamine isn't for the colder sections of Tennessee, but for gardeners in Zone 7, it's a delight.

Bloom Period and Color
Yellow in late winter and very early spring.

Mature Length × Spread
20 feet × 3 to 4 feet

Zone
7

When, Where, and How to Plant
Plant container-grown vines anytime from spring until fall. Although Carolina Jessamine will grow in most well-drained soils, it performs best in moist, fertile soil. Similarly, while tolerating some shade, it grows most vigorously and flowers heaviest when in full sun. Carolina Jessamine climbs by twining, so it is ideal for posts, chain-link fences, and trellises.

Growing Tips
Water regularly when rainfall is less than an inch per week, or temperatures remain over 90 degrees Fahrenheit. If the vine isn't growing as well as you'd like, fertilize in spring with a pelleted, slow-release fertilizer for flowering plants.

Care
Pinch off ends of stems in late spring to encourage bushy growth. After severe winters, wait for the vine to leaf out before removing damaged growth. When Carolina Jessamine gets top-heavy, with sparse growth at the base, cut it back to 2 feet high just after blooming ends. Then apply a slow-release fertilizer at half the rate recommended on the label; water well. You may also choose to cut one-third of the stems back to the ground each year for three years. Insects and diseases aren't troublesome.

Companion Planting and Design
This is a vine for trellises, arbors, lampposts, and mailboxes. It can also be used as a groundcover. Use the vine's evergreen foliage as a backdrop for a variety of annuals and summer-flowering perennials.

My Personal Favorite
'Pride of Augusta' has double, nonfragrant flowers and often blooms in fall as well as spring.

Clematis

Clematis species and hybrids

When, Where, and How to Plant

Clematis likes its "head in the sun, feet in the shade." The roots should stay cool, while the vine requires sun. Plant in a sunny spot, but use a thick mulch. In spring, plant in light, well-drained soil. Place the stem 2 inches deeper than it grew in the container. Young stems are fragile; protect them from being bumped.

Growing Tips

Water regularly when rainfall is below normal. Don't let the vine dry out. Apply a slow-release fertilizer for flowering plants every April.

Care

Without pruning, Clematis become a tangled mess and won't bloom well. When and how you prune depends on the type you have. This is easy to figure out by observing how your plant blooms. If it blooms in spring or summer on vines that grew last year, prune lightly right after flowering to keep it in shape. If flowers appear in late summer on stems that have grown since spring, cut young plants to 14 inches and mature plants to 2 feet in early spring. If the vine flowers twice, cut out weak growth or dead stems in spring. After flowering, shorten stems that bloomed.

Companion Planting and Design

Let Clematis scamper across shrubs and up trees, or let it cover a decorative trellis. Plant a row of Clematis vines of varying colors and bloom times for months of enjoyment.

My Personal Favorites

Clematis armandii (Zone 7) is evergreen and blooms in early spring. 'Carnaby' has rosy flowers twice a year on a compact vine.

It's interesting to watch Clematis spread through neighborhoods. One homeowner plants one on his mailbox and, as soon as the big blooms appear, all the neighbors rush to plant Clematis on their mailboxes, too. It offers much beauty for very little care, displaying a profusion of spectacular flowers against dark green foliage. After the blooms fade, the fluffy seedpods add interest to the vine, or they may be cut off to use in flower arrangements. In fall, Sweet Autumn Clematis (Clematis terniflora) produces masses of small, white flowers.

Bloom Period and Color

Summer to fall in white, pink, red, blue-violet, purple, and bicolor.

Mature Length × Spread

6 to 10 feet × 2 feet

Climbing Hydrangea

Hydrangea anomala petiolaris

People are intrigued when they see the 6- to 10-inch flowers of this vine and want to know what it is and where to get one. As a newspaper garden editor in Chattanooga, I regularly received calls about it from readers. Identifying the plant was easy; telling them where to find one locally wasn't always so simple. Hydrangeas have long been favorite shrubs in Tennessee, so it's puzzling that the climbing version isn't more widely available. Even if it takes effort to locate one, you'll be glad you did.

Bloom Period and Color
Late spring to early summer in white.

Mature Length × Spread
50 to 60 feet × 10 to 20 feet

When, Where, and How to Plant
This is a very large vine, so give it plenty of room to roam when you choose its site. Plant in spring or, if you can water frequently, in summer. Climbing Hydrangea likes a shady or partially sunny spot with rich, moist, well-drained soil. If your soil doesn't match that criteria, mix it liberally with compost, peat moss, and finely shredded bark.

Growing Tips
Climbing Hydrangea grows very slowly during the first few years. Don't worry that you've done something wrong—it's perfectly normal. To help it along, water regularly to keep the soil moist. Fertilize each spring with 2 pounds of 10-10-10 granular fertilizer.

Care
The more sun the vine receives, the more likely that Japanese beetles may be a pest. Pick them off by hand or spray them with an insecticide recommended by your local Extension Service office. Little pruning is necessary. If you inherit an overgrown vine, cut it back by one-fourth each year for four years. You may also cut severely overgrown vines to 3 feet tall, but the vine won't bloom for several years and getting rid of all the dead branches will be quite a chore.

Companion Planting and Design
Plant evergreen shrubs at the base of this deciduous vine, such as white-flowered Azaleas and Rhododendrons, Hostas that have green and white leaves, or variegated groundcovers like *Vinca minor* or *Liriope*.

My Personal Favorite
If you don't have much room but have fallen in love with this impressive vine, try 'Brookside Littleleaf', which is just right for smaller spaces.

Climbing Rose
Rosa species and hybrids

When, Where, and How to Plant
Plant bare-root Roses in early spring—from late February in Zone 7b to the end of March in Zone 6. Set out container-grown Roses in late spring, after roots have filled the pot. All Roses prefer full sun and soil that's been liberally enriched with organic matter. Also see page 251.

Growing Tips
Unless an inch of rain has fallen, soak the soil around your Rose once—or in very hot, dry weather twice—a week. (Poke a stick into the ground to make sure soil is moist to 14 inches deep.) If possible, use a soaker hose so you don't splash water on the leaves (causing fungus diseases). Use a granular rose fertilizer monthly around Climbing Roses that flower repeatedly. For more blooms, spray twice a month with a water-soluble fertilizer for blooming plants. For plants that flower once, feeding in April and May is adequate.

Care
Prune off flowers right after they fade, cutting to ¼ inch above a five-leaf cluster with a bud pointing outward. Keep canes tied to the supports. Roses growing horizontally will bloom better than canes growing straight up. Roses attract many pests, from aphids to blackspot, a fungus that disfigures the leaves.

Companion Planting and Design
Let Climbing Roses wrap around pillars and posts, scramble up a stone wall, soften the lines of a split-rail fence, and cover arbors and pergolas. I always plant mine with silver-hued *Artemisia* 'Powis Castle'.

My Personal Favorites
'Altissimo' has large, single, red blooms. Disease-resistant 'Berries 'n' Cream' produces yummy raspberry and white flowers.

A fragrant pink Rose scampering up a trellis or across a picket fence is such a romantic image. And it's an easy dream to transform into reality. Climbing Roses love to grow up and over any structure—and even beyond, if you don't pull out your pruners occasionally. I've been hunting for an archway to place at the entrance to my back garden. When I find it, I'll plant a Climbing Rose on each side and let them meet at the top—what prettier way to welcome guests?

Bloom Period and Color
May or June until frost in red, pink, orange, yellow, white, and bicolors.

Mature Length × Spread
8 to 30 feet × 4 to 10 feet

Crossvine
Bignonia capreolata

Hummingbirds love this fast-growing evergreen vine. U.T. fans should, too. Orange, tubular flowers (often yellow inside) are especially attractive against the glossy green foliage that turns reddish-purple in winter. When I let Crossvine ramble across a rustic rail fence— not paying attention to it except to cut it back when it went too far—I often got questions about its identity. Non-gardeners don't seem to know it at all, and gardeners sometimes confuse it with Trumpet Creeper, which blooms June to September. But Crossvine doesn't try to take over, as Trumpet Creeper may.

Bloom Period and Color
Reddish-orange flowers from late April into summer.

Mature Length × Spread
20 to 40 feet × 5 to 15 feet

When, Where, and How to Plant
Plant container-grown vines anytime from spring through early autumn, in a sunny or partially sunny place. To encourage vigorous new growth, cut the vine back by one-third to one-half when planting. Although Crossvine will grow in some shade, it blooms best in full sun. It prefers moisture-holding but well-drained soil that contains plenty of organic matter (compost, peat moss, or well-rotted leaves).

Growing Tips
You shouldn't have to fertilize Crossvine since it's a vigorous grower that doesn't usually need any boost. You *will* need to water regularly while the vine is becoming established and during dry spells.

Care
To keep the plant in good shape, prune out weak or winter-damaged growth in spring. Once it has reached the length you want, cut back one-half to two-thirds of the previous year's growth each spring. This encourages the vine to flower more profusely. Crossvine has no serious insect or disease problems.

Companion Planting and Design
Crossvine produces tendrils that are backed by holdfasts, so it readily climbs walls, but it is also suitable for chain-link fences. Good companions are *Potentilla*, Butterfly Weed, Shasta Daisy 'Becky', and Goldenrod, which bloom at different times in complementary colors.

My Personal Favorites
'Jekyll' blooms sporadically throughout the summer. Its flowers are orange on the outside with yellow inside. 'Tangerine Beauty' produces large quantities of spectacular flowers. Neither is fragrant.

Fiveleaf Akebia

Akebia quinata

When, Where, and How to Plant
There are very few situations where you cannot grow Fiveleaf Akebia. Although it prefers well-drained soil and full sun, I've grown it in hard clay and shade. Set out a container-grown plant anytime during the growing season—spring and early fall are best. It climbs by twining, so it is suitable for stout poles of all sorts, trellises, and arbors, as well as fences.

Growing Tips
When the plant is young, water it often enough to prevent wilting. Once established, it tolerates drought—as well as those times when the skies drop 15 inches of rain in March. Don't waste your time or money buying fertilizer for Fiveleaf Akebia—it grows fast and far without it.

Care
Keep your pruning shears or loppers sharpened because you'll need them. In late winter, cut the vine back by half or more to help control size. An overgrown *Akebia* also recovers quickly if cut almost back to the ground. This vine has no insect or disease problems of note.

Companion Planting and Design
Continue the purple theme with annuals such as Petunias or perennials such as Joe-Pye Weed or purple-flowered Butterfly Bush. To span the seasons, use Lenten Roses, *Heuchera* 'Palace Purple', *Echinacea purpurea* 'White Swan', and 'Jolly Joker' Pansies (which are an eye-popping orange and purple).

My Personal Favorites
Everyone admires 'Alba', which produces white flowers and fruit, and 'Variegata', which has green and white foliage and pink flowers.

Anyone who's ever visited the North Carolina State Arboretum in Chapel Hill has seen this vine covering the pergola at the entrance. Look carefully and you'll find numerous other species and hybrids of Akebia throughout the famous garden. You don't often see it in home landscapes—and that's a shame. Admittedly, you have to keep it inbounds, but it's an easy-to-grow plant for the gardener who likes something different and favors the color purple, which this deciduous vine offers in three seasons with flowers, new leaves, and cigar-shaped pods.

Bloom Period and Color
Lavender, white and pink flowers in April; purple, cigarlike pods in October.

Mature Length × Spread
20 to 40 feet × 10 to 15 feet

Gold Flame Honeysuckle

Lonicera × heckrottii

Thanks to Japanese Honeysuckle (Lonicera japonica), *which smells sweet and runs rampant over everything in its path, many people look askance at any vine with Honeysuckle in its name. Never fear—Gold Flame Honeysuckle is a well-behaved member of the clan. It's so nonaggressive that it's mostly used to decorate suburban mailboxes, although I like to grow it up lampposts, too. Wherever you put this twining deciduous vine with the ever-blooming habit, be sure it's a spot you'll walk by frequently to sniff the fragrance and enjoy the flowers.*

Bloom Period and Color
Late spring until frost in coral or maroon (and creamy yellow interior).

Mature Length × Spread
10 to 15 feet × 3 to 4 feet

When, Where, and How to Plant
Plant container-grown vines from spring, after chance of frost has past, until late summer in a sunny or mostly sunny spot. This vine tolerates any average soil. However, since it will be in the same place for many years, it's smart to mix organic matter in the hole.

Growing Tips
To encourage more vigorous growth, fertilize in April with a pelleted, slow-release 14-14-14 fertilizer, or use half the recommended amount of a granular fertilizer made for flowering shrubs. Water regularly when weekly rainfall totals less than an inch.

Care
Aphids may cause misshapen leaves or blossoms. If that happens, stop fertilizing to slow the rapid growth that attracts aphids. Knock off aphids with a strong stream of water, or spray with insecticidal soap. The Extension Service can recommend a chemical control in the rare occurrence that the problem gets out of hand. Gold Flame Honeysuckle isn't usually bothered by other pests. Do any necessary pruning or pinching back after the main flush of blooms fades. To keep the plant inbounds, cut the longest stems back by one-fourth. To renovate an overgrown vine, cut all stems back by one-fourth each year for four years.

Companion Planting and Design
Gold Flame Honeysuckle is a good subject to espalier. I've made a design out of heavy wire, placed it up against a fence, and trained the vine along it.

My Personal Favorites
I like 'Mardi Gras', which has deep maroon flowers, and 'Pink Lemonade', which is a lighter color.

Hardy Kiwi

Actinidia species

When, Where, and How to Plant

Kiwi vines aren't fussy about soil, as long as it's well-drained. But if you want good fruit production, plant container-grown vines (one male to every seven females) in spring along a sunny edge of the vegetable garden. Mix 2 to 4 ounces of timed-release fertilizer into the planting hole. Stake the vines and set up a sturdy, 20-foot wire trellis for them to climb. Grow *A. kolomikta* in partial sun on a decorative trellis.

Growing Tips

The first year is the most critical for Hardy Kiwis; water regularly and protect the vines from late spring frosts. After they've become established, spread 2 pounds of 10-10-10 fertilizer evenly in a circle on the ground around the vine in early spring before growth begins, and 1 pound after flowering. Lack of water causes fruit and leaf drop.

Care

Start pruning female vines in February after they have produced their first fruit the summer before. Prune off broken canes and three-fourths of the stems that bore fruit. Cut back male vines by one-fourth after they flower in spring. (The Extension Service has a pamphlet on pruning fruits that provides greater detail.) If plants wilt, pull them up. Cut back *Actinidia kolomikta* in early spring to keep it inbounds. All species have few pest problems.

Companion Planting and Design

Plant anywhere you need a vigorous deciduous vine for screening, to clamber across a rock pile, or to grow on a fence.

My Personal Favorites

'Issai' is self-pollinating, and 'Purpurea' has purple fruit.

Tennessee gardeners have a choice of Kiwi vines. Actinidia deliciosa is the Kiwi you know from the grocery store; it's for Zone 7. Hardy Kiwi (Actinidia arguta) produces sweet, juicy fruit the size of a large cherry, with smooth, edible skin. It survives temperatures of -25 degrees Fahrenheit, which aren't likely in Tennessee. As it ages, it has peeling bark, adding interest to the winter landscape. An even more attractive relative is Actinidia kolomikta (sometimes, it's called Hardy Kiwi and sometimes it's called Kolomikta Vine), which has heart-shaped pink, green, and white variegated leaves.

Bloom Period and Color

White in late spring.

Mature Length × Spread

15 to 30 feet × 3 to 5 feet

Hyacinth Bean
Dolichos lablab

My introduction to Hyacinth Bean was on a hot day at the Antique Rose Emporium in Texas. I was admiring the Roses and snapping photographs when I spied glowing purple beans up in the air. The glossy pods and pinkish-purple blossoms silhouetted against a clear blue sky made a memorable photo, and the vine made an indelible impression. It can be started from seed inexpensively, it will quickly grow up to 20 feet high, and it doesn't mind steamy summer weather. What more could you ask from a vine?

Bloom Period and Color
Purple-tinged blooms followed by shiny purple fruits all summer long.

Mature Length × Spread
10 to 20 feet × 5 to 8 feet

When, Where, and How to Plant
In late spring, after the soil has warmed up, choose a sunny spot with average, well-drained soil in which to plant seeds 1 foot apart. Mix a pelleted, slow-release fertilizer in the planting hole. Mulch to hold in moisture. The vines, which climb by twining, will grow up strings, much as pole beans do. They look best rambling over a decorative trellis. You can plant the seeds in midsummer if you need a replacement for a plant that didn't make it.

Growing Tips
Hyacinth Bean demands little except regular watering. Ample moisture is necessary to sustain the fast growth, especially in hot weather. Supplement the slow-release fertilizer used at planting time with an additional application at the end of July. Place it under the mulch, near the base of the stems, and water well.

Care
Because Hyacinth Bean is an annual, no pruning is required. If the plant gets out of bounds, cut it to the length you want. There's no need to keep an eye out for pests since this vine rarely attracts any. When beans mature, save some of the seeds to plant next year and to share.

Companion Planting and Design
Hyacinth Bean complements silver- or gray-foliaged plants, such as *Artemisia*, Lamb's Ears, and *Lamium masculatum* 'White Nancy' and 'Silver Beacon'. You may also enjoy the contrast that orange plants provide. Try Butterfly Weed, orange Sunflowers, and *Rudbeckia hirta* 'Marmalade'.

My Personal Favorite
One I've tried and liked is 'Ruby Moon', which produces intensely purple pods.

Mandevilla

Mandevilla × amoena

When, Where, and How to Plant

Mandevilla is usually grown as an annual. But if you plant it in a large pot, it can go indoors in fall and back out again the next spring. In May, fill a container about the size of a half barrel with high-quality potting mix that you've moistened well and mixed with a pelleted, slow-release fertilizer and a water-holding super-absorbant polymer. (Ask about these at a nursery.) Set the vine at the same depth it was growing before. Water well and place in a sunny spot next to a support.

Growing Tips

Like most tropicals, Mandevilla likes plenty of water and fertilizer. That's why it's wise to incorporate long-lasting fertilizer and the water-holding polymer when you plant—it will save you much time in the dog days of August. Don't let the soil dry out. Beginning in July, use a water-soluble fertilizer for flowering plants twice a week.

Care

Remove faded flowers. Pinch the tips of the stems occasionally throughout the growing season to encourage dense growth. In spring, prune back all stems of overwintered vines just before taking the container back outdoors.

Companion Planting and Design

To let Mandevilla be the star of the show, don't put it near other flowers. Instead, place it in the middle of a shrub border or among your foundation plantings by training it on a trellis that's been set up against the house or a fence.

My Personal Favorites

'Alice du Pont' has clear pink blooms. 'Janell' has rose-pink flowers, while 'Leah' is pale pink with a darker pink throat.

With the boom in tropical plants, we're seeing lots more of Mandevilla. It's a vine that anyone has room for—even a townhouse owner with a small patio or an apartment dweller with a sun-soaked porch. While most vines resemble Superman, Mandevilla behaves more like mild-mannered Clark Kent, growing only 10 feet or so during a season. The showy trumpet-shaped flowers will remind you of Lois Lane—they're beautiful. Put this vine by your mailbox, and your neighbors will be envious when it starts to bloom.

Bloom Period and Color

Large flowers in shades of pink or red (depending on cultivar) from spring until fall.

Mature Length × Spread

10 to 20 feet × 2 to 3 feet

Moonflower

Ipomoea alba

Many people who grew up in the South have fond memories of Moonflower. Before air conditioning was universal, families sat out on the porch in the evening to catch any cooling breeze that might be blowing. They chatted with neighbors, told stories, and watched white Moonflowers unfurl in the dark. If you were a kid, the way these white blossoms swirled open and filled the air with a sweet perfume seemed almost magical, especially if you happened to spy one of the hawk moths that pollinate the beautiful blooms.

Bloom Period and Color
White blooms at night during summer.

Mature Length × Spread
10 to 12 feet × 5 feet

When, Where, and How to Plant

Start seeds indoors in pots in April, or sow them outdoors in May after the weather is reliably warm both day and night. They do best in hot weather. The seeds have a hard covering, so you'll need to nick them with a knife to speed germination, or place them in warm water and soak overnight before planting. Mix fertilizer made for flowering plants with the soil in the planting hole. Place in a sunny spot by an arbor, fence, or trellis that's near a deck or porch so you can enjoy the nightly show. If necessary, help the vine get started up the support.

Growing Tips

Water regularly if rainfall is less than an inch per week. To keep the vine actively growing and blooming, mix a water-soluble fertilizer for flowering plants in a hose-end sprayer and spray on the vine every two weeks during the summer.

Care

Since Moonflower is an annual vine, you won't need to prune or shape it. You'll rarely find any pests bothering the plant. You can save some of the seeds for next year, but you might also discover that the vine self-seeds—although these volunteer vines may begin blooming rather late in the summer.

Companion Planting and Design

For a night-and-day combination that's hard to beat, interplant Moonflower with a Morning Glory, such as 'Crimson Rambler' or 'Heavenly Blue'.

My Personal Favorite

'Calonyction' climbs to only 6 feet or so, making it a nice choice for townhouse patios or other spots with limited space.

Passionflower
Passiflora species

When, Where, and How to Plant

In fall or midspring, thickly sow seeds of *Passiflora incarnata* 1/2 inch deep in any well-drained, moist soil. Expect spotty germination. Plant containers of *Passiflora caerulea*, Blue Passionflower, after there's no longer any chance of frost. Although both prefer full sun, they will do fine in afternoon shade.

Growing Tips

Water deeply whenever an inch of rain doesn't fall during the week. At the end of April, fertilize established vines with two handfuls of 10-10-10 spread in a circle at the base of the plant; water well.

Care

In Zone 6a and in cold winters elsewhere in the state, *Passiflora incarnata* may die back to the ground. Since it's root-hardy to at least -10 degrees Fahrenheit, it grows back the next year. When this happens, cut back stems by two-thirds in late winter. Once the vine is growing again, remove the rest of the dead stems. Dig up suckers anytime. Don't remove caterpillars from the vine; they're the larvae of the Fritillary butterfly, for which this is an important food source. Expect *Passiflora caerulea* to be an annual, although in Zone 7, it may return after mild winters.

Companion Planting and Design

Place Passionflower in front of shrubs or trees with dark green foliage so that its unusual blossoms can be seen to greatest advantage. I also like to allow Passionflower to grow up through and scamper across Yews.

My Personal Favorite

Although it's not hardy, I occasionally like to grow *Passiflora coccinea*, Red Passionflower, a tropical plant that laughs at hot weather.

This attractive vine is Tennessee's official wildflower. It's a native plant with instantly recognizable and appealing violet flowers. Passionflower is appealing only not to humans—it's an important host plant for Fritillary butterflies. Wildflower folklore relates each part of Passionflower to the passion of Christ Jesus. The fringed crown symbolizes the crown of thorns, the ovary represents the hammer, and the three styles represent the nails. Maypop, another common name, refers to the little yellow fruits that the vine produces, from which generations of kids have sipped sweet juice.

Bloom Period and Color

White or pale lavender from mid-June until October. Yellow fruits form in late summer.

Mature Length × Spread

15 to 25 feet × 5 to 8 feet

Trumpet Creeper
Campsis species and hybrids

Trumpet Creeper is a good example of a deciduous vine that combines some excellent qualities (showy flowers that attract hummingbirds and stay in bloom for several months) with some traits that aren't so wonderful (it grows vigorously and will often pop up elsewhere in your yard, via suckers or bird-sown seed). If you have a hot, dry spot with poor soil beside a long fence, and you don't mind the inevitable maintenance that this vine requires, it's a fabulous choice. Just don't think you can plant it and forget it.

Bloom Period and Color
Orange, red, or yellow from midsummer to fall.

Mature Length × Spread
30 feet × 15 feet

When, Where, and How to Plant
In early spring, plant bare-root vines in a sunny spot. Set out container-grown plants from midspring until early fall in any average to poor soil. Don't put Trumpet Creeper in rich soil because that will encourage it to grow too aggressively. This vine climbs by twining and also through aerial holdfasts, so it will cover a wall easily.

Growing Tips
If ever there was a plant that wants to grow, Trumpet Creeper is it. Although you should keep the vine watered its first year, rarely will you need to do so again. Never fertilize—that causes faster growth, which you will eventually regret.

Care
Pruning and digging up suckers are the big chores with Trumpet Creeper, and these must be performed regularly or the vine will get out of hand. In late winter or early spring, before the plant leafs out, cut it back by half or more. If you have an overgrown vine, hack it back to 3 feet long. During the growing season, pinch out the tips of the stems to encourage branching. Dig up suckers whenever you see them, being careful to do a thorough job—any piece that's left behind will sprout.

Companion Planting and Design
For a natural look that produces months of color, combine Trumpet Creeper with *Coreopsis grandiflora*, several cultivars of Shasta Daisy that bloom at different times, "wild" orange Daylilies, and Goldenrod.

My Personal Favorites
For big, show-stopping flowers, *Campsis* × *tagliabuana* 'Mme. Galen' is the hands-down choice. 'Flava' has eye-catching yellow blooms.

Trumpet Honeysuckle

Lonicera sempervirens

When, Where, and How to Plant

Plant Trumpet Honeysuckle in any moist, well-drained soil from spring until late summer. It will tolerate shade, but won't bloom well in it. Because the vine is much favored by hummingbirds, you'll want to place it in a spot where you can observe their antics. An ideal location is where it can be easily seen from inside the house or from a porch, deck, or patio. A twining vine, Trumpet Honeysuckle will grow on trellises, chain-link fences, lattice, or netting.

Growing Tips

Fertilizer usually isn't needed by this fast-growing, deciduous vine. Should you feel it needs nourishment, use a liquid plant food made for flowering plants. Water during dry spells.

Care

Aphids are the major pests, particularly in spring. Hose them off or spray with insecticidal soap. Because the vine blooms mostly on old wood (last year's growth), it is important to prune it after the main flush of flowering—not in winter, when pruning will prevent flowering. An exception is an overgrown vine, which can be cut back to the ground in early spring.

Companion Planting and Design

Trumpet Honeysuckle looks best on a fence with annuals and perennials at the base to hide its lower stems. Coordinate the color of the flowers in the bed to the blooms on the vine.

My Personal Favorites

Three good choices that bloom over and over are 'Alabama Scarlet' (red flowers), 'John Clayton' (yellow), and 'Blanche Sandman' (orange-red).

Trumpet Honeysuckle, also called Coral Honeysuckle, is guaranteed to attract birds to your yard. Throughout the summer, it's a hummingbird magnet. In autumn, it produces an abundance of red berries much appreciated by other birds. The vine is covered with clusters of tubular flowers in spring before most hummers arrive in Tennessee, and continues blooming sporadically until frost. Once I had it growing on a solid wood fence. When it reached the top, instead of falling to the other side, it puffed out and became almost shrublike—an interesting look.

Bloom Period and Color

Yellow, red, or orange-red from spring until fall.

Mature Length × Spread

10 to 25 feet × 10 feet

Wisteria

Wisteria species and hybrids

Wisteria in full bloom is a sight to behold. The long, lilac-colored flower clusters emit a sweet fragrance and are a sure sign of spring in the Volunteer State. Throughout the South, Japanese Wisteria can often be spied climbing to the tops of tall trees. Just as attractive and less aggressive, but hard to find, is Kentucky Wisteria (Wisteria macrostachys), a native. If you confine Japanese or Chinese Wisteria to a sturdy arbor or stone wall and don't mind pruning it frequently, there's no more rewarding or beautiful vine.

Bloom Period and Color
Purplish, white, or pink in mid-spring.

Mature Length × Spread
40 to 50 feet × 10 to 15 feet

When, Where, and How to Plant
Because seed-grown Wisteria may take as long as five to ten years to bloom, it's best to buy grafted plants or named cultivars. For a tree Wisteria, purchase one that has already begun to be trained. In spring, plant the vine in well-drained, acidic soil near a very strong arbor or pergola since Wisteria becomes heavy when it matures. Use a strong stake for support. A sunny spot is best. Do not fertilize at planting.

Growing Tips
Wisteria rarely needs fertilizing, but sometimes gardeners do it because they hope feeding will cause flowering. Actually, fertilizing just encourages the vine to grow more. (This is especially true of high-nitrogen fertilizers.) Water regularly the first two years. When mature, it survives nicely on rainfall.

Care
Pruning is the key to a happy relationship with Wisteria. After planting, train the vine to a single stem or to several stems, as you prefer, removing other growth. Once it reaches the desired size and begins to bloom, prune every winter, considerably shortening side shoots off the main stem and cutting back the flower spurs to two or four buds. In summer, cut out shoots that didn't produce leaves. If insects or diseases become a problem, consult the Extension Service.

Companion Planting and Design
Pair Wisteria with *Vinca minor*—try a white-flowered cultivar with lavender Wisteria.

My Personal Favorites
Wisteria floribunda 'Macrobotrys' has huge flower clusters almost 36 inches long. *Wisteria macrostachys* 'Clara Mack' has large white blooms.

Water Gardens *for Tennessee*

The soothing sound of water trickling over stones or rushing down a stream brings back delightful memories for me of the wonderful creek on my grandparents' farm that I loved to wade in, as a little girl. Also, when my husband and I lived overseas, we always enjoyed the ubiquitous fountains found in even small European towns.

I'm not the only one with memories of aquatic pleasures—or with an appreciation of the tranquility a water garden brings to the home landscape. For the past few years, the building of ponds, decorative pools, streams, and fountains has become the most popular backyard gardening project. Many a homeowner has gotten interested in gardening after installing a water garden and discovering that a little pond or stream looks prettier with plants in and around it.

Location, Location, Location

Because you can't just move a water garden, you'll want to plan its placement carefully. If possible, choose a spot where you can see— and hear—the water garden from inside the house or at least from a porch or deck. Although a place that gets an hour or two of afternoon shade is fine, avoid putting your water garden near trees. Sure, it will look cool and inviting—until autumn arrives and you have to spend days removing leaves from the pond or pool. (Not only do those leaves disrupt the balance of the water, too many can kill your fish.)

Another reason to favor a sunny site is that Waterlilies don't like shade. Most need a minimum of six hours of sunshine to bloom well. An aquatic plant dealer should have a few Waterlilies that will do well in about four hours of direct sun, but the size of the selection won't be as large as for sun-loving varieties.

The Cast of Characters

It's natural to want to concentrate on Waterlilies and other colorful floating plants—the beauty queens of the water garden—but to keep the water in your pond from turning green with algae, you'll want to use a variety of aquatic plants. The least assuming, but most valuable of these are called *submerged*, or *oxygenating, plants*. You've probably never heard of *Anacharis, Cabomba,* or *Myriophyllum,* but think of them as supporting players who silently and out of sight go about their work of absorbing minerals and giving off oxygen, thus helping prevent algae in your pond. Water garden retailers sell them by the bunch. They're green and won't be much to look at, but you should buy one bunch for every two to three square feet of water surface.

Waterlilies come in two types: *hardy,* which are perennial, and *tropical,* which are killed by hard freezes. It might seem obvious in Tennessee, where our winter weather rarely approaches tropical, that hardy Waterlilies are the way to go. And certainly you may want the bulk of them to be hardy. But there are other considerations.

Tropical Waterlilies are more spectacular than hardy ones—they have larger, more impressive flowers in a wider array of colors. And they continue flowering up to a month and a half longer in the fall. Randall Tate of The Water Garden in Red Bank says that the typical hardy Waterlily finishes blooming about the end of September or the first of October, but he often has tropical Waterlilies in flower at Thanksgiving, even after a cold spell or two (since it takes repeated freezes to kill them).

Hardy Waterlilies usually finish flowering about 3 p.m. (In the morning, they open when the sun hits them.) So, if you work nine-to-five, you probably won't get to enjoy the show, except on weekends. Tropicals, on the other hand, have blooming periods that are ideal for those who are away from home during most of the day. Tropical Waterlilies are divided into two groups: day-blooming and night-blooming. Day-bloomers stay in flower until about 6 p.m. Night-bloomers, whose blossoms begin opening when the sun goes down, stay open till 10 a.m. or even noon the next day, making them a real conversation piece for evening parties on the patio.

Don't go wild buying aquatic plants, though. You should aim to have plants covering about half the water's surface; when two-thirds is filled with plants, you should remove some.

How to Create a Water Garden

Many people are surprised to discover that water garden plants are grown in pots, instead of on the bottom of the pond. Because of the robust growth that's typical of many Waterlilies, you may want to use plastic tubs made especially for aquatic plants. But old metal dishpans, wooden buckets, and heavy plastic pots (*without* holes in the bottom) will work fine, too. Avoid redwood, new lumber, and half barrels that smell of whiskey. When you're starting out, the most useful container is about twelve inches wide and six inches deep.

If you have clay soil, your water garden pots are the place for it, mixed with heavy loam. The reason you don't use packaged potting soil is that it's so light it will float away. For the same reason, avoid manure, wood chips, and any kind of fertilizer except the tablets sold specifically for use in water gardens.

Wet the soil and fill the container two-thirds to three-fourths full. Place the plant's roots or rootstock on top of the soil. Cover Waterlilies with a bit more soil so that the crown is slightly above soil level; Lotus roots should be three inches below the soil's surface. Following label instructions, poke one or more fertilizer tablets into the soil, then cover the soil's surface with a layer of pea gravel. The listings on the following pages will tell you how deep in the water the various plants need to be placed. Set the pots on bricks to bring them to the correct height.

In autumn, after the plants have stopped blooming, remove the bricks from beneath the containers of all aquatic plants except tropical Waterlilies and let them sink to the bottom of the pool; this will protect them from freezing. Tropicals can be discarded after they've been killed by cold, or you can try to overwinter them indoors. First, allow the tubers to dry in fall, and then place them in a plastic tub between layers of damp sand. Keep the container in a frost-free place, and check occasionally to make sure the sand hasn't dried out completely.

It's a good idea to wait a couple of days after filling your pool with water before you add plants and to wait ten to fourteen days before introducing fish. This allows chemicals in the water to dissipate. Hardy Waterlilies may be planted in mid-spring, but wait until the weather is reliably warm—early

May in the southern parts of the state, late May in upper East Tennessee—before planting tropicals.

Sometimes gardeners complain that the colorful Japanese fish called *koi* that they've introduced to their ponds don't mix well with water garden plants. It varies, Tate says. In one garden, they may munch a Waterlily down to the soil level. In another, they may root in the pots your plants are growing in, looking for worms and small crustaceans—a messy business! If you have the latter problem, use larger gravel on top of the soil and visit a water garden dealer to pick up netting to place around the pots.

Growing Memories

Watering garden is a bit different from other kinds of gardening, but the results—the tranquil pond, the refreshing sound of water cascading from a fountain—make it one of the most satisfying backyard projects you can undertake. Think of it as growing memories.

Cattail

Typha species

You'll spy tall Cattails waving in the breeze in almost every Tennessee wetland, including boggy spots on the sides of roadways. That's a clue this graceful plant is easy to grow. But you'll want to be careful with your selection. Some species may be too large for a small pond. Also Typha latifolia *can be invasive, although it's usually not a problem in containers. I think* Typha angustifolia, *which reaches 4 feet tall, is ideal for all but the smallest pond. All species of Cattail have narrow, green leaves.*

Bloom Period and Color
Slender, velvety-brown catkins appear in midsummer.

Mature Height
18 inches to 8 feet

When, Where, and How to Plant
Plant regular-sized Cattails in spring so that the top of the container is covered by 2 to 6 inches of water; 2 to 3 inches for dwarf Cattail. On pages 219 and 220, you'll find directions on how to pot up aquatic plants. Cattails are usually happiest along the shallow edges of ponds and where they will be in sunshine half a day or more.

Growing Tips
Once a month during the growing season, fish the container out of the water and insert a fertilizer tablet made for water gardening into the soil. Replace any pea gravel that has washed away.

Care
Cut the "pokers" at the base of the stems to use in fresh or dried flower arrangements. It's best to cut them while the catkins are still firm and not past their prime. In fall, remove the bricks the container has been placed on to regulate the depth and let the pot (complete with plant) sink to the bottom of the pool. This will help it survive winter weather. Divide Cattails in spring. You should experience few pest problems.

Companion Planting and Design
Cattails present an opportunity for the gardener to add height to the water garden, balancing the Waterlilies that float on the surface of the water. Mass several plants or intersperse with Water Cannas and Pickerel Weed.

My Personal Favorite
Dwarf Cattail, *Typha minima*, which grows to 18 inches high, has small catkins and leaves that are narrow and grasslike. It's a tiny jewel that enhances any water garden.

Lotus
Nelumbo species

When, Where, and How to Plant

After weather has warmed up in spring, plant in a tub that's about 18 inches around and 10 inches deep, following the directions given on pages 219 and 220. Be sure the green or white tip (the growing tip) is about a half inch *above* the soil. Place a flat rock on top of the root to prevent it from floating, but make sure the rock doesn't touch the tender growing tip. After inserting a fertilizer tablet in the soil, place pea gravel on top of the soil (but not touching the growing tip). Lower into the pond so that the container is covered by 6 to 18 inches of water. Place so that the plant will be in full sun.

Growing Tips

Fertilize monthly with tablets available at water garden retailers. Your Lotus may not experience full growth its first season; it often takes a year to get established.

Care

In winter, lower the plant, still in its pot, to the bottom of the pond. As long as the growing tip doesn't freeze, the plant will survive; it's quite hardy. When the plant has outgrown its container, you can divide the root, replanting each section in a separate pot. The best time to do this is in early spring, when you see the first leaf.

Companion Planting and Design

Lotus is at home with tropical and hardy Waterlilies of complementary colors.

My Personal Favorites

'Momo Botan' is excellent for smaller ponds and even container water gardens. 'Mrs. Perry Slocum' is red when it opens, then gradually fades to cream.

Lotus isn't just a large, more spectacular version of the Waterlily; it actually grows much differently, beginning with floating pads that are bluish-green and up to 2 feet across. Then come aerial leaves that often stand up 5 feet and can reach 8 feet. Covered with wax, these aerial leaves sparkle with dew and rain. Flowers open over a period of four days and may be a foot in diameter. Later, the well-known seedpods—great for flower arranging—are the "icing on the cake."

Bloom Period and Color

White, yellow, pink, or red flowers beginning in midsummer.

Mature Height

18 inches to 3 feet

Pickerel Weed

Pontederia cordata

Not all water garden plants are showy and exciting. Some, like Pickerel Weed, are quiet and charming. A clumping plant, it has glossy heart-shaped leaves accented by spikes of long-lasting blue flowers. It's also quite hardy. While no one is going to build a water garden in order to plant Pickerel Weed—as they might for Waterlilies—everyone who sees the plant loves it. Think of it as the unassuming "bridesmaid" to your glamorous Waterlilies—a decorative accent that adds an attractive touch to any size water garden.

Bloom Period and Color
Blue, purple, or white flowers from spring into fall.

Mature Height
2 to 3 feet

When, Where, and How to Plant
Plant anytime in spring after all chance of frost is past. You can also add Pickerel Weed to the water garden in summer. Pickerel Weed is a marginal or bog plant, so place it—in its container—along the shallow inside edge of the water garden, covered by 3 to 5 inches of water. It prefers to be in full or mostly sun. See pages 219 and 220 for directions on how to pot up water garden plants. Stick a fertilizer tablet made for water gardens into the soil in the container before placing it in the water.

Growing Tips
Each month during the growing season, remove the container from the pond and insert another fertilizer tablet into the soil.

Care
When plants become crowded in their pots and bloom less than before, divide Pickerel Weed in spring, and repot the divisions. This ensures more vigorous growth. When blossoms finally fade, cut off the flower stalks at their base. Sink plant and container to the bottom of the pond during winter to protect from freezing. Pests should not present a problem with Pickerel Weed.

Companion Planting and Design
Mix blue- and white-flowered Pickerel Weed, or combine with Flowering Rush (*Juncus subnodulosus*).

My Personal Favorite
White Pickerel Weed, which grows to about 28 inches tall, tolerates partial shade and blooms a long time.

Waterlily

Nymphaea species

When, Where, and How to Plant

See pages 219 and 220 for complete instructions on planting. You may place hardy Waterlilies in the pond as soon as the chance of frost has passed and on into summer. Wait until temperatures are reliably warm before setting out tropicals (about the same time that melons would be planted). Both prefer a sunny location. Insert fertilizer tablets made for aquatic plants into the soil. Cover tropical Waterlilies with 6 to 12 inches of water; place hardies about 18 to 24 inches deep.

Growing Tips

Monthly during the growing season, remove the container from the water and insert a fertilizer tablet into the soil. To keep Waterlilies open as cut flowers, refrigerate several hours before using or place a drop or two of melted paraffin or candle wax where the petals and sepals are attached to the base.

Care

After frost, lower hardy Waterlilies—in their containers—to the bottom of the pond until spring to prevent freezing. Treat tropical Waterlilies as annuals or, if desired, overwinter them in damp sand in a basement or garage. (See page 220.) Divide in spring, as needed, by cutting the rhizome into 4- to 6-inch sections, each with a growing tip and several eyes.

Companion Planting and Design

For a longer period of bloom, combine hardy Waterlilies with at least one night-blooming and one day-blooming tropical type in coordinating colors.

My Personal Favorites

'Comanche Pink Sensation' (hardy) is always among the first to bloom. 'White Delight', a tropical day bloomer, has enormous flowers.

Waterlilies are one of the main reasons to have a water garden. They're beautiful, they bloom a long time, and many have an enticing fragrance—even the foliage is interesting! The flowers of hardy Waterlilies usually float on the surface of the water, while those of tropical types are held on stems above water level. (See page 219 for a discussion of the differences between hardies and tropicals.) Even if you don't have room for an in-ground pond, it's worth filling a half-barrel with water just to grow fabulous Waterlilies.

Bloom Period and Color

Hardy Waterlilies begin blooming in mid-spring and continue to early autumn in white, red, pink, yellow, and copper. Tropical Waterlilies flower from late spring through late fall in all shades but green.

Mature Height

Varies greatly.

Gardening Basics

Gardening isn't difficult; even small children are successful gardeners. But, as with other hobbies, gardening requires paying attention to the basics—soil, water, fertilizer, mulch, and weather. Pay attention to those, and you'll have a landscape to be proud of. Here's what you need to know.

Soil

Soil Is the Foundation
It's hard to get excited about dirt. It's not as interesting as plants. It doesn't bloom; it just sits there, underfoot. But the soil is the foundation for all your gardening. If the soil is good (either naturally or you've improved it), then plants are going to be happy. If the soil is poor, plants won't grow well and will develop problems.

So the first step is to learn what your soil is like. Your nearby neighbors can probably tell you; so can the Soil Conservation Service office in your county. A simple home test is to pick up a golf-ball-sized piece of moist but not wet soil. Squeeze and then release it. If the ball of soil crumbles, it has a balanced texture. If it holds its shape, it's clay.

The Importance of the Right Conditions
If you've read about gardening at all, you've heard the advice about having your soil tested. That's wise counsel. All it involves is digging up small samples of soil from various parts of your yard, mixing them together well, and turning them in to your County Extension Service to be sent off for testing. The best time to do this is fall, when the labs aren't so busy and when—if your soil needs lime—there's plenty of time to apply it and for it begin to take effect.

When your soil test results come back, you'll learn if your soil is deficient in any nutrients (and consequently what kind and how much fertilizer to use) and also the pH of your soil. What's pH? It's the measure of acidity or alkalinity of your soil. A pH of 7 is neutral—below that is acidic, above that is alkaline. In Tennessee, most of our soils are acidic, but some of us do live on properties with alkaline soil. Because plants have definite preferences for one type or the other, it's important to know your soil's pH level.

Because the ideal soil for most plants is moist and well drained, it's good to know whether your soil tends to stay wet or dry and whether it drains well. Clay soils stay wet longer than loam; sandy or rocky soils drain much faster than other types of soil—which is often good—but they need watering more frequently. Plants that are able to live in especially wet or dry conditions are noted in the descriptions throughout this book.

If you suspect that drainage is poor at a site in your yard, test to be sure. Dig a hole 6 to 12 inches deep and as wide. Fill the hole with water and time how long it takes for the water to drain completely. If it takes 15 minutes to half an hour, drainage is good. Faster means the soil doesn't hold moisture well, and slower means clay.

Improving Your Soil

Just because your yard has a particular type of soil doesn't mean you have to live with it. Instead, improve it with soil amendments. Organic matter, such as compost, not only lightens heavy clay soil and improves its drainage, but it also boosts the water-holding capability of lighter soil.

Other good soil amendments include rotted leaves, rotted sawdust, composted manure, fine bark, old mushroom compost, and peat moss.

If you're digging a new bed, spread 3 or more inches of compost or other soil amendment on top of the soil and till it into the top 8 inches of soil. Otherwise, improve the soil as you plant.

Water

How Much Is Enough?

The rule of thumb says most popular garden plants need 1 inch of water per week in the growing season, and many need its equivalent all year long. Unfortunately, the amount of rain that fell at your city's airport, or other official weather station, may not be the amount that fell on your plants. The only way to know for sure is to put up a rain gauge to assist in obtaining a specific measurement. In summer, when "scattered showers" are always in the forecast, I find that the "official" rainfall and what fell on my yard are rarely the same. If I had watered—or not watered—on the basis of the totals given by the National Weather Service, I would almost always either overwater or under-water my plants. Instead, I save time and money—as well as protect my plants—by knowing exactly how much rainfall they receive.

When and How to Water

In general, plants respond best to thorough but occasional soakings rather than daily spurts of smaller amounts of water. Regulate water pressure to reduce runoff so more water gets into the soil. Such good garden practices as these encourage plants to develop deeper roots, which provide greater stability; that's especially important for shrubs and trees. Deep roots also make plants more drought-tolerant.

The worst thing you can do for your plants in a drought is to stand over them with a hose for a few minutes each evening. Most of the water runs off instead of soaking in, and what does penetrate the soil doesn't usually go deeply enough. The soil should be wet to at least 8 to 10 inches deep for perennials and other flowers; 12 to

24 inches deep for trees and shrubs. Insert a dry stick into the soil to be sure how far the water has penetrated. It's impossible to say how long watering will take, because water absorption rates vary by soil type. An inch of water will penetrate fastest into sandy soil and slowest into clay. Time your watering the first few times and then you'll have a guide for future watering.

If you use sprinklers or an irrigation system, set out coffee cans at intervals to measure the amount of water delivered in 30 minutes. That will show you how long it will take the system to deliver an inch of water to your plants.

Too little water causes plants to perform poorly. Small leaves, pale or no flowers, stunted size, wilting, little or no fruit formation, and premature leaf drop can all be signs of water stress. Soil surfaces may dry out and even crack, destroying feeder roots near the surface; their loss can be fatal to annual flowers and vegetables. If watering seems adequate and plants still wilt daily, they may be located in too much sun. If such beds are deeply mulched, check to be certain that the water is getting down into the soil.

The best time of day to water is early morning; late afternoon is second best. No one wants to get up at 4 a.m. to turn on a lawn sprinkler. But there's an easy way out. Water timers can be attached to any hose and faucet to regulate sprinklers and soaker hoses; their effective use is the hallmark of in-ground irrigation systems. Soaker hoses—which don't wet foliage—may be used any time day or night.

The Right Tools

As with all gardening activities, watering is more efficient with the right equipment. Small gardens and containers of plants can be watered efficiently with only a garden hose and watering can—use a water-breaking nozzle to convert the solid stream of water into smaller droplets that will not damage plants. When watering container plants, irrigate until water flows out the drain hole in the bottom of the pot, and then cover the soil with water once again. This practice keeps the root zone healthy by exchanging gases in the soil.

Larger garden beds require sprinklers, either portable or in-ground systems. Sprinklers spread plenty of water around and most of it gets to soil level; the rest is lost to evaporation but does provide a playground and essential moisture for birds. Adjustable sprinkler heads are a good investment; the ability to set the pattern specifically to increase the size of the water droplets gives the gardener more control over irrigation.

Where water is precious or pricey, drip watering systems and soaker hoses offer very efficient irrigation. They're especially useful around plants, such as Roses and Zinnias, that develop mildew or other fungus diseases easily. These hoses apply much smaller amounts of water at one time than you may be used to. To measure output, let the water run for an hour, then turn the soaker hose off. Dig down into the soil to see how deeply it is wet. That will help you gauge how long to keep soaker hoses or drip systems on. For the health of your plants, when watering this way, occasionally supplement with overhead watering (either sprinklers or hand-held hoses) to clean the leaves and deter insects.

Watering Plants in Containers

Because hanging baskets and annuals in small pots often become rootbound by midsummer—when temperature and humidity levels are high—they may need watering once or even twice daily. You can lessen this chore slightly by mixing a super-absorbent polymer into the soil at planting time. When mixed, these look like Jell-O®. They absorb moisture, and then release it as the plants need it. Although they're pricey, only a tiny amount is needed (never use more than what is recommended, or you'll have a mess on your hands), and they last in the soil for up to five years. My experience is that they just about double the length of time between waterings. That is, if I would water a container plant without the polymer once a day, then with the polymer, I can usually water every other day. That may not sound like a big deal, but in the dog days of August it's a blessing! These super-absorbent polymers are sold under a number of trade names; ask for them at garden centers and nurseries.

Why Is Watering Important?

Water is vital because it makes up at least 95 percent of a plant's mass, and its timely supply is crucial to healthy growth. It is literally the elixir of life, moving from the root zone and leaf surfaces into the plant's systems, carrying nutrients and filling cells to create stems, leaves, flowers, and fruit. Without ample water for roots to work efficiently, nutrients go unabsorbed, growth is stunted, and plant tissues eventually collapse, wilt, and die. Ironically, too much water creates equally disastrous conditions. When soils are flooded, the roots suffocate, stop pumping water and nutrients, and the plant eventually dies.

Watering Tips

- Shrubs and other plants growing under the overhang of the roof may need more frequent watering than those planted out in the yard. Foundation shrubs often don't get much water from precipitation, and they also have to contend with the reflected heat from the house.
- Raised beds, berms, and mounds also need watering more often.
- Watch out for excessive runoff when watering. If the soil isn't absorbing the moisture, slow down the rate of water application.
- Never fertilize without watering thoroughly afterward. Fertilizer salts can damage the roots if moisture is lacking.

Fertilizer

Nutrition in appropriate amounts is as important as sunlight and water to plant growth. Three elements—nitrogen, phosphorus, and potassium—are essential to plants and are called *macronutrients*. Some of these nutrients are obtained from the soil, but if they're not available in the amounts needed, the gardener must provide them through fertilizer.

The Role of Nutrition

Each nutrient plays a major role in plant development. Nitrogen produces healthy, green leaves, while phosphorus and potassium are responsible for strong stems, flowers, and fruit. Without enough of any one of the macronutrients, plants falter and often die. Other elements, needed in much smaller amounts, are known as *trace elements, minor elements,* or *micronutrients*. Included in most complete fertilizers, the minor elements are boron, iron, manganese, zinc, copper, and molybdenum.

Fertilizers come from two basic sources: organic materials and manufactured ones. Organic sources include rocks, plants, and animals; fertilizers are extracted or composted from them. The advantages of organics affect both plants and people: centuries of history to explain their uses, slow and steady action on plants and especially soils, and the opportunity to put local and recycled materials to good use. Manufactured sources are the products of laboratories. Nutrients are formulated by scientists and produced in factories. The advantages of commercially prepared inorganic fertilizers are consistency of product, formula diversity, definitive analysis of contents, and ready availability. Most gardeners use a combination of the two, but purely organic enthusiasts use natural products exclusively.

Speaking the Language

Every fertilizer sold must have a label detailing its contents. Understanding the composition and numbers improves the gardener's ability to provide nutrition. The three numbers on a fertilizer label relate to its contents; the first number indicates the amount of nitrogen, the second number the amount of phosphorus, and the third the amount of potassium. For example, if the numbers are 20-15-10, it means the product has 20 percent nitrogen, 15 percent phosphorus, and 10 percent potassium. Their relative numbers reveal their impact on plants—a formula high in nitrogen greens-up the plant and grows leaves, ones with lower first and higher second and third numbers encourage flowers and fruits.

A good rule of thumb is to use a balanced fertilizer (one where all the numbers are equal, as in 10-10-10) to prepare new soil. Then fertilize the plants with a formula higher in nitrogen at the beginning of the growing season to get plants up and growing; switch to special formulas (that is, those formulated specifically for flowers and fruiting) later in the season.

Fertilizers can be water-soluble or granular; both types have advantages and appropriate uses. Soluble formulas are mixed in water. They are available in very specific formulas, compact to store, fast acting, and can be used either as a soil drench or to spray the leaves (plants will absorb them through foliage or soil). Solubles work quickly (leaves will often green up overnight—great if you want the yard to look good for a cookout), but their effects do not last long and they must be reapplied frequently. They are especially useful in growing container plants, which need more frequent watering as well as fertilizing.

Granular fertilizers can be worked into the soil when tilling or used as a top dressing around established plants. They incorporate easily into soils, and their effects may last for several weeks. Slow-release fertilizers, which are usually pelleted, keep working for three to nine months depending on the formula. The coated pellets of these popular fertilizers (with names like Osmocote, Polyon, and Once) decompose slowly with water or temperature changes over time. They cost more than granular fertilizers but save much time for the gardener because they're usually applied just once a season. Their other big advantage over granular fertilizers is that it's almost impossible for gardeners to "burn" plant foliage when using them; whereas, great care must be taken to keep granular fertilizers off plant parts.

Organic fertilizers also work very slowly, over a long period of time. They usually have lower ratios of active ingredients (nitrogen, phosphorus, and potassium) and so provide steady nutrition, rather than a quick green-up. Organic fertilizers that provide nitrogen are bloodmeal, fishmeal, soybean meal, and cottonseed meal. Organic phosphorous fertilizers include bonemeal and rock phosphate. To provide potassium, use greensand or sulfate of potash-magnesia.

Although soil may contain many nutrients, most gardeners find applying fertilizer makes growing plants more satisfactory. However, many tend to overdo it. Too much fertilizer can harm plants, just as too little does. Excessive nitrogen often leads to attacks of aphids, which appreciate the tender young growth that's being produced, and to floppy stems in perennial plants.

Rules to Remember
- Never fertilize a dry plant. Water the day before you fertilize at least, or several hours before.
- Always use products at the recommended rate or a bit lower. Never use more than what is recommended.
- Rinse stray granules off plant leaves to prevent burning.

The following recommendations for lawn fertilization are adapted from those made by the University of Tennessee Agricultural Extension Service. You may not want to fertilize your lawn this frequently. Many people don't. If you do fertilize, the most valuable time for cool-season grasses is fall.

When to Fertilize Your Lawn

COOL-SEASON GRASSES (Fescues, Perennial Ryegrass, Kentucky Bluegrass)

Application Dates	Amount of Fertilizer per 1,000 Square Feet
March 15	4 to 5 pounds of high-nitrogen fertilizer (such as 24-4-12; may be a pre-emergent crabgrass control formula) or 17 pounds of Milorganite (organic sewage sludge)
May 1	Same as March
September 1	10 to 15 pounds of granular 6-12-12 (for healthy root growth going into winter)
October 15	Same as March and May

WARM-SEASON GRASSES (Bermuda and Zoysia)

Application Dates	Amount of Fertilizer per 1,000 Square Feet
April 15	4 to 5 pounds of high-nitrogen fertilizer (24-4-8, for example) or 17 pounds of Milorganite
June 1	Same as April
July 15	Same as April and June
September 1	10 to 15 pounds of granular 6-12-12 (for healthy root growth going into winter)

Mulch

One important thing you can provide your plants—which may mean the difference between success and failure—is mulch.

Mulch Matters

Mulch is the most useful material in your garden. A blanket of mulch keeps soil warmer in winter and cooler in summer, prevents erosion, and doesn't allow the soil surface to develop a hard crust. When heavy rain or drought causes water stress, mulch ameliorates both situations, acting as a barrier to flooding and conserving water in dry soil. Mulch suppresses weed growth and prevents soil from splashing onto leaves (and thus reduces the spread of soilborne diseases). A neat circle of mulch around newly planted trees offers a physical barrier to keep lawnmowers and string trimmers away from tender trunks. (Such trunk damage is one of the leading causes of death for young trees.) Mulch also makes a garden look neater than it does with just bare soil.

What Mulch Is

Mulch can be any material, organic or inorganic, that covers the soil's surface. Popular organic mulches include hardwood barks (ground, shredded, or nuggets), pine and wheat straws, shredded leaves and leaf mold, and shredded newsprint and other papers. Your excess grass clippings also make a great mulch, provided you let them age a week or so (until they're no longer hot) before using, so they don't burn plants. Organic mulches gradually break down and enrich the soil.

If you can find a source of free organic material in your area—peanut hulls, ground-up corncobs, waste from an old cotton gin, or similar materials—so much the better. I have a friend who's a high school industrial arts teacher, and several times a year he brings me enormous bags of sawdust, left over from his students' projects. Some of it I let rot and use as a soil amendment, but I also spread quite a bit of the fresh sawdust around all sorts of plants as mulch.

And, of course, don't overlook rotted leaves as an excellent no-cost mulch. I've often wondered why some homeowners lug bags of leaves to the curb in fall, then, in spring, turn around and spend money to buy bags and bales of mulch material from a nursery.

Inorganic mulches can be made from pea gravel, crushed lava rock, marble chips, crushed pottery chards, and clear or black plastic. Also available in garden centers to be used as mulch are rolls of landscape fabric, which look like a thick cloth. Both plastic and landscape fabric need to be covered with a layer of an organic mulch for appearance's sake, unless used in the vegetable garden.

In general, organic mulches are best around your yard's ornamental plantings. Black plastic and some landscape fabrics can prevent air, water, and nutrients from readily reaching the roots of your plants. They also cause shallow root growth, which makes the plants more susceptible to drought.

Because pea gravel and other stone mulches are difficult to move if you decide you don't like the way they look, you may want to try them in a small spot first. They're ideal, however, for pathways and other permanent areas, because they don't rot or float away.

What Can Mulch Do?

Beyond practical considerations, you may want to think about what different mulch materials offer the landscape aesthetically. The color and texture of many mulches can be attractive and offer contrast to green plants and lawns. Used on walkways and paths, mulch should provide a comfortable walking surface in addition to adding color and weed control to high-traffic areas. Mulch adds definition to planting areas and can be extended to neatly cover thinning lawn areas under trees. Mulch also works as a landscape-unifying element—use the same mulch material throughout the garden to tie diverse plantings together visually and to reduce maintenance at the same time.

Mulch Dos and Don'ts

- Apply mulch to a depth of about 3 inches when planting new trees and shrubs.
- Replenish mulch around perennials each year when tending established beds in spring or fall. Apply pine straw to a depth of about 5 inches because it quickly settles.
- Use pine straw to mulch plantings on slopes or hills, where other mulches may be washed away in hard rains.
- Don't pile mulch up against a plant's stem or trunk; that can cause damage. Instead, start spreading mulch about 2 inches away from the plant.
- Don't pile mounds of mulch around trees; it's not good for them.
- When setting out small bedding plants, you may find it easier to mulch the entire bed first—then dig individual holes—rather than to try to spread mulch evenly around tiny seedlings.
- Don't spread mulch over weed-infested ground, thinking it will kill the weeds. Generally, they'll pop right through. Instead, weed before mulching.
- Add to the organic mulch around each plant yearly—9 to 12 months after you originally mulched. Think of this mulch renewal not as a chore, but as a garden job that pays rich dividends.
- In fall always add more mulch around plants that may be damaged by an extra-cold winter.
- Wait until the soil has reliably warmed up (usually in May sometime) before mulching heat-loving plants, such as Perennial Hibiscus, Caladium, and Madagascar Periwinkle. If they're mulched too early, the soil will remain cool and they'll get off to a very slow start.
- Don't mulch ground that stays wet all the time; it only aggravates the situation.
- Don't over-do the mulch. More than 4 or 5 inches of mulch may prevent water from penetrating to the soil below.

Compost

Creating Black Gold in the Garden

Compost is a boon to your garden, your pocketbook, and the environment. It's one of the simplest and least expensive ways to add nutrients to your garden. And it puts yard and kitchen waste to good use, while also keeping it out of landfills.

Making compost can be as simple as piling up autumn's leaf harvest and leaving it behind the shrubs until it decomposes naturally over the next year or so. The result will either be leaf mold (the leaves have rotted, but pieces are still distinguishable) or true compost, which has no distinct leaves remaining.

Better compost comes by mixing other organic materials with the leaves, then aerating and moistening the pile. In warm weather and with less than an hour's attention each week, a 3-foot pile of leaves can produce about 2 gallons of screened compost in less than three months. The average backyard composter builds a pile, then tends it once a month and has compost in six months. The choice is yours— slow and steady, or tending the pile for faster results.

Bins for making compost are available commercially and offer the advantage of being attractive and self-contained—a definite plus in many neighborhoods. But almost any material can be used to make a compost container so long as it holds a pile about 3 feet square (the smallest size that consistently heats up well), allows air and water to pass through, and offers some way to turn the pile. Wooden slats, rings of wire fencing, or recycled wooden pallets make practical and inexpensive compost bins.

But be a good neighbor about your pile. Many people put their compost at the far reaches of their yard, right up against the property line. If you don't want to look at it, your neighbor won't either. Try moving it to a site that's handier for scooping out the compost and screen the bin with shrubs or vines to improve its appearance.

Care and Feeding of Compost

Yard materials appropriate for composting—besides fallen leaves—include lawn clippings (as long as the grass hasn't been treated with chemicals); frost-killed annuals, perennials, and vegetable plants; and rotting or damaged fruits or vegetables. Woody materials (stems and branches from shrubs and trees) can be used in limited amounts if they're ground up. Small pieces always compost faster. Chop and shred before adding to the pile, if possible.

The ideal ratio of materials for compost is two parts "brown" (or high carbon) material (such as leaves, hay, straw, sawdust, and chopped cornstalks) to one part green (or high nitrogen) material (such as kitchen scraps, grass clippings, fresh leaves blown down in a storm, fresh weeds, and fresh manure). This allows the material to decompose at an optimum rate. Layer the materials brown/green/brown and repeat. At every foot of height, sprinkle on a cup of good garden soil and half a cup of organic nitrogen to inoculate, or start, the pile cooking. Kitchen debris—from vegetable trimmings to egg shells and coffee grounds—make excellent additions to the pile. Keep a stick handy and bury those wet materials deep in the compost pile. A good size for a pile is 4 feet high by 3 to 4 feet wide.

The composting process depends on organic materials working together in the presence of microorganisms and minimal amounts of nitrogen and water to produce heat. Active compost can measure up to 150 degrees Fahrenheit or higher at the center of the pile. This heating action sterilizes many pests, but there are still materials to leave out of the compost pile because their ultimate safety cannot be insured. Avoid these materials in compost piles: animal waste including cat litter; meat of any sort, raw or cooked; weeds with seedheads attached; diseased plant debris; and lawn clippings recently sprayed with weed-control products.

Tending the pile is a simple matter of turning the compost with a spading fork to aerate the mixture. A two-bin system simplifies this task (the gardener moves the mix from one bin into the other and back again), but so long as the compost is turned over or into another pile even briefly, aeration is accomplished. In the absence of regular rainfall, water the pile occasionally to keep it moist.

Occasionally, a pile that is left unturned or is built with excessive fresh, green matter will develop the unpleasant odor of anaerobic bacteria at work; turn the compost immediately and add some dry brown material or a sprinkling of horticultural lime to control the smell.

If you can't make enough compost for all your needs, purchasing bagged compost has three advantages. First, it is readily available on demand; unlike waiting for the backyard pile to mature, bagged products are at the garden center. Second, the material is consistent and thus reliable in its performance. Finally, bagged products have been analyzed for fertilizer content more precisely than homemade composts. That information reveals what nutrients will be available to growing plants and what additional fertilizer elements to add for balanced soil fertility.

Compost Tea

Soaking finished compost in water creates "compost tea," which has been shown to control some bacterial diseases, such as mildew, leaf spot, blight, rust, wilts, and some rots.

There are various ways to make compost tea, and different gardeners recommend varying ratios of compost to water. Experiment a bit and see what works best for you. Fill a bucket or barrel with water and let it stand overnight. Fill pantyhose or a burlap sack with rotted compost and tie at the top. (You can also just dump compost into the water, but then you'll have to strain your "tea.") I use about one part compost to two parts water. Others like to mix them half and half. Let steep for at least 24 hours or up to a week. (The longer the compost soaks, the stronger the mixture.) Then spray or pour over affected plants.

Pruning

While winter—when plants are dormant—is often seen as the ideal time to prune, both late and early spring are also good times to prune some plants.

General Guidelines

- Prune spring-flowering shrubs and trees as soon as they finish blooming.
- Prune shrubs that flower after July 1 in late winter or early spring.
- When shrubs are grown for their berries, wait to prune them until after the berries are gone.
- Broadleafed evergreens may be pruned whenever their stems and branches are not frozen. December is an excellent time so that they may be used for holiday decorations.

What to Prune in Early Spring

- Summer-flowering shrubs and trees that bloom on new growth
- Roses (Hybrid Teas, Grandifloras, Polyanthas, and Miniatures)
- Winter damage from all shrubs and trees
- Shrubs that produce berries

What to Prune in Late Spring

- Spring-flowering shrubs
- Hedges

What to Prune in Summer

- Climbing or Rambling Roses (after flowering)
- Dogwood, Maple, Walnut, and Yellowwood trees
- Hedges may be sheared

What to Prune in Fall

- Trim back any long Rose canes that would whip in the wind over winter

What to Prune in Winter

- Shrubs with berries and evergreen shrubs for holiday decoration (if desired)
- Deciduous trees (except those noted under Summer)

Pest Problems

Most gardeners see bugs as "the enemy." Sometimes that's true, but sometimes it isn't. Beneficial insects, such as ladybugs and praying mantis, often control other insects that do cause damage in the garden. (This is an area in which scientists—and home gardeners—are learning more and more.)

In the not-so-distant past, the main decision about pest control was: Do I use an organic method, or do I spray with a chemical? Now, even those who don't consider themselves strictly organic gardeners may not pick up an insecticide from the start of the growing season until the end. There are so many other effective controls available that spraying may not be necessary.

There may be a simple solution for the problem—such as picking bagworms off shrubs by hand in the evening after the caterpillars have returned "home," or using physical barriers to block access. Another example is placing Tulip bulbs in a "cage" made of chicken wire so that moles and field mice can't dig them up. Or placing floating row covers (available at garden centers) over tender young plants to keep out insects.

An Ounce of Prevention

One solution that's often overlooked is prevention. If you keep lawn mowers and string trimmers away from the trunks of Dogwoods, for instance, you probably won't have to worry about dogwood borers. And if you seal the ends of the canes (with white glue, shellac, or candle wax) when you prune Roses, rose borers won't be able to tunnel into the stems.

But the biggest preventative of all is a healthy plant that's been placed in the conditions it prefers (sun or shade, moist or dry soil). A plant that needs sun isn't going to grow well in shade, and if you put a plant that needs well-drained soil in a spot that rarely dries out, the plant may develop root rot and die. If a plant is watered regularly and receives the nutrients it needs, insects and diseases are much less likely to be a problem.

Some plants are more susceptible to insects and diseases than others. The majority of plants listed in this book are seldom targets for insects or diseases. That's one reason they're included; few of us want to spend our time in the garden fighting pests. But that doesn't mean you have to avoid plants that are subject to a particular insect or disease. Instead, look for disease-resistant varieties of those plants. Find these by reading catalog and label descriptions, and ask knowledgeable gardeners, as well as nursery personnel. Why grow Garden Phlox, Zinnias, and Beebalm that look awful halfway through the summer because of powdery mildew when you can find cultivars that rarely develop it? Similarly, don't choose a Rose just because it has a pretty flower; make sure it's resistant to blackspot—then you won't be spending your summer with a sprayer in your hands.

Cleanliness Is Next To . . .

Gardening practices can also make a big difference as to whether or not plants are free of diseases and insects. If you use a hose or overhead sprinkler to water plants that are subject to mildew, blackspot, and other fungus diseases, the wet leaves will probably become diseased. But if you water at the base of the plants (such as with soaker hoses), you may be able to prevent fungus problems.

In the same way, if a Rose develops blackspot and sheds the affected leaves, the fungus spores will stay in the ground litter to trouble the plant again the next year—unless you rake up all the diseased leaves and remove them from the garden.

I recall a business management technique called "Managing by Walking Around." What it meant was that there was no substitute for what a manager saw and learned on daily visits to all parts of a company or office. This also applies to gardeners. Most good growers walk through their yards, looking at their plants, once a day. If something is wrong, they quickly notice and take care of it before it gets out of hand. (All insects and diseases, as well as weeds, are more easily controlled if caught early.)

Using Caution with Chemicals

No specific chemical controls are mentioned in this book, because the recommended products change frequently. Old products are taken off the market as new ones are developed. This is also true of organic products. Your local office of the University of Tennessee Agricultural Extension Service will have the most up-to-date advice on any plant problem. Personnel at a good nursery often can also point you to an effective control.

But you also have to do your part. You've heard it a million times, but how often do you actually read every word on the label of a pesticide? It's the smart thing to do—yes, even if it is an organic product—and it can save you from making mistakes. When you follow label instructions that tell you not to spray the product when temperatures are above 85 degrees Fahrenheit, for example, you can avoid needlessly damaging your plants. Or maybe the label offers a hint that you had not heard—such as watering weeds the day before spraying a herbicide makes the product more effective. You'll learn that some products are toxic to bees and, therefore, shouldn't be sprayed until dusk when honeybees aren't likely to be in the garden. You'll also discover that insecticidal soap and horticultural oil are toxic to fish, so they shouldn't be used near a water garden.

Common Pests in Tennessee

Some problems pop up over and over in Tennessee gardens. Here are the most common insect and disease problems that you'll face, along with some possible solutions.

INSECTS

Aphids

Description: Tiny, pear-shaped insects (1/8- to 1/4-inch long) that are found on new growth, sucking out the juices.

Signs: Foliage and flowers (particularly Roses) may look distorted; plants become weakened. They exude a sticky, sweet substance on the plants (called honeydew), which attracts ants.

Prevention: Stop fertilizing (to slow new growth). On Roses, shrubs, or trees that have had continuing problems with aphids, spray with a dormant oil in winter.

Control: Knock aphids off plants with a strong blast of water from the hose. Spray with insecticidal soap. (Both methods may need to be repeated.)

Bagworms

Description: A caterpillar that resides inside a tiny conical-shaped brown bag that, in small numbers, looks as though it's part of the needled evergreen on which it's found.

Signs: Little brown bags that resemble small pinecones; or defoliated shrub or tree needles.

Prevention: No prevention.

Control: In early evening, pick off and destroy all the bags you can find. Do this several nights in a row because it's difficult to see them all. Afterward, check the affected shrub or tree (and those nearby) once a week. You can also spray with *Bacillus thuringiensis* (*B.t.*), although you have to be sure the caterpillars are in the bags before spraying—they are usually "out" during the day.

Caterpillars

Description: There are many different caterpillars that munch their way through your yard. Remember, though, that caterpillars are future butterflies or moths, and decide accordingly if the damage is serious enough to warrant control.

Signs: Skeletonized leaves. Usually you will see the caterpillars, if you look carefully.

Prevention: No prevention.

Control: Handpick them off. Spray with *Bacillus thuringiensis*.

Hemlock Woolly Adelgids

Description: This insect, which is becoming quite serious on Canadian Hemlocks, looks like an aphid and sucks sap from the stems. It kills the needles, while also giving off a substance that prevents the tree from growing new ones.

Signs: White, wooly egg sacs on stems and needles; needles discolor and fall off.

Prevention: No prevention.

Control: Spray tree thoroughly with horticultural oil once in summer and with a dormant oil in fall or winter.

Japanese Beetles

Description: A 1/2-inch beetle with a metallic green coat and copper-colored wings. They emerge from the ground in late spring and return to the soil in late summer.

Signs: Groups of beetles; flowers and foliage eaten away.

Prevention: Kill the grubs, in the soil, that become beetles. Provide some shade. (Japanese beetles are worse in full sun.) Spread Milky Spore, *Bacillus popillae*, on the lawn to kill the larvae (this is relatively expensive and takes several years to be fully effective, but one treatment lasts up to fifteen years. Best results are obtained when your neighbors use Milky Spore, too.)

Control: Handpick beetles. Spray with Neem.

Lace Bugs

Description: A boxy insect, about 1/8-inch long, with lacy wings.

Signs: Splotched or bleached-looking leaves that may have small, shiny dark spots underneath. Tree leaves fall off in summer, rather than autumn; flowering plants don't bloom well.

Prevention: Plant Azaleas in shade and moist soil since lace bugs like sun and dryness. Use horticultural oil in spring on plants that were affected the previous year.

Control: Spray with insecticidal soap or light horticultural oil, or wash off with a strong blast of water from the hose. Be sure to spray beneath the leaves as well as on top.

Scale
Description: Small brown bumps on stems, leaves, or bark. Some have soft coatings; others have a hard coating that is difficult to penetrate with insecticides.
Signs: Leaves or needles turn yellow, then brown. A black sooty mold may be present, as well as a sticky substance called honeydew.
Prevention: Use a dormant oil spray on susceptible plants in winter.
Control: Scrape off scales with fingernails, a nail file, or a plastic dish scrubber. Or use a horticultural oil beginning in spring as growth begins and monthly throughout the growing season.

Slugs, Snails
See page 243.

Spider Mites
Description: Spider mites are so small they're often confused with dust. One way to know if you have them is to hold a piece of white paper beneath a leaf as you shake it; if dots show up on the paper, they're mites.
Signs: Speckled or yellowed leaves; buds that dry out instead of opening.
Prevention: Water plants regularly—particularly those in hot, dry locations—and hose down the foliage of susceptible plants weekly.
Control: Hit undersides of leaves with a hard blast of water from the hose. Introduce ladybugs or lacewings into the garden. Because mites are not technically insects, a general insecticide will not kill them. If you want to use a chemical, get a miticide.

Spittlebugs
Description: Green or brown, triangular-shaped insects.
Signs: Gobs of white foam, which look as though someone has just spit on the plant.
Prevention: No prevention.
Control: Hose off the foam; repeat as necessary.

Tent Caterpillars
Description: These 2-inch-long caterpillars build white gauzy nests where tree branches join the trunk.
Signs: You will see the white, gauzy tents before you notice any damage.
Prevention: Check the bark or twigs of fruit trees, ornamental fruit trees, and other susceptible plants in winter for egg masses and remove them.
Control: Remove by hand (always wear gloves); spray nests in early evening with *Bacillus thuringiensis* (caterpillars leave the nests during the day). Do *not* burn the tents; this can harm the tree.

Thrips
Description: Thrips are almost too tiny to be seen with the naked eye. They suck the juices from foliage and flowers.
Signs: Leaf surface becomes silvery or bronzed and may be speckled; flowers are distorted or don't open; black flecks may appear on the underside of leaves.
Prevention: Keep plants well watered and hose the foliage weekly (except on plants, such as Roses and Zinnias, that easily develop mildew).
Control: Place sticky yellow traps (available at garden centers) near infested plants. Pick off affected flowers and remove them from the garden. Introduce beneficial insect predators, such as parasitic wasps or green lacewings.

Whiteflies

Description: Tiny, white flying insects.

Signs: When you brush against an infected plant, a cloud of whiteflies arises. Leaves may turn dappled yellow, then curl up. Sticky substance on the foliage may turn black.

Prevention: No prevention.

Control: Hose down with a strong blast of water; spray with insecticidal soap, horticultural oil, or Neem; or introduce natural enemies, such as parasitic wasps or lacewings.

White Grubs

Description: The larvae of beetles (including Japanese beetles); they're white with brown heads.

Signs: Usually you will see them when you dig up the soil. Because they eat the roots of grass, sections of the lawn may turn brown and die. Grubs attract moles.

Prevention: The only prevention is to kill the beetles that produce them; however, it is not possible to kill them all.

Control: Release beneficial nematodes. Spread Milky Spore to control Japanese beetle grubs. If you use a chemical insecticide to control grubs, apply it in spring, before the grubs have become beetles but when they are close to the soil's surface, and in early fall, shortly after the beetles have laid eggs.

DISEASES

Azalea Leaf Gall

Description: When young, these galls look like cotton or tiny cauliflowers on the stems of Evergreen Azaleas and possibly on Rhododendrons. (A different gall can appear on Camellias.) They turn brown as they age.

Symptoms: Distorted leaves; flowers may appear to be covered with a fungus.

Prevention: Water at the base of the plant so that the leaves don't get wet. Make sure Azaleas aren't crowded; move a few elsewhere to improve air circulation.

Control: Pick off galls by hand and remove from the garden.

Blackspot

Description: Round black spots on leaves, caused by a fungus that overwinters in mulch and fallen leaves as well as canes.

Symptoms: Spots grow larger; leaves turn yellow and fall off. (Leaves will grow back, but repeated loss and regrowth weakens the bush.)

Prevention: Plant Roses that are resistant to blackspot. Don't use sprinklers or other watering systems that splash water on leaves. In late fall, rake up and remove from the garden all leaves and mulch at the base of affected plants; replace with fresh, clean mulch. Spray plants with lime sulfur in winter. Grow plants farther apart to improve air circulation.

Control: It's important to recognize that the following recommendations, as well as chemical controls, are preventative, not curative. They must be used every seven to ten days (and reapplied after rain) from the beginning of the season and they may not always work. Spray with one part compost tea to five parts water. Or mix 1 tablespoon baking soda and 1 tablespoon horticultural oil in 1 gallon of water, and spray weekly. Make compost tea by steeping 1 cup of finished compost in 1 gallon of water for a week; strain before use.

Powdery Mildew

Description: White or gray splotches that eventually, if not checked, cover leaves and buds.

Symptoms: New growth is stunted; flowers may not open or will be covered with mildew.

Prevention: Plant mildew-resistant cultivars. Water at the base of the plant so leaves don't get wet. Improve air circulation. Give plants more sun. Mix 1 tablespoon baking soda with 1 tablespoon horticultural oil (or dishwashing soap) in a gallon of water, and spray weekly. Sulfur-based fungicides work until temperatures climb over 75 degrees Fahrenheit; then they will damage leaves.

Control: May be controlled by hosing the plant weekly but this treatment may cause blackspot on Roses.

Root Rot

Description: Root rot can be the result of bacteria, a fungus, overwatering, or poor drainage.

Symptoms: Foliage, or entire plant, wilts and turns brown; stems and branches die. When plant is dug up, roots are rotting.

Prevention: Mix heavy clay soil with plenty of organic matter, such as fine bark, compost, or rotted leaves. Plant in raised beds. Don't crowd plants. Don't overfertilize. Don't buy damaged bulbs or tubers, and handle them carefully to prevent injuring them during planting. Don't replant in affected areas. Switch to plants that can tolerate wet soil.

Control: Divert drainage from drain pipes and channel to other areas.

Slugs and Snails

Slugs and snails have voracious appetites and may gnaw ragged holes in the leaves of almost any plant in the garden—they seem especially attracted to the most expensive ones! You'll know the damage was caused by slugs or brown snails because of the slimy trail they leaves behind on the plants, the ground, and any nearby walkway. Slugs like moist conditions and are troublesome during rainy spells and in shady gardens.

I prefer to deal with brown snails rather than slugs, because I can pick snails off the plant or ground and crush them underfoot. Some people (wearing rubber gloves) are able to do the same with slugs, but they're less squeamish than I. Because these slimy creatures come out mostly after dark, the best time to find them is around 10 P.M. (you have to use a flashlight) or just after daybreak. Always peek beneath leaves and under stones or boards that may be serving as walkways in the garden.

Because slugs and snails are such a constant problem in the garden, gardeners have devised numerous ways of getting rid of them. Here are a few:

Crying in Their Beer

You've probably heard the trick of pouring beer into a saucer and placing it in the garden to attract slugs, which will then drown in the brew. But studies at the University of Colorado have shown that it wasn't the alcohol that attracted the slugs; it was brewer's yeast used in the beer. In fact, in a test of a number of brands of beer, the one that attracted the most slugs was nonalcoholic. A drawback of beer, besides the cost, is that some dogs, cats, and other small animals are attracted to it. But never fear, you can mix your own bait by dissolving $1/4$ teaspoon yeast and 1 teaspoon sugar in 1 cup of water. Fill jar lids and shallow saucers with the mixture and place in areas where slug damage has been observed. Remove drowned slugs each morning. This is most effective the first two days it's out. During rainy spells, use covered traps sold at garden centers, so your beer or yeast bait doesn't get diluted.

Dissolve 'em or Make It Hard on Them

Although not a suitable control around plants that need acidic soil, a 3- to 4-inch-wide band of lime dissolves slugs on contact. Salt also dissolves slugs, but isn't good for plants, so use it only on sidewalks or driveways. Some people also sprinkle rock salt beneath pavers and pathway stones where slugs have been known to hide.

Knowing that the soft-bodied slugs don't like to slither over rough terrain, gardeners often use prickly mulch—such as straw, cocoa hulls, or sharp stones—and save their eggshells or wood ashes until they have enough to make a 2-inch barrier around plants that seem to attract slugs and snails.

Strip Them Out

Why not keep slugs and snails from entering the garden in the first place? One popular control is a copper strip barrier that's placed around affected plants. It's very effective and unlike the other controls, continues working in rainy weather and can be used for containers. Unfortunately, the copper strips have sharp edges and can cut unwary hands and bare feet. The copper barriers sold in garden centers are also expensive, but there is a type sold in hobby shops that costs much less.

Ducking the Problem

One slug-free gardener told me she got rid of slugs permanently in her Hosta garden by sprinkling birdseed on the ground among the plants. She already had the birds in the yard at a feeder, so she made a birdseed trail to encourage her avian friends to visit the shady garden and consume its slugs and insects.

If all else fails, invite a duck to visit for a month or two. They're supposed to be wonderful de-sluggers!

Weeds

There's an old saying that points out the most important thing you need to know about weeds: "One year of seeds, seven years of weeds." If you let weeds go to seed, you'll have them around for years to come. For that reason, I've gone around the yard cutting off weed seedheads when I knew I wouldn't be able to weed for a few days, such as before a vacation.

Weeds Are Competitors

Weeds are the bullies of the garden. They compete with your desirable plants for water, space, sun, and nutrients. A few here and there probably won't make much difference, but if left unchecked, they can take over—making much more work for the gardener.

Like flowers, weeds may be annuals, perennials, or, occasionally, biennials. Crabgrass and chickweed are summer annuals, which sprout from seed that has lain dormant since the previous year. Henbit is a winter annual; it pops up in your yard in fall and drops its seeds over winter. Knowing this life cycle, it's easier for you to understand when the critical times to control weeds are.

Perennial weeds—nutgrass, kudzu, plantain, and curly dock—are the hardest to control once mature. Always get them out of the garden when they're young, and the job will be easier. If you hoe or dig weeds with deep taproots, be sure you grub out the entire thing; otherwise, it will sprout from the piece that was left in the ground.

Where do weeds come from? Birds drop the seeds, and you may bring them into the garden in straw mulch or fresh manure. Whenever you dig or till the soil, you bring weed seeds to the surface, where they can germinate and grow. (A thick layer of mulch can prevent this.)

Getting Rid of Weeds

Remove weeds by pulling, digging, or hoeing—it's better exercise than going to the health club! If you choose to use a chemical control, be certain that you understand how the product works (some are selective—they kill only weeds and not grasses; others kill everything they touch; still others prevent weed seeds from germinating, but don't affect weeds that are already present). Be cautious about using a fertilizer that contains weedkiller in a lawn that has trees or shrubs in or next to it. Gardeners have reported damage to good plants that absorbed the weedkiller through their roots.

Never ever spray a herbicide when there's the least little breeze stirring or when temperatures are high—you may find damage to nearby plants if you do. Also ask at your favorite full-service garden center about organic weedkillers and organic pre-emergent weed preventers.

Sowing Seeds

Thrifty gardeners enjoy growing plants from seeds—collected from plants grown the previous year, shared by friends, or purchased. If you want to get a head start on the season and have plants to set out as soon as the chance of frost has passed, you'll need to start them indoors in containers. But if you don't mind having flowers that begin blooming in midsummer, you can sow them directly in the garden where you want them to grow.

Starting Seeds Indoors

For indoor planting, you may use wooden or plastic flats, peat pots, cell packs, or any number of homemade containers, such as Styrofoam cups, egg cartons, or cut-down half-gallon orange juice cartons. Just about anything will work, as long as it's clean and you can punch drainage holes in it. Soak previously used pots in a mixture of one part liquid bleach to nine parts water, and then let them dry for several days before using.

While any high-quality potting soil may be used for starting seeds, I prefer to use a commercial potting mix that's sold as a seed starter because it doesn't contain perlite (which tends to float to the surface and get in the way). Always moisten the mix thoroughly with warm water at least a few hours ahead of time. Fill the container to within 1/2 to 1 inch from the top (leaving the larger amount of room on bigger containers) and pat down gently to level the surface.

Read the packet label to see how deeply the seeds should be planted and if they should be covered or not (a few seeds require light to germinate). The packet will also tell you about how long it will take the seeds to grow into plants large enough to go outdoors into the garden. If it says eight weeks, then count back from your average date of last frost to see the best time to sow the seeds. Doing it too early generally leads to leggy plants (those that are tall and spindly) instead of the desired short and stocky.

Scatter the seeds evenly over the surface of the potting mix, or scratch light furrows or rows into the soil and sow the seeds in those. Cover with clean builder's sand, press down gently, and then water lightly. Some gardeners like to cover the flat or container with plastic until the seeds germinate. Place the container where the temperature is about 70 degrees Fahrenheit. In a house that's kept cooler than that, try putting a few seed containers on top of a water heater or refrigerator. (You can also buy special heating mats to place under flats that will keep the soil warm.) Don't let the soil dry out, but don't let it get soggy either.

When the seeds have sprouted and started growing, give them strong light (from sun or fluorescent fixtures left on 12 to 14 hours a day). Wait until they've developed their second set of true leaves (these will look different from the first set of leaves that develop) and transplant them into individual containers of moist potting soil into which you've poked small holes for the plants. Use a spoon or fork to gather up the small seedlings and place them in their new homes. If you have to touch the seedlings (to separate those that have become intertwined), always hold them by the leaves, never the stem—which can easily be crushed and kill the young plant. Again, keep the soil in the individual containers moist and provide plenty of light for the plants. Temperatures may be cooler than those needed for seed germination. Use water-soluble fertilizer at half-strength every other week.

Transplant seedlings into the garden as you would purchased bedding plants, after the chance of frost has past—unless the plant is hardy and able to withstand cold weather.

Sowing Seeds Outdoors

There are several ways to sow seeds where you want the plants to grow. The simplest—often used when someone gives you a handful of Poppy or Bachelor Button seeds—is to mix them with an equal amount of clean builder's sand and scatter them on top of prepared soil. Rake them lightly and water. They'll take care of themselves until spring blooming time.

A more formal method, to be used in mid- to late spring after the weather has warmed, is to prepare a plot of ground for a flower bed or vegetable garden. Remove all weeds and grass, and till or dig the soil 8 inches deep. Add soil amendments and granular or pelleted fertilizer, if desired, and till or mix together again. Smooth the top of the soil and water well. Wait a day before planting.

If you want to plant in a straight row, take the corner of a hoe and scratch a line in the soil. Sow the seeds in the row, trying to space them evenly. Next, using the hoe, pull a small amount of soil over them (cover so that they're no deeper than twice the diameter of the seed). Water gently. When seedlings appear, you'll probably need to thin them by pulling out the ones that are growing too close to others. This is hard for most gardeners, but it makes a big difference—crowded seedlings remain small and don't perform well. If you didn't mix fertilizer with the soil before planting, feed the young plants now. Spread fertilizer no closer than 1 inch from the stems and follow label instructions for the amount to use.

The easiest flowers to grow from seeds sown outdoors are Cleome, Cosmos, Marigold, and Zinnia. Many vegetables—beans, cucumbers, melons, and squash, for example—are started from seeds planted where they are to grow. Planting from seed is fun for both kids and adults.

USDA Cold Hardiness Zone Map

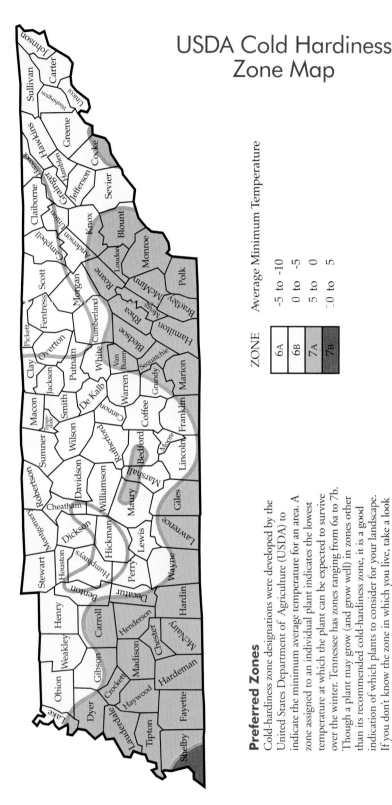

ZONE		Average Minimum Temperature
6A		-5 to -10
6B		0 to -5
7A		5 to 0
7B		10 to 5

Preferred Zones

Cold-hardiness zone designations were developed by the United States Department of Agriculture (USDA) to indicate the minimum average temperature for an area. A zone assigned to an individual plant indicates the lowest temperature at which the plant can be expected to survive over the winter. Tennessee has zones ranging from 6a to 7b. Though a plant may grow (and grow well) in zones other than its recommended cold-hardiness zone, it is a good indication of which plants to consider for your landscape. If you don't know the zone in which you live, take a look at this map.

248

Frost Data

How to Use the Frost Probability Table

To use this table, locate the recording station nearest you. The stated date indicates the likelihood, at 50%, that a freeze will occur *on or after* the indicated date for spring. Conversely, for fall, the stated date indicates the probability, at 50%, that a freeze will occur *on or before* the stated date. A probability of 50% means the odds are 1 to 1.

Probability (50%)

Station	Spring	Fall
Ashwood	April 8	October 24
Bolivar	April 3	October 23
Bristol	April 16	October 23
Brownsville	March 28	October 31
Carthage	April 7	October 28
Chattanooga WB Airport	March 26	November 9
Clarksville	April 4	October 29
Coldwater	April 11	October 21
Copperhill	April 11	October 23
Covington	March 27	November 3
Crossville	April 21	October 14
Dale Hollow Dam	April 13	October 21
Decatur	April 14	October 24
Dickson	April 10	October 23
Dover	April 15	October 19
Franklin	April 12	October 21
Gatlinburg	April 29	October 16
Greeneville Exp. Sta.	April 20	October 17
Jackson Exp. Sta.	April 6	October 23
Kenton	April 1	October 24

Probability (50%) (continued)

Station	Spring	Fall
Knoxville WB Airport	March 31	November 6
Lewisburg	April 14	October 20
Loudon	April 10	October 24
Lynnville	April 13	October 20
McMinnville	April 8	October 28
Memphis WB Airport	March 20	November 12
Milan	April 4	October 26
Moscow	April 2	October 24
Murfreesboro	April 5	October 25
Nashville WB Airport	March 28	November 7
Newbern	March 27	October 31
Newport	April 11	October 24
Norris Dam	April 16	October 27
Palmetto	April 10	October 24
Paris	April 12	October 31
Rogersville	April 17	October 24
Rugby	May 3	October 8
Samburg Wildlife Rfg.	March 29	November 2
Savannah	April 4	October 28
Springfield Exp. Sta.	April 7	October 30
Tullahoma	April 10	October 23
Union City	March 31	October 28
Waynesboro	April 18	October 15

Credit: Pickett, B. S. and M. H. Bailey. 1964. Freeze probabilities in Tennessee. University of Tennessee Agric. Exp. Station and Weather Bureau, U.S. Dept. of Commerce cooperating, Bulletin 374.

More About Roses

How to Plant a Bare-Root Rose

You buy a Rose in early spring and it's all canes and roots. That's called a *bare-root Rose*, and it's typically the way they're sold by mail-order catalogs. They are also available this way at the correct planting time for your area. Although the Rosebush doesn't come in a container of soil—as you're used to with flowers, shrubs, and trees—it's not really difficult to plant. It is, however, a good investment to buy a pair of thorn-proof gloves just for working with Roses.

First, fill a large bucket or tub with water to which you've added transplant solution or several stems cut from a Weeping Willow tree (both encourage rooting). Soak the roots of the bush in the water for 8 to 24 hours.

Dig a hole that's wider and deeper than the roots, at least 12 to 18 inches wide and deep. Mix the soil that's removed from the hole with a generous amount of fine bark, peat moss, compost, rotted leaves, composted sawdust, or other organic material.

Prune any canes or roots that are broken and seal the end of the canes with white glue or shellac. Build a mound of the amended soil in the middle of the hole. Place the Rosebush on top, spreading out the roots on all sides of the cone of soil. Make sure the bud union (the knobby part of the lower stem) will be at ground level or 1 inch above (the former for colder parts of the state, the latter for warmer climates).

Holding the bush in place with one hand, use the other hand to partially replace the soil that was removed from the hole. Water, then fill the hole to the top with the remaining amended soil. Spread a heavy layer of mulch around the newly planted Rose, starting about 2 inches from the bush.

If you've planted the Rose when cold weather may still be ahead in your area, you'll need to protect it by covering the canes with garden soil, potting soil, or shredded leaves. Gradually uncover the bush as new growth emerges in the spring.

Pruning Roses

Start all Rose pruning by cutting back diseased, deformed, broken, or winterkilled canes and stems. Also remove all stems that are smaller than the diameter of a pencil and all crisscrossing canes. Cut off any growth that's coming from beneath the bud union. Many Roses are grafted onto the rootstock of another type of Rose, usually one that's a vigorous grower. If Roses suddenly appear on your bush that are different from the others, they're from the rootstock and the canes on which they're growing should be removed immediately; otherwise, they will take over.

Always use sharpened pruners or loppers and make your cuts at a 45-degree angle about $1/4$ inch above an outward-facing swollen bud. The angle of the cut will help prevent the cane from rotting, and cutting above a bud that faces the outside of the bush will direct new growth in that direction. (Discourage growth toward the interior of the bush since it interferes with air circulation, which helps keep fungus diseases at bay.)

Seal the ends of all canes after pruning with shellac, white glue, or commercial sealant. This prevents borers from getting into the canes and causing considerable damage.

When you finish pruning a Hybrid Tea Rose, you should have three to six good-sized canes that are evenly spaced in a vase shape. Leave them about 18 to 24 inches tall. On Floribundas and Grandifloras, the rule of thumb is to cut the canes back to about half the size they were the previous summer. Or you may leave the canes about 24 inches high. If you have a lot of Miniature Roses, it's okay to save time and prune them after flowering with hedge shears.

When to Prune

- Hybrid Teas, Floribundas, Miniatures, Polyanthas, and Species Roses are pruned in early spring, about two months before you expect the first blooms (i.e., March 15 for flowers by May 15). Then remove faded flowers and prune back lightly after each blooming.
- Climbing Roses and Ramblers aren't pruned until they're at least two to three years old. After that, they're pruned as necessary to keep them in bounds, after they finish blooming.
- Prune Shrub or Old Garden Roses lightly to shape or shorten vigorous growth right after they finish flowering. If they bloom several times during the season, remove faded flowers and prune as needed after each flush of blossoms.

Made in the Shade

When I moved to a new house in the middle of an acre of enormous trees (mostly Oaks), I got the feeling I was going to have to learn to garden all over again. While I'd always had shady corners in other yards, now I had only a few sunny spots. I wondered if I was going to be limited to growing mostly Hostas and Ferns.

As it turned out, I needn't have worried. A wide variety of plants enjoy woodland sites. But I did have to get to know my yard better, and then I had to do some experimenting to find out what plants grew well where.

First, I mapped out the various types of shade in different parts of the yard. How many hours a day did this spot or that receive direct sunlight? Was there occasional dappled light falling through the leaves of trees overhead? Did the sun shine on the area in the morning or the afternoon? (The afternoon sun is hotter and brighter, and each hour of it equals 2 hours of morning sun.) I penciled my discoveries on the survey map of our property and made several copies.

All Shade Isn't Created Equal

The two main things to remember about shade gardening are that all shade isn't equal and that there's no standard definition of what shade is. Maybe, in thinking about your own yard, you've become confused by terms such as dappled shade, high shade, and bright shade. *Dappled shade* receives spotty sunlight through the leaves of trees. *Bright shade* and *high shade* refer to areas that receive no direct sunlight, but are brightly lit (in the case of high shade, because tree limbs have been removed to a height of 10 feet or more). *Dense shade* is heavy shade, such as beneath evergreen trees with low limbs.

In this book, *full sun* means full sun, all day, with the possible exception of an hour of shade in the morning or afternoon. *Part sun* is about 6 hours of direct sun during the day or 4 or 5 hours of afternoon sun. *Part shade* is dappled shade or high shade with 5 or fewer hours of morning sun (3 or less in the afternoon). *Full shade* is mostly shade all the time.

In most shady yards, there are plenty of in-between spots and that's where some experimenting may be called for. Start with the chart on page 255, which lists plants that will grow in full or partial shade. Then turn to the pages that describe those plants and learn more about their other requirements (moist soil, well-drained soil), matching them with the conditions in your yard.

But don't stop there. You may find that some of the plants listed in this book as "part sun" do just fine in your partly shady garden. After all, plants don't read garden books. Many Daylilies grow well in partial shade, for instance. (But if blooms get fewer and fewer, you'll know they need to be moved into more light.)

You don't necessarily have to accept what Mother Nature has dished out in the way of shade. I had several trees that weren't in good condition removed and many others were "limbed up" so that their lowest branches were 20 to 25 feet high. You may also want to have an experienced professional arborist thin some limbs to allow more sunlight to pass through.

Expanding Your Shade Garden

When I began to make lists of plants that thrived in shade, I learned that spring was going to be the most colorful time in my shade garden, but that, with some planning, I would be able to have something in bloom throughout the growing season (and even in cold weather).

I also began to appreciate plants for their interesting and varied foliage, rather than judging them strictly on their flowers. I searched out plants with variegated leaves and gold foliage, which almost seem to glow in shady spots. I looked for Evergreen Ferns and groundcovers so that the yard wouldn't look so brown in winter.

The nicest discovery was how cool and serene a shade garden was on the sultriest summer days. With a sunny garden, there was almost always something that needed doing, even on sweltering August days—especially watering. Not so with shade. I could just sit back and take it easy, enjoying the garden instead of constantly working in it.

I'm still learning, still experimenting, and still moving plants around the garden to find just the amount of shade they like. And, do you know what? I've decided that gardening in shade is a lot of fun!

Shade Plants for Tennessee

Following is a list of plants that will grow in full or partial shade (the designation listed first—shade or part shade—is the plant's main preference).

Annuals
Coleus: part shade, shade (page 24)
Geranium: part shade (page 26)
Impatiens: shade, part shade (page 28)
Pansy: part shade (page 36)
Petunia: part shade (page 38)
Wax Begonia: shade, part shade (page 45)

Bulbs
Arum: shade, part shade (page 52)
Caladium: shade, part shade (page 53)
Siberian Iris: part shade (page 59)
Spanish Bluebell: part shade (page 62)

Grasses
Mondo Grass: shade, part shade (page 76)
Monkey Grass: shade, part shade (page 77)
Tall Fescue: part shade (page 80)

Groundcovers
Bugleweed: shade, part shade (page 84)
Creeping Phlox: part shade (page 86)
English Ivy: shade, part shade (page 88)
Foamflower: shade, part shade (page 89)
Pachysandra: shade, part shade (page 90)
Spotted Dead Nettle: shade, part shade (page 91)
Strawberry 'Pink Panda': part shade (page 92)
Sweet Box: shade, part shade (page 93)
Vinca: shade, part shade (page 94)
Wild Ginger: shade, part shade (page 95)

Perennials
Anemone (or Japanese Anemone): part shade (page 100)
Bleeding Heart: part shade, shade (page 104)
Cardinal Flower: part shade (page 108)
Columbine: part shade (page 110)
Deciduous Ferns: shade, part shade (page 113)
Evergreen Ferns: shade, part shade (page 115)
Foxglove: part shade (page 116)
Hardy Begonia: shade, part shade (page 119)
Heuchera: part shade, shade (page 120)
Hosta: shade, part shade (page 121)
Lenten Rose: shade, part shade (page 123)

Shrubs
Aucuba: shade, part shade (page 138)
Boxwood: part shade (page 140)
Camellia: part shade (page 144)
Carolina Allspice: part shade (page 145)
Evergreen Azalea: part shade, shade (page 149)
Hydrangea *Hydrangea arborescens* 'Anabelle': part shade, shade (page 155)
Kerria: part shade, shade (page 156)
Leucothoe: part shade, shade (page 157)
Loropetalum: part shade (page 158)
Nandina: shade, part shade (page 159)
Oakleaf Hydrangea: part shade, shade (page 155)
Rhododendron: part shade (page 161)
Summersweet: part shade (page 165)
Viburnum: part shade (page 166)
Virginia Sweetspire: part shade (page 167)
Witch Hazel: part shade (page 168)

Trees
Canadian Hemlock: part shade (page 174)
Carolina Silverbell: part shade (page 175)
Dogwood: part shade (page 177)
Japanese Maple: part shade (page 183)
Serviceberry: part shade (page 193)

Vines
Climbing Hydrangea: shade, part shade (page 204)

What's in a Name?

Sometimes gardeners feel uncomfortable with botanical names. The words are unfamiliar and sometimes long and hard to pronounce. Why don't garden books just use common names instead?

There are several reasons why books and catalogs give both botanical and common names. Mostly, it's to avoid confusion. Common names for a plant vary from place to place. You and a neighbor, who grew up in a different state, may call the same plant by different common names. One plant may also have collected a number of different common names, adding to the confusion.

So every plant has a botanical name—usually Latin, occasionally Latinized Greek—that belongs to it and it alone. If you are looking for a particular plant at a local garden center or from a mail-order nursery, you'll find it by the botanical name. If you need to ask advice about a plant from the Extension Service or another expert, they can readily identify your plant by its botanical name.

Another reason for using botanical names is that, once you look at them carefully, you'll pick up clues to what the plant is like. *Alba* means white, for instance. *Japonica* tells you that the plant originated in Japan, while *canadensis* tells you the plant was originally found in Canada. *Citrina* indicates lemony yellow. In leaf shapes, *lancifolia* is lance-leafed, *crispula* may be curled, *undulata* may be wavy, and *serrata* indicates serrated leaves. *Variegata* obviously indicates variegation (more than one color on a leaf). *Sempervirens* is evergreen. As part of a species name, *micro* means very small, *grandis* is large, and *gracilis* is slender or graceful.

The first word in a plant's botanical name (which is always capitalized and italicized) is the genus name; think of it as a family name. It's a group of plants that are closely related—*Hosta*, for instance. The second name (which begins with a lowercase letter and is also italicized) is the species, which identifies a distinct type of individual plant, such as *Hosta fortunei*. The third name (which may be more than one word) is the variety or cultivar name. In botanical terms, there are differences between varieties and cultivars, but in popular gardening parlance, they're used interchangeably. Cultivar stands for cultivated variety. It's a plant that was selected for its desirable qualities from a larger group of plants. The cultivar name is usually enclosed in single quotation marks. For example, *Hosta fortunei* 'Albopicta' further identifies our Hosta as a particular cultivar.

What Did You Say?

But how do you pronounce all those tongue-twisting words? That's why the following pronunciation guide is provided—to give you the confidence to ask for a plant and talk about it by its botanical name. Consider it a guide only. Different experts have varying ways of pronouncing some of these names. In most of the U.S., for example, we say "Stokesia" as Stow-KEY-zee-uh. In England, and among some professionals in this country, it's pronounced STOKES-ee-uh, after the man for whom the plant was named. So you'll hear it both ways.

Not to worry. You already know how to pronounce many more botanical names than you think. You're not so sure? Well, what about these—Impatiens, Petunia, Salvia, Begonia, Zinnia, Canna, Crocus, Dahlia, Iris, Zoysia, Phlox, Vinca, Sedum, Camellia, Forsythia, Hibiscus, Nandina, Rhododendron, Viburnum, Magnolia, Hydrangea, and Wisteria? See, you already have a head start on pronouncing botanical names.

Pronunciations

Annuals
Ageratum, *Ageratum houstonianum* (ah-jer-AY-tum hous-tone-ee-AN-um)
Angel Trumpet, *Datura wrightii* (dah-TOUR-ah RIGHT-ee-eye)
Celosia, *Celosia argentea plumosa* (seh-LOW-see-uh r-JEN-tee-uh plew-MO-suh)
Cleome, *Cleome hasslerana* (klee-OH-mee hass-ler-AH-nuh)
Coleus, *Solenostemon scutellarioides* (sol-eh-no-STEH-mon scoo-tuh-LOID-eez)
Cosmos, *Cosmos bipinnatus* (KOZ-mose bi-pin-NAY-tus)
Geranium, *Pelargonium* species and hybrids (pel-ar-GO-nee-um)
Globe Amaranth, *Gomphrena globosa* (gom-FREE-nah glow-BOE-sah)
Impatiens, *Impatiens walleriana* (im-PAY-shens wall-er-ee-AY-nuh)
Madagasgar Periwinkle, *Catharanthus roseus* (cath-ah-RAN-thus ROE-see-us)
Marigold, *Tagetes* species and hybrids (TAH-jeh-teez)
Melampodium, *Melampodium paludosum* (mel-um-PO-dee-um pal-you-DOE-sum)
Moss Rose, *Portulaca grandiflora* (por-tyew-LACK-uh gran-dih-FLOOR-uh)
New Guinea Impatiens, *Impatiens hawkeri* (im-PAY-shens HAWK-er-eye)
Ornamental Cabbage, *Brassica oleracea* (BRASS-ih-kah ohl-er-AY-cee-uh)
Ornamental Pepper, *Capsicum annuum* (CAP-sih-come AN-you-um)
Pansy, *Viola* x *wittrockiana* (vy-OH-lah wit-rock-ee-AY-nuh)
Pentas, *Pentas lanceolata* (PEN-tas lan-cee-oh-LAY-tah)
Petunia, *Petunia* x *hybrida* (peh-TUNE-ee-uh Hy-BRED-uh)
Red Salvia, *Salvia* species and hybrids (SAL-vee-ah)
Scaveola, *Scaveola* x 'Blue Wonder' (skuh-VOH-lah)
Snapdragon, *Antirrhinum majus* (an-tir-RHY-num MAY-jus)
Snow-on-the-Mountain, *Euphorbia marginata* (you-FORB-ee-uh mar-gin-AY-tuh)
Sunflower, *Helianthus annus* (hee-lee-AN-thuss AN-yew-us)
Sweet Alyssum, *Lobularia maritima* (lob-you-LAIR-ee-uh mah-RIT-ih-mah)

Wax Begonia, *Begonia* x *semperflorens-cultorum* (beh-GOAN-ee-uh sem-per-FLOR-ens cull-TORE-um)

Zinnia, *Zinnia* species and hybrids (ZIN-nee-uh)

Bulbs

Arum, *Arum italicum* (AIR-um i-TAL-i-cum)
Caladium, *Caladium bicolor* (kuh-LAY-dee-um BYE-cull-er)
Canna, *Canna* species and hybrids (KAN-nuh)
Crocus, *Crocus* species and hybrids (CROW-kus)
Daffodil, *Narcissus* (nar-SIS-sus)
Dahlia, *Dahlia* species and hybrids (DAL-ya)
Grape Hyacinth, *Muscari* species and hybrids (mus-CARE-ee)
Iris, *Iris* species and hybrids (EYE-ris)
Lily, *Lilium* species hybrids (LIL-ee-um)
Lycoris, *Lycoris* species (lie-KORR-is)
Spanish Bluebell, *Hyacinthoides hispanica* (hy-ah-sin-THOY-deez his-PAN-ih-kuh)
Tulip, *Tulipa* species and hybrids (TOO-lih-pa)

Grasses

Bermuda Grass, *Cynodon dactylon* (SIGH-no-don DACK-tih-lon)
Carex, *Carex* species and hybrids (CARE-ex)
Feather Reed Grass, *Calamagrostis acutiflora* (kal-a-ma-GROS-tiss ah-ku-ti-FLOOR-uh)
Fountain Grass, *Pennisetum* species and hybrids (pen-ni-SEE-tum)
Japanese Blood Grass, *Imperata cylindrica* 'Rubra' ('Red Baron') (im-per-AH-tuh si-LIN-drih-kuh)
Miscanthus, *Miscanthus sinensis* (mis-KAN-thus si-NEN-sis)
Mondo Grass, *Ophiopogon japonicus* (oh-fee-oh-PO-gon ja-PON-ih-cus)
Monkey Grass, *Liriope* species and hybrids (li-RIE-oh-pee)
Pampas Grass, *Cortaderia selloana* (kor-ta-DEE-ree-a sel-low-AN-nuh)
Switch Grass, *Panicum virgatum* (PAN-i-kum ver-GAY-tum)
Tall Fescue, *Festuca arundinacea* (fes-TOO-ka a-RUN-de-nay-see-uh)
Zoysia, *Zoysia* species (ZOY-ziah)

Groundcovers

Bugleweed, *Ajuga reptans* (a-JOO-guh REP-tans)
Creeping Juniper, *Juniperus* species and hybrids (jew-NIP-er-us)
Creeping Phlox, *Phlox* species and hybrids (flocks)
Creeping Thyme, *Thymus praecox* (TIME-us PRE-cox)
English Ivy, *Hedera helix* (HED-er-uh HE-licks)
Foamflower, *Tiarella* species and hybrids (tee-a-REL-a)
Pachysandra, *Pachysandra* species and hybrids (pack-ih-SAN-dra)
Spotted Dead Nettle, *Lamium maculatum* (LAY-mee-um mac-u-LA-tum)
Strawberry 'Pink Panda', *Fragaria frel* 'Pink Panda' (fra-GAY-ree-uh frel)
Sweet Box, *Sarcococca hookeriana humilis* (sar-koh-KOH-uh hook-er-ih-A-nuh hum-uh-lis)

Vinca, *Vinca minor* (VING-ka MY-ner)
Wild Ginger, *Asarum* species and hybrids (a-SAIR-um)

Perennials

Anemone, *Anemone × hybrida* (uh-NEM-o-nee high-BRED-duh)
Artemisia, *Artemisia* 'Powis Castle' (ar-te-MEEZ-ee-uh)
Baptisia, *Baptisia* species and hybrids (bap-TIZ-ee-uh)
Black-Eyed Susan, *Rudbeckia* species and hybrids (rood-BEK-ee-uh)
Bleeding Heart, *Dicentra spectabilis* (die-SEN-tra spek-TAH-bil-iss)
Boltonia, *Boltonia asteroides* (bowl-TONE-ee-uh as-ter-OY-deez)
Butterfly Weed, *Asclepias tuberosa* (as-KLEE-pee-us too-buh-RO-suh)
Candytuft, *Iberis sempervirens* (eye-BEER-is sem-per-VIE-renz)
Cardinal Flower, *Lobelia cardinalis* (lo-BEE-lee-a kar-di-NAH-lis)
Chrysanthemum, *Dendranthema × grandiflorum* (Den-DRAN-thuh-muh
  gran-dih-FLOOR-um)
Columbine, *Aquilegia* species and hybrids (ack-wi-LEE-gee-uh)
Coreopsis, *Coreopsis grandiflora* (ko-ree-OP-sis gran-di-FLOOR-uh)
Daylily, *Hemerocallis* hybrids (hem-er-oh-KAL-iss)
Dianthus, *Dianthus* species and hybrids (die-AN-thus)
Foxglove, *Digitalis* species and hybrids (di-ji-TAL-liss)
Gaillardia, *Gaillardia grandiflora* (gay-LAR-dee-uh gran-di-FLOOR-uh)
Goldenrod, *Solidago* species and hybrids (sol-ih-DAY-go)
Hardy Begonia, *Begonia grandis* (beh-GOAN-ee-a GRAN-dis)
Heuchera, *Heuchera* species and hybrids (HEW-ker-uh)
Hosta, *Hosta* species and hybrids (HOSS-tuh)
Joe-Pye Weed, *Eupatorium purpureum* (you-pa-TOE-ree-um pur-pu-REE-um)
Lenten Rose, *Helleborus orientalis* (hell-e-BORE-us or-ih-en-TAL-iss)
Peony, *Paeonia lactiflora* (pee-OH-nee-uh lac-ti-FLOOR-uh)
Perennial Hibiscus, *Hibiscus* species and hybrids
Phlox, *Phlox* species and hybrids (flocks)
Purple Coneflower, *Echinacea purpurea* (ek-ih-NAY-see-uh pur-pu-RE-uh)
Red Valerian, *Centranthus ruber* (ken-TRAN-thus ROO-ber)
Salvia, *Salvia* species and hybrids (SAL-vee-uh)
Sedum 'Autumn Joy', *Sedum × telephium* 'Autumn Joy' (SEE-dum the-LEF-ee-um)
Shasta Daisy, *Leucanthemum × superbum* (loo-KAN-thuh-mum × soo-PER-bum)
Sundrops, *Oenothera fruticosa* (ee-NOTH-er-a fru-ti-CO-suh)
Verbena, *Verbena* species and hybrids (ver-BEE-nuh)
Yarrow, *Achillea* species and hybrids (a-kil-LEE-uh)

Shrubs

Aucuba, *Aucuba japonica* (ah-Q-bah juh-PON-ik-uh)
Beautyberry, *Callicarpa* species and hybrids (kal-i-CAR-puh)
Boxwood, *Buxus* species and hybrids (BUCKS-us)
Buckeye, *Aesculus* species and hybrids (ESS-ku-lus)
Burning Bush, *Euonymus alatus* (u-ON-e-mus a-LAY-tus)
Butterfly Bush, *Buddleia davidii* species and hybrids (BUD-lee-uh day-VID-ee-eye)

Camellia, *Camellia* species and hybrids (ka-MEAL-yuh ja-PON-ick-uh)
Carolina Allspice, *Calycanthus floridus* (kal-i-KAN-thus FLOOR-i-dus)
Crape Myrtle, *Lagerstroemia* species and hybrids (lay-gear-STRO-me-uh)
Deciduous Azalea, *Rhododendron* species and hybrids (row-doe-DEN-dron)
Deciduous Holly, *Ilex* species and hybrids (EYE-lex)
Evergreen Azalea, *Rhododendron* hybrids (row-doe-DEN-dron)
Evergreen Holly, *Ilex* species and hybrids (EYE-lex)
False Cypress, *Chamaecyparis* species and hybrids (kam-uh-SIP-a-ris)
Flowering Quince, *Chaenomeles* species and hybrids (key-NOM-uh-leez)
Forsythia, *Forsythia* species and hybrids (for-SITH-ee-uh)
Fothergilla, *Fothergilla* species (father-GILL-uh)
Hydrangea, *Hydrangea* species and hybrids (high-DRAN-gee-uh)
Kerria, *Kerria japonica* (KER-ee-uh ja-PON-ick-uh)
Leucothoe, *Leucothoe* species and hybrids (loo-KOTH-oh-ee)
Loropetalum, *Loropetalum chinense* (lor-row-PET-a-lum chi-NIN-see)
Nandina, *Nandina domestica* (nan-DEE-nuh do-MES-ti-cuh)
Redvein Enkianthus, *Enkianthus campanulatus* (en-key-AN-thus kam-pan-u-LAY-tus)
Rhododendron, *Rhododendron* species and hybrids (row-doe-DEN-dron)
Rose, *Rosa* species and hybrids (RO-zuh)
Smoke Tree, *Cotinus coggygria* (ko-TIE-nus ko-GIG-ree-uh)
Spirea, *Spiraea* species and hybrids (spy-REE-uh)
Summersweet, *Clethra alnifolia* (KLETH-ruh al-ni-FO-lee-uh)
Viburnum, *Viburnum* species and hybrids (vie-BURR-num)
Virginia Sweetspire, *Itea virginica* (eye-TEE-uh ver-GIN-i-kuh)
Witch Hazel, *Hamamelis* species and hybrids (ham-uh-MEL-is)

Trees
American Holly, *Ilex opaca* (I-lex o-PAY-kuh)
Bald Cypress, *Taxodium distichum* (tax-O-dee-um DIS-ti-kum)
Canadian Hemlock, *Tsuga canadensis* (TSOO-gah can-uh-DEN-sis)
Carolina Silverbell, *Halesia tetraptera* (huh-LEE-zi-uh tee-TRAP-ter-uh)
Chaste Tree, *Vitex agnus-castus* (VIE-tex AG-nus-KAS-tus)
Dogwood, *Cornus* species and hybrids (KOR-nus)
Flowering Cherry, *Prunus* species and hybrids (PROO-nus)
Fringe Tree, *Chionanthus virginicus* (ki-o-NAN-thus ver-GIN-i-kus)
Ginkgo, *Ginkgo biloba* (GING-ko bi-LOW-buh)
Golden Rain Tree, *Koelreuteria paniculata* (kol-roo-TEER-ee-uh pan-ick-you-LAY-tuh)
Japanese Cryptomeria, *Cryptomeria japonica* (krip-toe-MEER-ree-uh ja-PON-i-cuh)
Japanese Maple, *Acer palmatum* (Ace-er pall-MAY-tum)
Japanese Zelkova, *Zelkova serrata* (zel-KO-vuh ser-RAY-tuh)
Lacebark Elm, *Ulmus parvifolia* (UL-mus par-vi-FO-lee-uh)
Oak, *Quercus* species and hybrids (KWER-kus)
Ornamental Pear, *Pyrus calleryana* (PIE-rus kal-er-ee-A-nuh)
Paperbark Maple, *Acer griseum* (Ace-er GRIS-ee-um)
Redbud, *Cercis canadensis* (SER-sis kan-a-DEN-sis)
Red Maple, *Acer rubrum* (Ace-er RU-brum)

River Birch, *Betula nigra* (BET-u-la NIGH-gra)
Saucer Magnolia, *Magnolia soulangiana* (mag-NO-lee-uh sue-lan-gee-A-nuh)
Serviceberry, *Amelanchier* species and hybrids (am-e-LANG-kee-er)
Sourwood, *Oxydendrum arboreum* (ox-ee-DEN-drum ar-BO-re-um)
Southern Magnolia, *Magnolia grandiflora* (mag-NO-lee-uh gran-di-FLOOR-uh)
Sweet Gum, *Liquidambar styraciflua* (lick-wid-AM-bar sti-rah-see-FLOW-uh)
Tulip Poplar, *Liriodendron tulipifera* (leer-ee-oh-DEN-dron two-lih-PIF-er-uh)
Yellowwood, *Cladrastis kentukea* (klad-RAST-iss ken-TUK-ee-uh)

Vines

Carolina Jessamine, *Gelsemium sempervirens* (jell-SEE-mee-um sem-per-VIE-renz)
Clematis, *Clematis* species and hybrids (KLEM-a-tis)
Climbing Hydrangea, *Hydrangea anomala* (hy-DRAN-gee uh-NOM-uh-luh)
Climbing Roses, *Rosa* species and hybrids (RO-zuh)
Crossvine, *Bignonia capreolata* (big-KNOWN-ee-uh cap-ree-o-LA-tuh)
Five-Leaf Akebia, *Akebia quinata* (a-KEE-bi-a kwi-NAY-tuh)
Gold Flame Honeysuckle, *Lonicera × heckrottii* (lon-ISS-er-a hek-ROT-ti-eye)
Hardy Kiwi, *Actinidia* species (ak-ti-NID-ee-uh)
Hyacinth Bean, *Dolichos lablab* (DOL-li-kos LAB-lab)
Mandevilla, *Mandevilla × amoena* (man-dee-VIL-luh a-MEE-na)
Moonflower, *Ipomoea alba* (ip-po-MEE-uh AL-ba)
Passionflower, *Passiflora* species (pas-si-FLOOR-uh)
Trumpet Creeper, *Campsis* species and hybrids (KAMP-sis)
Trumpet Honeysuckle, *Lonicera sempervirens* (lon-ISS-er-a sem-per-VI-renz)
Wisteria, *Wisteria* species and hybrids (wis-TEE-ree-uh)

Water Gardens

Cattail, *Typha* species (TIE-fuh)
Lotus, *Nelumbo* species (nee-LUM-bo)
Pickerel Weed, *Pontederia cordata* (Pon-the-DEE-ree-uh kor-DAY-tuh)
Waterlilies, *Nymphaea* species (nim-FAY-a)

Glossary

Alkaline soil: soil with a pH greater than 7.0. It lacks acidity, often because it has limestone in it.

All-purpose fertilizer: powdered, liquid, or granular fertilizer with a balanced proportion of the three key nutrients—nitrogen (N), phosphorus (P), and potassium (K). It is suitable for maintenance nutrition for most plants.

Annual: a plant that lives its entire life in one season. It is genetically determined to germinate, grow, flower, set seed, and die the same year.

Balled and burlapped: describes a tree or shrub grown in the field whose soilball was wrapped with protective burlap and twine when the plant was dug up to be sold or transplanted.

Bare root: describes plants that have been packaged without any soil around their roots. (Often young shrubs and trees purchased through the mail arrive with their exposed roots covered with moist peat or sphagnum moss, sawdust, or similar material, and wrapped in plastic.)

Barrier plant: a plant that has intimidating thorns or spines and is sited purposely to block foot traffic or other access to the home or yard.

Beneficial insects: insects or their larvae that prey on pest organisms and their eggs. They may be flying insects, such as ladybugs, parasitic wasps, praying mantids, and soldier bugs, or soil dwellers such as predatory nematodes, spiders, and ants.

Berm: a narrow, raised ring of soil around a tree, used to hold water so it will be directed to the root zone.

Bract: a modified leaf structure on a plant stem near its flower, resembling a petal. Often it is more colorful and visible than the actual flower, as in Dogwood.

Bud union: the place where the top of a plant was grafted to the rootstock; usually refers to roses.

Canopy: the overhead branching area of a tree, usually referring to its extent including foliage.

Cold hardiness: the ability of a perennial plant to survive the winter cold in a particular area.

Composite: a flower that is actually composed of many tiny flowers. Typically, they are flat clusters of tiny, tight florets, sometimes surrounded by wider-petaled florets. Composite flowers are highly attractive to bees and beneficial insects.

Compost: organic matter that has undergone progressive decomposition by microbial and macrobial activity until it is reduced to a spongy, fluffy texture. Added to soil of any type, it improves the soil's ability to hold air and water and to drain well.

Corm: the swollen energy-storing structure, analogous to a bulb, under the soil at the base of the stem of plants such as crocus and gladiolus.

Crown: the base of a plant at, or just beneath, the surface of the soil where the roots meet the stems.

Cultivar: a CULTIvated VARiety. It is a naturally occurring form of a plant that has been identified as special or superior and is purposely selected for propagation and production.

Deadhead: a pruning technique that removes faded flower heads from plants to improve their appearances, abort seed production, and stimulate further flowering.

Deciduous plants: unlike evergreens, these trees and shrubs lose their leaves in the fall.

Desiccation: drying out of foliage tissues, usually due to drought or wind.

Division: the practice of splitting apart perennial plants to create several smaller-rooted segments. The practice is useful for controlling the plant's size and for acquiring more plants; it is also essential to the health and continued flowering of certain ones.

Dormancy: the period, usually the winter, when perennial plants temporarily cease active growth and rest. Dormant is the verb form, as used in this sentence: *Some plants, like spring-blooming bulbs, go dormant in the summer.*

Established: the point at which a newly planted tree, shrub, or flower begins to produce new growth, either foliage or stems. This is an indication that the roots have recovered from transplant shock and have begun to grow and spread.

Evergreen: perennial plants that do not lose their foliage annually with the onset of winter. Needled or broadleaf foliage will persist and continues to function on a plant through one or more winters, aging and dropping unobtrusively in cycles of three or four years or more.

Foliar: of or about foliage—usually refers to the practice of spraying foliage, as in fertilizing or treating with insecticide; leaf tissues absorb liquid directly for fast results, and the soil is not affected.

Floret: a tiny flower, usually one of many forming a cluster, that comprises a single blossom.

Germinate: to sprout. Germination is a fertile seed's first stage of development.

Graft (union): the point on the stem of a woody plant with sturdier roots where a stem from a highly ornamental plant is inserted so that it will join with it. Roses are commonly grafted.

Hands: the female flowers on a banana tree; they turn into bananas.

Hardscape: the permanent, structural, nonplant part of a landscape, such as walls, sheds, pools, patios, arbors, and walkways.

Herbaceous: plants having fleshy or soft stems that die back with frost; the opposite of woody.

Hybrid: a plant that is the result of intentional or natural cross-pollination between two or more plants of the same species or genus.

Low water demand: describes plants that tolerate dry soil for varying periods of time. Typically, they have succulent, hairy, or silvery-gray foliage and tuberous roots or taproots.

Mulch: a layer of material over bare soil to protect it from erosion and compaction by rain, and to discourage weeds. It may be inorganic (gravel, fabric) or organic (wood chips, bark, pine needles, chopped leaves).

Naturalize: (*a*) to plant seeds, bulbs, or plants in a random, informal pattern as they would appear in their natural habitats; (*b*) to adapt to and spread throughout adopted habitats (a tendency of some nonnative plants).

Nectar: the sweet fluid produced by glands on flowers that attract pollinators such as hummingbirds and honeybees, for whom it is a source of energy.

Organic material, organic matter: any material or debris that is derived from plants. It is carbon-based material capable of undergoing decomposition and decay.

Peat moss: organic matter from peat sedges (United States) or sphagnum mosses (Canada), often used to improve soil texture. The acidity of sphagnum peat moss makes it ideal for boosting or maintaining soil acidity while also improving its drainage.

Perennial: a flowering plant that lives over two or more seasons. Many die back with frost, but their roots survive the winter and generate new shoots in the spring.

pH: a measurement of the relative acidity (low pH) or alkalinity (high pH) of soil or water based on a scale of 1 to 14, 7 being neutral. Individual plants require soil to be within a certain range so that nutrients can dissolve in moisture and be available to them.

Pinch: to remove tender stems and/or leaves by pressing them between thumb and forefinger. This pruning technique encourages branching, compactness, and flowering in plants, or it removes aphids clustered at growing tips.

Pollen: the yellow, powdery grains in the center of a flower. A plant's male sex cells, they are transferred to the female plant parts by means of wind or animal pollinators to fertilize them and create seeds.

Raceme: an arrangement of single-stalked flowers along an elongated, unbranched axis.

Rhizome: a swollen energy-storing stem structure, similar to a bulb, that lies horizontally in the soil, with roots emerging from its lower surface and growth shoots from a growing point at or near its tip, as in Bearded Iris.

Rootbound (or potbound): the condition of a plant that has been confined in a container too long, its roots having been forced to wrap around themselves and even swell out of the container. Successful transplanting or repotting requires untangling and trimming away of some of the matted roots.

Root flare: the transition at the base of a tree trunk where the bark tissue begins to differentiate and roots begin to form just before entering the soil. This area should not be covered with soil when planting a tree.

Self-seeding: the tendency of some plants to sow their seeds freely around the yard. It creates many seedlings the following season that may or may not be welcome.

Semievergreen: tending to be evergreen in a mild climate but deciduous in a rigorous one.

Shearing: the pruning technique whereby plant stems and branches are cut uniformly with long-bladed pruning shears (hedge shears) or powered hedge trimmers. It is used when creating and maintaining hedges and topiary.

Slow-acting fertilizer: fertilizer that is water insoluble and therefore releases its nutrients gradually as a function of soil temperature, moisture, and related microbial activity. Typically granular, it may be organic or synthetic.

Succulent growth: the sometimes undesirable production of fleshy, water-storing leaves or stems that results from overfertilization.

Sucker: a new-growing shoot. Underground plant roots produce suckers to form new stems and spread by means of these suckering roots to form large plantings, or colonies. Some plants produce root suckers or branch suckers as a result of pruning or wounding.

Tuber: a type of underground storage structure in a plant stem, analogous to a bulb. It generates roots below and stems above ground (example: Dahlia).

Variegated: having various colors or color patterns. The term usually refers to plant foliage that is streaked, edged, blotched, or mottled with a contrasting color—often green with yellow, cream, or white.

White grubs: fat, off-white, wormlike larvae of Japanese beetles. They reside in the soil and feed on plant (especially grass) roots until summer when they emerge as beetles to feed on plant foliage.

Wings: (*a*) the corky tissue that forms edges along the twigs of some woody plants such as Winged Euonymus; (*b*) the flat, dried extension of tissue on some seeds, such as Maple, that catch the wind and help them disseminate.

Bibliography

Reference Books

Armitage, Allan M. *Herbaceous Perennial Plants*. Champaign, Illinois: Stipes Publishing, 1997.

Bender, Steve, editor. *The Southern Living Garden Problem Solver*. Birmingham, Alabama: Oxmoor House, 1999.

Darke, Rick. *Color Encyclopedia of Ornamental Grasses*. Portland, Oregon: Timber Press, 1999.

Dirr, Michael A. *Manual of Woody Landscape Plants*. Champaign, Illinois: Stipes Publishing, 1998.

DiSabito-Aust, Tracy. *The Well-Tended Perennial Garden*. Portland, Oregon: Timber Press, 1998.

Heriteau, Jacqueline and Marc Cathey, editors. *The National Arboretum Book of Outstanding Garden Plants*. New York, New York: Simon & Schuster, 1990.

Hoshizaki, Barbara Joe and Robbin C. Moran. *Fern Grower's Manual*. Portland, Oregon: Timber Press, 2001.

General Reading

Bender, Steve and Felder Rushing. *Passalong Plants*. Chapel Hill, North Carolina: The University of North Carolina Press, 1993.

Hodgson, Larry. *Perennials for Every Purpose*. Emmaus, Pennsylvania: Rodale Press, 2000.

Holmes, Roger, editor. *Taylor's Guide to Ornamental Grasses*. Boston, Massachusetts: Houghton Mifflin Co., 1997.

Ogden, Scott. *Garden Bulbs for the South*. Dallas, Texas: Taylor Publishing, 1994.

Roth, Susan A. *The Four-Season Landscape*. Emmaus, Pennsylvania: Rodale Press, 1994.

Sedenko, Jerry. *The Butterfly Garden*. New York, New York: Villard Books, 1991.

Xerces Society, The, and The Smithsonian Institution. *Butterfly Gardening*. San Francisco, California: Sierra Club Books, 1998.

Photography Credits

Thomas Eltzroth: pages 16, 17, 19, 24, 26, 27, 28, 29, 30, 33, 36, 38, 39, 40, 41, 44, 45, 47, 50, 54, 56, 60, 62, 63, 64, 68, 72, 75, 80, 82, 84, 87, 90, 92, 94, 96, 99, 100, 101, 103, 107, 108, 109, 110, 114, 116, 118, 120, 121, 126, 130, 131, 132, 134, 135, 136, 137, 142, 147, 155, 159, 163, 164, 170, 174, 196, 197, 199, 201, 202, 211, 214, 218, 220, 221, 223, 225 and the first photo on the back cover

Liz Ball and Rick Ray: pages 10, 13, 14, 18, 20, 23, 32, 42, 43, 46, 53, 57, 58, 77, 83, 86, 89, 95, 104, 106, 112, 113, 123, 127, 133, 141, 144, 150, 161, 165, 173, 178, 180, 183, 187, 189, 190, 192, 203, 204, 205, 216, 217, 222 and the second through the fourth photos on the back cover

Pamela Harper: pages 31, 34, 71, 74, 76, 85, 91, 93, 102, 117, 128, 139, 143, 145, 148, 149, 154, 156, 160, 168, 175, 176, 179, 181, 182, 185, 186, 188, 191, 193, 206, 207, 212, 215

Dency Kane: pages 21, 22, 35, 37, 52, 59, 73, 79, 105, 115, 122, 124, 129, 140, 151, 152, 167, 172, 177, 194, 208, 210, 213

Lorenzo Gunn: pages 25, 111, 125, 138, 146, 169, 195

William Adams: pages 78, 81, 119, 158, 224

Mike Dirr: pages 61, 157, 184, 198, 209

Ralph Snodsmith: pages 55, 88, 153, 162, 166

Robin Conover: The front cover, pages 8, 15

Clint Waltz: page 70

T. Fred Miller: page 272

The following products are trademarked: Osmocote™, Polyon™, Once™, Milorganite™, and Holly Tone™.

Index

Acer griseum, 188
Acer palmatum, 183
Acer rubrum, 190
Achillea species and
  hybrids, 134
Actinidia arguta, 209
Actinidia deliciosa, 209
Actinidia kolomikta, 209
Actinidia species, 209
Aesculus parviflora, 141
Aesculus pavia, 141
Aesculus species and
  hybrids, 141
African Marigolds, 30
Agapanthus, 33
Agarista populifolia, 157
Ageratum, 20
*Ageratum
  houstonianum*, 20
Ajuga reptans, 84
Akebia, Fiveleaf, 207
Akebia quinata, 207
Allegheny
  Serviceberry, 193
  Spurge, 90
Allspice, Carolina, 145
Allwood Pinks, 114
Alpine Strawberry, 92
Alumroot, 120
Alyssum, Sweet, 44
*Amelanchier
  arborea*, 193
*Amelanchier
  canadensis*, 193
Amelanchier laevis, 193
Amelanchier species and
  hybrids, 193
American
  Beautyberry, 139
  Holly, 150, 172
  Marigolds, 30
Anacharis, 218
Anemone, 100
  Japanese, 100
Anemone tomentosa, 100
Anemone × hybrida, 100
Angel Trumpet, 21
Angel-Wing Begonia, 119
Annual
  Rye, 70, 81
Annuals, 17
Antique Rose, 100, 131
Antirrhinum majus, 41
Aquilegia species and
  hybrids, 110
Artemisia, 23, 44, 73
*Artemisia
  schmidtiana*, 101

Artemisia, 129, 130, 133,
  162, 205, 210
Arum, 48, 52
Arum italicum, 52
Asarum canadense, 95
*Asarum
  shuttleworthii*, 95
Asarum species and
  hybrids, 95
Asclepias incarnata, 106
Asclepias tuberosa, 106
Asiatic Lily, 60
Asparagus Fern, 37
Aster, 79, 105, 109,
  110, 118
Astilbe, 71, 76, 90,
  92, 174
*Athyrium
  felix-femina*, 113
*Athyrium
  nipponicum*, 113
Aucuba, 138
Aucuba japonica, 138
Aurelian Lily, 60
Autumn
  Crocus, 55
  Fern, 115
Azalea, 58, 86, 89, 95,
  135, 136, 149,
  154, 204
  Cumberland, 147
  Deciduous, 147, 160
  Evergreen, 147, 149,
    161, 174, 175, 177
  Pinkshell, 147
  Swamp, 147
  Sweet, 147
Bald Cypress, 173
Baptisia, 102, 132
Baptisia alba, 102
Baptisia australis, 102
Baptisia pendula, 102
Baptisia species and
  hybrids, 102
Barberry, 72
Bean, Hyacinth, 210
Bearded Iris, 13, 47, 51,
  59, 102, 131
Beautyberry, 139
  American, 139
  Japanese, 139
  Purple, 139
Begonia
  Angel-Wing, 119
  Hardy, 119
  Wax, 17, 29, 45
Begonia grandis, 119
Begonia sinensis, 119

*Begonia × semperflorens-
  cultorum*, 45
Bermuda Grass, 10, 14,
  66, 67, 69, 70, 80
Betula nigra, 191
Bigleaf Hydrangea, 155
Bignonia capreolata, 206
Birch, River, 191
Black Mondo Grass, 76
Black-eyed Susan, 31, 72,
  73, 75, 98, 102, 103,
  106, 117, 118, 122,
  127, 134
Black-Flowering
  Sedge, 71
Blanketflower, 117
Bleeding Heart, 90, 92,
  104, 116, 120
  Fringed, 104
Blue
  False Indigo, 102
  Rug, 85
  Salvia, 129
Bluebell, Spanish, 48,
  62, 86
Bluegrass,
  Kentucky, 65, 66
Boltonia, 105, 118, 134
Boltonia asteroides, 105
Bottlebrush
  Buckeye, 141
Bougainvillea, 21
  Golden Rain Tree, 181
Box, Sweet, 93
Boxwood, 11, 136,
  140, 150
Brassica oleracea, 34
Bridal Wreath, 164
Buckeye, 141
  Bottlebrush, 141
  Red, 141
Buddleia davidii, 143
Bugleweed, 84
Bulbs, 47
Burning Bush, 142
Busy Lizzie, 28
Buttercup, 156
Butterfly Bush, 143, 207
Butterfly Weed, 43, 103,
  106, 206, 210
Buxus sempervirens, 140
Buxus species and
  hybrids, 140
Cabbage, Ornamental, 34
Cabomba, 218
Cactus, 57
Caladium, 47, 48, 53,
  90, 91, 121

Caladium bicolor, 53
*Calamagrostis ×
  acutiflora*, 72
Callicarpa americana, 139
Callicarpa dichotoma, 139
Callicarpa japonica, 139
Callicarpa species and
  hybrids, 139
Calycanthus floridus, 145
Camellia, 135, 144
Camellia japonica, 144
Camellia sasanqua, 144
Camellia species and
  hybrids, 144
Campsis species and
  hybrids, 214
*Campsis ×
  tagliabuana*, 214
Canadian
  Ginger, 95
  Hemlock, 78, 169, 174
Candytuft, 96, 107, 114
Canna, 33, 47, 54
Canna species and
  hybrids, 54
Canna, Water, 122, 222
Capsicum annuum, 35
Cardinal Flower, 92, 108,
  116, 174
Carex, 64, 71, 100
Carex elata, 71
Carex conica, 71
Carex morrowii, 71
Carex nigra, 71
Carex species and
  hybrids, 71
Carolina
  Allspice, 145
  Jessamine, 157, 202
  Phlox, 126
  Silverbell, 175
Cast-Iron Plant, 62
Catharanthus roseus, 29
Cattail, 122, 222
  Dwarf, 222
Cedar, Japanese, 182
Celosia, 22, 40
  Plumed, 22
Celosia argentea, 22
*Celosia argentea
  cristata*, 22
*Celosia argentea
  plumosa*, 22
Centranthus ruber, 128
Cercis canadensis, 189
Cercis texensis, 189
Chaenomeles species and
  hybrids, 152

Chamaecyparis obtusa, 151
Chamaecyparis pisifera, 151
Chamaecyparis species and hybrids, 151
Chaste Tree, 176
Cheddar Pinks, 114
Chelone, 100
Cherry
  Flowering, 178
  Ornamental, 171
  Sargent, 178
Cherry Tomato, 35
Chinese
  Elm, 185
  Fringe Tree, 179
  Holly, 150
  Pennisetum, 23
  Wisteria, 216
Chionanthus retusus, 179
Chionanthus virginicus, 179
Christmas Fern, 115
Chrysanthemum, 34, 57, 99, 105, 109, 118
Chrysanthemum rubellum, 109
Cinnamon Fern, 113
Cladrastis kentukea, 198
Cladrastis platycarpa, 198
Clematis, 203
  Sweet Autumn, 203
Clematis armandii, 203
Clematis species and hybrids, 203
Clematis terniflora, 203
Cleome, 23, 54, 102
Cleome hasslerana, 23
Clethra alnifolia, 165
Climbing
  Hydrangea, 200, 201, 204
  Rose, 205
Clover, Red, 27
Cockscomb, 22
Colchicum, 55
Coleus, 17, 24, 60, 91, 93, 103
Colorado Blue Spruce, 16
Columbine, 86, 110, 119
Coneflower, 103
  Cutleaf, 103
  Purple, 122, 127, 128, 134
Coral
  Bells, 120
  Honeysuckle, 215
Coreopsis, 20, 37, 43, 98, 111, 117, 118, 133
  Threadleaf, 111
Coreopsis, 60

Coreopsis grandiflora, 111, 214
Coreopsis verticillata, 111
Cornus florida, 177
Cornus kousa, 12, 177
Cornus species and hybrids, 177
Cortaderia jubata, 78
Cortaderia selloana, 78
Cosmos, 20, 25
Cosmos bipinnatus, 25
Cosmos sulphureus, 25
Cotinus coggygria, 163
Cottage Pinks, 114
Crape Myrtle, 9, 146
Creeper, Trumpet, 214
Creeping
  Fescue, 66
  Juniper, 85
  Phlox, 11, 73, 79, 86, 120
  Thyme, 82, 87,
Crocus, 47, 48, 50, 55, 62, 94, 168
  Autumn, 55
Crocus species and hybrids, 55
Crocus speciosus, 55
Crossvine, 206
Cryptomeria, Japanese, 182
Cryptomeria japonica, 182
Cumberland Azalea, 147
Cutleaf Coneflower, 103
Cynodon dactylon, 70
Cypress
  Bald, 173
  False, 136, 151
Cyrtomium falcatum, 115
Daffodil, 11, 13, 47, 48, 50, 52, 56, 58, 63, 86, 93, 94, 112, 153, 168, 177
Dahlia, 47, 48, 57
Dahlia species and hybrids, 57
Daisy, 25, 57
  Shasta, 31, 72, 102, 122, 131, 133, 206, 214
Datura wrightii, 21
Daylily, 13, 73, 75, 96, 112, 129, 164, 214
Dead Nettle, Spotted, 91
Deciduous
  Azalea, 147, 160
  Ferns, 113
  Holly, 148
Dendranthema × *grandiflorum*, 109
Dendranthema zawadskii, 109

Dianthus, 92, 107, 114
Dianthus barbatus, 114
Dianthus deltoides, 114
Dianthus gratianopolitanus, 114
Dianthus plumarius, 114
Dianthus species and hybrids, 114
Dianthus × *allwoodii*, 114
Dicentra eximia, 104
Dicentra spectabilis, 104
Digitalis grandiflora, 116
Digitalis × *mertonensis*, 116
Digitalis purpurea, 116
Digitalis species and hybrids, 116
Dogwood, 11, 12, 58, 95, 149, 169, 175, 177, 189
  Flowering, 177
  Kousa, 12, 177
Dolichos lablab, 210
Doublefile Viburnum, 166
Dryopteris erythrosora, 115
Dryopteris intermedia, 115
Dusty Miller, 24, 26, 39, 129, 130
Dutch Iris, 51, 59
Dwarf Cattail, 222
Echinacea purpurea, 207
Echinacea purpurea, 127
Egyptian Star Cluster, 37
Elm
  Chinese, 185
  Lacebark, 185
  Siberian, 185
English
  Ivy, 88, 201
  Rose, 73, 162
Enkianthus campanulatus, 160
Enkianthus, Redvein, 160
Euonymus alatus, 142
Eupatorium maculatum, 122
Eupatorium purpureum, 122
Euphorbia marginata, 42
Evergreen
  Azalea, 147, 149, 161, 174, 175, 177
  Fern, 115
  Holly, 148, 150
  Wood Fern, 115
False
  Cypress, 136, 151
  Hinoki, 151
  Sawara, 151
  Indigo, 102
  Blue, 102

  White, 102
Fan Flower, 40
Feather Reed Grass, 72
Fern, 28, 53, 89, 95, 100, 104, 110, 115, 116, 119, 120, 121, 161, 167, 174
  Asparagus, 37
  Autumn, 115
  Christmas, 115
  Cinnamon, 113
  Deciduous, 113
  Evergreen, 115
  Wood, 115
  Hart's Tongue, 115
  Japanese
    Holly, 115
    Painted, 113
  Korean Rock, 115
  Lady, 113
  Royal, 113
  Soft Shield, 115
Fescue, 10, 65, 66, 67, 69
  Creeping, 66
  Tall, 66, 80
Festuca arundinacea, 80
Fiveleaf Akebia, 207
Flag Iris, 108
Florida Leucothoe, 157
Flowering
  Cherry, 178
  Dogwood, 177
  Quince, 11, 152
  Rush, 224
Foamflower, 89, 104, 120
Forsythia, 11, 56, 153, 156
Forsythia species and hybrids, 153
Fothergilla, 154
Fothergilla gardenii, 154
Fothergilla major, 154
Fothergilla species, 154
Fountain Grass, 37, 54, 73
Foxglove, 36, 116
  Strawberry, 116
Fragaria frel
  'Pink Panda', 92
Fringe Tree, 179
  Chinese, 179
Fringed Bleeding Heart, 104
Gaillardia, 43, 96, 97, 117, 127
Gaillardia, 72
Gaillardia grandiflora, 117
Garden
  Mum, 109
  Phlox, 126
Gelsemium sempervirens, 202

Geranium, 24, 26
  Ivy, 26
German Iris, 59
Ginger
  Canadian, 95
  Wild, 95
Ginkgo, 12, 180
Ginkgo biloba, 180
Gladiolus, 47
Globe Amaranth, 27
Gold Flame
  Honeysuckle, 200
Golden Bells, 153
Golden Rain
    Tree, 12, 181
  Bougainvillea, 181
Goldenrod, 105, 111,
  117, 118, 206, 214
Gomphrena, 27, 42, 46
Gomphrena globosa, 27
Gomphrena haageana, 27
Grancy Graybeard, 179
Grape Hyacinth, 48, 46,
  56, 58, 93
Grass
  Bermuda, 10, 14, 66,
    67, 69, 70, 80
  Feather Reed, 72
  Fountain, 37, 54, 73
  Japanese Blood, 64, 74
  Mondo, 64, 76
  Monkey, 64, 77
  Pampas, 78
  Switch, 79
Grasses, 64
Groundcovers, 82
Gum, Sweet, 171, 196
Halesia tetraptera, 175
Hamamelis ×
  intermedia, 168
Hamamelis species and
  hybrids, 168
Hamamelis vernalis, 168
Hamamelis
  virginiana, 168
Hardy
  Begonia, 119
  Kiwi, 209
  Waterlily, 219
Hart's Tongue Fern, 115
Heavenly Bamboo, 159
Hedera helix, 88
Helianthus annus, 43
Hellebores, 123
Helleborus orientalis, 123
Hemerocallis hybrids, 112
Hemlock, Canadian, 78,
  169, 174
Heuchera, 91, 114, 120
Heuchera, 76, 207
Heuchera americana, 120
Heuchera sanguinea, 120

Heuchera species and
  hybrids, 120
Hibiscus, 125
  Perennial, 125
  Swamp, 125
Hibiscus coccineus, 125
Hibiscus species and
  hybrids, 125
Hibiscus syriacus, 125
Hinoki False
  Cypress, 151
Holly, 72, 135
  American, 150, 172
  Chinese, 150
  Deciduous, 148
  Evergreen, 148, 150
  Japanese, 150
Honeysuckle
  Coral, 215
  Gold Flame, 208
  Japanese, 199, 208
  Trumpet, 215
  Wild, 147
Hosta, 24, 28, 52, 53, 77,
  94, 98, 100, 104, 110,
  119, 120, 121,
  174, 204
Hosta species and
  hybrids, 121
Hyacinth, 58
  Grape, 48, 56, 93
Hyacinth Bean, 210
Hyacinthoides
  hispanica, 62
Hybrid Tea Rose, 162
Hydrangea, 155
  Bigleaf, 155
  Climbing, 200, 201,
    204
  Oakleaf, 155, 174
  Peegee, 155
  Smooth, 155
Hydrangea
  arborescens, 155, 164
Hydrangea
  macrophylla, 155
Hydrangea
  paniculata, 155
Hydrangea anomala
  petiolaris, 204
Hydrangea quercifola, 155
Hydrangea species and
  hybrids, 155
Hylotelephium
  spectabile, 130
Iberis
  sempervirens, 107
Ilex cornuta, 150
Ilex crenata, 150
Ilex decidua, 148
Ilex glabra, 150
Ilex opaca, 172

Ilex serrata, 148
Ilex species and
  hybrids, 148, 150
Ilex verticillata, 148
Impatiens, 28, 53,
  104, 121
  New Guinea, 33
Impatiens hawkeri, 33
Impatiens
  walleriana, 28, 33
Imperata cylindrica, 74
Indigo, 102
  False, 102
Inkberry, 150
Ipomoea alba, 212
Iris, 59
  Bearded, 13, 47, 51,
    59, 102, 131
  Crested, 59
  Dutch, 51, 59
  Flag, 59, 108
  German, 59
  Japanese, 59
  Louisiana, 51, 59
  Siberian, 13, 51, 59
Iris siberica, 59
Iris species and
  hybrids, 59
Itea virginica, 167
Ivy, 200
  English, 88, 201
Ivy Geranium, 26
Jack-in-the-Pulpit, 52
Japanese
  Anemone, 100
  Beautyberry, 139
  Blood Grass, 64, 74
  Cedar, 182
  Cryptomeria, 182
  Holly, 150
    Fern, 115
  Honeysuckle, 199, 208
  Iris, 59
  Maple, 183
  Pachysandra, 90
  Painted Fern, 113
  Spirea, 164
  Winterberry, 148
  Wisteria, 216
  Yellowwood, 198
  Zelkova, 12, 184
Jessamine,
  Carolina, 157, 202
Joe-Pye Weed, 122,
  133, 207
  Spotted, 122
Juncus subnodulosus, 224
Juneberry, 193
Juniper, Creeping, 85
Juniperus horizontalis, 85
Juniperus species and
  hybrids, 85

Jupiter's Beard, 128
Kale, Ornamental, 34
Kentucky
  Bluegrass, 65, 66
  Wisteria, 216
Kerria, 12, 56, 156
Kerria japonica, 156
Kiwi, Hardy, 209
Koelreuteria
  bipinnata, 181
Koelreuteria
  paniculata, 181
Kolomikta Vine, 209
Korean Rock Fern, 115
Kousa Dogwood, 12, 177
Kudzu, 199
Lacebark Elm, 185
Lacecap Hydrangea, 155
Lady Fern, 113
Lagerstroemia species and
  hybrids, 146
Lamb's Ear, 73, 87, 210
Lamium, 71
Lamium
  masculatum, 91, 210
Laurel, Mountain, 174
Lenten Rose, 89, 119,
  123, 207
Leucanthemum ×
  superbum, 131
Leucothoe, 157
  Florida, 157
Leucothoe axillaris, 157
Leucothoe
  fontanesiana, 157
Leucothoe populifolia, 157
Leucothoe species and
  hybrids, 157
Lilium species and
  hybrids, 60
Lily, 47, 48, 60
  Asiatic, 60
  Aurelian, 60
  Magic, 61
  Oriental, 60
  Surprise, 61
Lily of the Valley, 175
Liquidambar
  styraciflua, 196
Liriodendron
  tulipifera, 197
Liriope, 41, 76, 77, 204
Liriope muscari, 77
Liriope species and
  hybrids, 77
Liriope spicata, 77
Lobelia cardinalis, 108
Lobularia maritima, 44
Lonicera × heckrottii, 208
Lonicera japonica, 208
Lonicera sempervirens, 215
Loropetalum, 12, 158

Loropetalum chinense, 158
Lotus, 223
Louisiana Iris, 51, 59
Lycoris, 47, 48, 61, 93
Lycoris albiflora, 61
Lycoris aurea, 61
Lycoris radiata, 61
Lycoris species, 61
Lycoris squamigera, 61
Madagascar Periwinkle,
29, 35, 39, 128
Magic Lily, 61
Magnolia
Dedicuous, 12
Saucer, 192
Southern, 169, 171,
195
Magnolia grandiflora, 195
Magnolia
soulangiana, 192
Maiden Pinks, 114
Mandevilla, 211
Mandevilla ×
amoena, 211
Maple, 169
Japanese, 183
Paperbark, 188
Red, 12, 190
Marigold, 18, 20, 30, 46
African, 30
American, 30
Maypop, 213
Mealycup Salvia, 39
Melampodium, 31,
42, 46
Melampodium
paludosum, 31
Mexican Sunflower, 79
Miniature Rose, 162
Miscanthus, 64, 75
Miscanthus sinensis, 75
Mondo Grass, 64, 76
Black, 76
Monkey Grass, 64, 77
Moonflower, 199,
200, 212
Morning Glory, 22,
201, 212
Moss Rose, 32, 42
Mountain Laurel, 174
Mum, Garden, 109
Muscari armeniacum, 58
Muscari botryoides, 58
Muscari latifolium, 58
Muscari species and
hybrids, 58
Myriophyllum, 218
Naked Lady, 61
Nandina, 159
Nandina domestica, 159
Narcissus, 56
Narrowleaf Zinnia, 46

Nelumbo species, 223
New Guinea
Impatiens, 33
Nuttall Oak, 186
Nymphaea species, 225
Oak, 186
Nuttall, 186
Pin, 186
Scarlet, 186
Southern Red, 186
White, 186
Willow, 186
Oakleaf
Hydrangea, 155, 174
Oenothera fruticosa, 132
Old Garden Rose, 162
Ophiopogon japonicus, 76
Ophiopogon
planiscapus. 76
Oriental Lily, 60
Ornamental
Cabbage, 34
Cherry, 171
Kale, 34
Peach, 12
Pear, 11, 12, 187
Pepper, 35
Osmunda
cinnamonea, 113
Osmunda regalis, 113
Oxydendrum
arboreum, 194
Pachysandra, 90
Japanese, 90
Pachysandra
procumbens, 90
Pachysandra species and
hybrids, 90
Pachysandra
terminalis, 90
Paeonia lactiflora, 124
Pampas Grass, 78
Panicum virgatum, 79
Pansy, 34, 36, 63, 207
Paperbark Maple, 188,
Parrot Tulip, 63
Passiflora caerulea, 213
Passiflora coccinea, 213
Passiflora incarnata, 213
Passiflora species, 213
Passionflower, 200, 213
Red, 213
Peach, Ornamental, 12
Pear, Ornamental, 11,
12, 187
Peegee Hydrangea, 155
Pelargonium species and
hybrids, 26
Pennisetum
alopecuroides, 73
Pennisetum species and
hybrids, 73

Pentas, 37, 92
Pentas lanceolata, 37
Peony, 97, 124
Pepper,
Ornamental, 35
Perennial
Hibiscus, 125
Ryegrass, 65
Perennials, 96
Periwinkle, 29, 30
Madagascar, 29, 35,
39, 128
Petunia, 22, 35, 37, 38,
40, 92, 207
Floribunda, 38
Grandiflora, 38
Multiflora, 38
Petunia × hybrida, 38
Phlox, 122, 126, 132
Carolina, 126
Creeping, 11, 73, 79,
86, 120
Garden, 126
Summer, 126
Phlox divaricata, 86
Phlox maculata, 126
Phlox nivalis, 86
Phlox paniculata, 126
Phlox pilosa, 86
Phlox species and
hybrids, 86, 126
Phlox subulata, 86
Phyllitis
scolopendrium, 115
Pickerel Weed, 222, 224
Pin Oak, 186
Pine, 144, 170
Pineapple Sage, 145
Pinks, 114
Allwood, 114
Cheddar, 114
Cottage, 114
Maiden, 114
Pinkshell Azalea, 147
Plumed Celosia, 22
Poinsettia, 42
Polystichum
acrostichoides, 115
Polystichum
setiferum, 115
Polystichum
tsussimense, 115
Pontederia cordata, 224
Poplar, Tulip, 197
Portulaca, 32
Portulaca
grandiflora, 32
Possumhaw, 148
Potentilla, 206
Primrose, 132
Prunus sargentii, 178
Prunus serrulata, 178

Prunus species and
hybrids, 178
Prunus subhirtella, 178
Prunus × yedoensis, 178
Purple
Beautyberry, 139
Coneflower, 75,118,
122, 127, 128, 134
Pyrus calleryana, 187
Quercus alba, 186
Quercus coccinea, 186
Quercus falcata, 186
Quercus nuttallii, 186
Quercus palustris, 186
Quercus phellos, 186
Quercus species and
hybrids, 186
Quince,
Flowering, 11, 152
Red
Buckeye, 141
Clover, 27
Hot Poker, 106
Maple, 12, 190
Passionflower, 213
Salvia, 39
Valerian, 12, 128
Redbud, 175, 189
Redvein
Enkianthus, 160
Rhododendron, 89, 91,
95, 154, 157, 160, 161,
174, 175, 204
Rhododendron species and
hybrids, 147, 149, 161
Rhododendron
viscosum, 147
River Birch, 191
Rosa species and hybrids,
162, 205
Rose, 39, 44, 162,
199, 200
Antique, 131
Climbing, 205
English, 73, 62
Lenten, 89, 119, 123
Miniature, 162
Moss, 32, 42
Old Garden, 162
Shrub, 162
Rose of Sharon, 125
Rose Verbena, 133
Royal Fern, 113
Rudbeckia fulgida, 103
Rudbeckia hirta, 103, 210
Rudbeckia laciniata, 103
Rudbeckia nitida, 103
Rudbeckia species and
hybrids, 103
Rush, Flowering, 224
Russian Sage, 129
Rye, Annual, 70, 81

Ryegrass, Perennial, 65
Sage
  Pineapple, 145
  Russian, 129
  Scarlet, 39
  Texas, 39
Salvia, 18, 39, 40, 91,
  128, 129, 132
  Blue, 129
  Mealycup, 39
  Red, 39
Salvia coccinea, 39
Salvia species and
  hybrids, 39, 129
Salvia splendens, 39
Sarcococca hookerana
  digyna, 93
Sarcococca hookerana
  humilis, 93
Sargent Cherry, 178
Saucer Magnolia, 192
Sawara False Cypress, 151
Scarlet
  Oak, 186
  Sage, 39
Scaveola, 40
Scaveola ×
  'Blue Wonder', 40
Sedge,
  Black-Flowering, 71
Sedum 'Autumn Joy', 130
Sedum × telephium
  'Autumn Joy', 130
Serviceberry, 193
  Allegheny, 193
Shadbush, 193
Shasta Daisy, 31, 72, 102,
  106, 111, 122, 131,
  133, 206, 214
Shrub Rose, 162
Shrubs, 135
Siberian
  Elm, 185
  Iris, 13, 51, 59
Silverbell, Carolina, 175
Smoke Bush, 42, 163
Smoke Tree, 163
Smooth
  Hydrangea, 155
Snapdragon, 20, 29,
  36, 41
Snow-on-the
  Mountain, 42, 60
Snowball, 166
Snowdrops, 62
Snowflake, 94

Soft Shield Fern, 115
Solenostemon
  scutellarioides, 24
Solidago species and
  hybrids, 118
Solomon's Seal', 89
Sourwood, 194
Southern
  Magnolia, 171, 195
  Red Oak, 186
Spanish Bluebell, 48,
  62, 86
Spider Flower, 23
Spiraea japonica, 164
Spiraea prunifolia, 164
Spiraea × bumalda, 164
Spirea, 12, 164
  Japanese, 164
Spotted
  Dead Nettle, 91
  Joe-Pye Weed, 122
Spruce, Colorado
  Blue, 16
Spurge, Allegheny, 90
Star Flower, 37
Stokesia, 132
Stonecrop, 130
Strawberry
  'Pink Panda', 92
Strawberry
  Alpine, 92
  Foxglove, 116
Summer Phlox, 126
Summersweet, 165
Sundrops, 132
Sunflower, 31, 40, 43,
  54, 117, 134, 210
  Mexican, 79
Surprise Lily, 61
Swamp
  Azalea, 147
  Hibiscus, 125
  Milkweed, 106
Sweet
  Alyssum, 44
  Autumn Clematis, 203
  Azalea, 147
  Box, 12, 93
  Gum, 171, 196
  William, 114
Sweetspire,
  Virginia, 165, 167
Switch Grass, 79
Tagetes species and
  hybrids, 30
Tall Fescue, 66, 80

Taxodium distichum, 173
Tea Rose, Hybrid, 162
Texas
  Redbud, 189
  Sage, 39
Threadleaf
  Coreopsis, 111
Thrift, 11, 86
Thyme, Creeping, 82, 87
Thymus praecox, 87
Thymus serphyllum, 87
Tiarella species and
  hybrids, 89
Tithonia rotundifolia, 79
Tomato, Cherry, 35
Trees, 169
Trumpet
  Creeper, 199, 206, 214
  Honeysuckle, 215
Tsuga canadensis, 174
Tulip, 11, 12, 13, 47, 48,
  49, 50, 52, 58, 63, 86,
  93, 114, 149, 177
  Poplar, 197
Tulip, Parrot, 63
Tulipa species and
  hybrids, 63
Turtlehead, 100
Typha angustifolia, 222
Typha latifolia, 222
Typha minima, 222
Typha species, 222
Ulmus parvifolia, 185
Ulmus pumila, 185
Valerian, Red, 12, 128
Verbena, 53, 128, 133
Verbena, Rose, 133
Verbena
  bonariensis, 41, 133
Verbena canadensis, 133
Verbena species and
  hybrids, 133
Viburnum, 166
  Doublefile, 166
Viburnum ×
  burkwoodii, 166
Viburnum × pragense, 166
Viburnum plicatum
  tomentosum, 166
Viburnum species and
  hybrids, 166
Vinca, 29, 62, 94
Vinca major, 94
Vinca minor, 26, 82, 94,
  146, 204. 216
Vines, 199

Viola, 63
Viola × wittrockiana, 36
Virginia
  Sweetspire, 165, 167
Vitex agnus-castus, 176
Vitex negundo, 176
Water Canna, 122, 222
Water Gardens, 217
Waterlily, 57, 63, 218,
  219, 220, 222, 223,
  224, 2257
Waterlily, Hardy, 219
Wax Begonia, 17, 29, 45
Weeping Willow, 186
White
  False Indigo, 102
  Oak, 186
Wild
  Ginger, 95
  Honeysuckle, 147
Willow Oak, 186
Willow, Weeping, 186
Windflower, 100
Winterberry, 148
  Japanese, 148
Wisteria, 201, 216
  Chinese, 216
  Japanese, 216
  Kentucky, 216
Wisteria floribunda, 216
Wisteria macrostachys, 216
Wisteria species and
  hybrids, 216
Witch Hazel, 12,
  135, 168
Yarrow, 72, 127, 134
Yellow Rose of Texas, 156
Yellowwood, 198
  Japanese, 198
Zelkova,
  Japanese, 12, 184
Zelkova serrata, 184
Zinnia, 18, 23, 30, 31,
  46, 57, 128
  Narrowleaf, 46
Zinnia elegans, 46
Zinnia species and
  hybrids, 46
Zoysia, 10, 14, 66, 67,
  69, 80, 81
Zoysia species, 81

Meet Judy Lowe

Judy Lowe has been active in gardening all her life, starting as a child working with her mother, also an accomplished gardener. Lowe began her garden writing career more than twenty years ago as Garden Editor at the *Chattanooga Free Press* (now, the *Chattanooga Times-Free Press*). Judy has shared her gardening wisdom with thousands of readers over the years, and currently is the Garden Editor at *The Christian Science Monitor*. She also is president of the Garden Writers Association of America, and has held many other offices in that organization over the years.

Lowe's other credits include contributing articles to *Woman's Day* and *Southern Living* magazines. She was the Southern Gardening Editor for www.suite101.com and appeared weekly in a gardening segment on Chattanooga station WDEF-TV.

Judy Lowe has received numerous awards and honors from prestigious organizations. She has received four Quill and Trowel Awards from the Garden Writers Association of America; a Special Communication Award for Tennessee Horticulture from the Tennessee Fruit and Vegetable Growers; the Best Article on Trees from the American Society of Consulting Arborists; the Exemplary Journalism for Home Garden Communication Award from the National Garden Bureau, and many others.

Judy is married to an electrical engineer who doubles as the "official hole digger" in their garden. Judy has lived in several different regions of Tennessee and has experience growing plants in everything from hard red clay to shady sites with rocky soils. She and her husband currently live in Soddy Daisy and have two sons. Her proudest "gardening moment" was having a daylily named after her.